CENOTAPH SOUTH

Chris McCabe's poetry collections are *The Hutton Inquiry, Zeppelins, THE RESTRUCTURE* and, most recently, *Speculatrix* (Penned in the Margins, 2014). He has recorded a CD with the Poetry Archive and was shortlisted for The Ted Hughes Award in 2013 for his collaborative book with Maria Vlotides, *Pharmapoetica*. His plays *Shad Thames, Broken Wharf* and *Mudflats* have been performed in London and Liverpool, and he is the co-editor of *The New Concrete: Visual Poetry in the 21st Century* (Hayward Publishing, 2015) with Victoria Bean. His short story *Mud* was published in the Galley Beggar Digital Singles series and his book *Real South Bank* was published by Seren in 2016. McCabe has read at venues including the British Library, the BFI, the Whitechapel Gallery, the Wellcome Collection, Latitude Festival and Ledbury Poetry Festival.

McCabe's creative non-fiction book *In the Catacombs: a Summer Among the Dead Poets of West Norwood Cemetery* was an LRB Bookshop Book of the Year. This is the first part of an epic project that aims to discover a great lost poet in one of London's Victorian cemeteries. He works as the Poetry Librarian at The National Poetry Library, Southbank Centre, and teaches for the Poetry School.

ALSO BY CHRIS MCCABE

CREATIVE NON-FICTION

*In the Catacombs: A Summer Among the Dead Poets of West
    Norwood Cemetery* (Penned in the Margins, 2014)
Real South Bank (Seren, 2016)

POETRY COLLECTIONS

The Hutton Inquiry (Salt Publishing, 2005)
Zeppelins (Salt Publishing, 2008)
THE RESTRUCTURE (Salt Publishing, 2012)
Speculatrix (Penned in the Margins, 2014)
As editor: *The New Concrete: Visual Poetry in the 21st Century*,
    with Victoria Bean (Hayward Publishing, 2015)

DRAMA

Shad Thames, Broken Wharf (Penned in the Margins, 2010)

Cenotaph South

Mapping the Lost Poets of Nunhead Cemetery

Chris McCabe

Penned in the Margins

LONDON

PUBLISHED BY PENNED IN THE MARGINS
Toynbee Studios, 28 Commercial Street, London E1 6AB
www.pennedinthemargins.co.uk

First published in hardback in 2016

This edition published in 2017

Printed in the United Kingdom by Bell & Bain

ISBN
978-1-908058-57-7

Supported by the Friends of Nunhead Cemetery and Arts Council England

CONTENTS

ACKNOWLEDGEMENTS

I am hugely grateful to Arts Council England for awarding me Grants for the Arts funding to allow me to write this book and to Southbank Centre for giving me a six-month sabbatical. I would like to thank Jude Kelly and Shân Maclennan for their support, all my colleagues at Southbank Centre and, in particular, all the staff at The National Poetry Library.

This book couldn't have been written without the help of the Friends of Nunhead Cemetery. Tim Stevenson has been the most fascinating of guides into the wilderness of the Cemetery, tirelessly responding to emails and meeting me at the gates. Tim was a fantastic collaborator on my poetry tour of Nunhead Cemetery in August 2016. I have been inspired by Ron Woollacott's wellspring of books about Nunhead Cemetery and his deep knowledge of its history. His tour de force *Investors in Death* provided me with many of the facts about Nunhead Cemetery which have been drawn on for my distinct purpose. I would like to thank Tim and Ron for their suggestions on an early draft of this book. Thanks too to Jeff Hart for offering the support of the Friends towards my project. I would like to thank Tom Phillips for permission to use an image from his work *A Humument.*

As always I'd like to thank my editor Tom Chivers at Penned in the Margins whose instinctive reaction to the early drafts of *Cenotaph South* was spot-on and who has helped to shape the book into its final form here. Working with Tom always feels like more of an artistic collaboration.

And thank you to my wife Sarah and son Pavel who have created a supportive environment for me to work in: Sarah for encouragement and support along the way and Pavel for letting me work at his desk through the long days of the summer holiday, ready for the 5pm finishes when the bike and football could see the light of day!

This book is dedicated to my mum,
whose strength and perseverance
has amazed everyone who knows her.

Cenotaph South

Mapping the Lost Poets of Nunhead Cemetery

A fool sees not the same tree that a wise man sees.
William Blake, 'Proverbs from Hell'

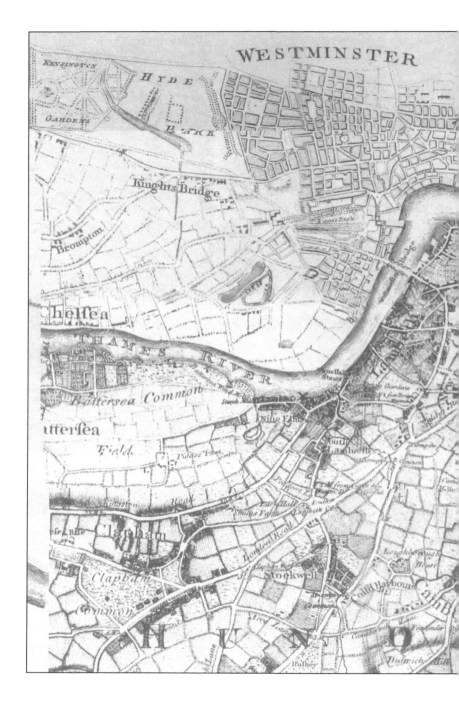

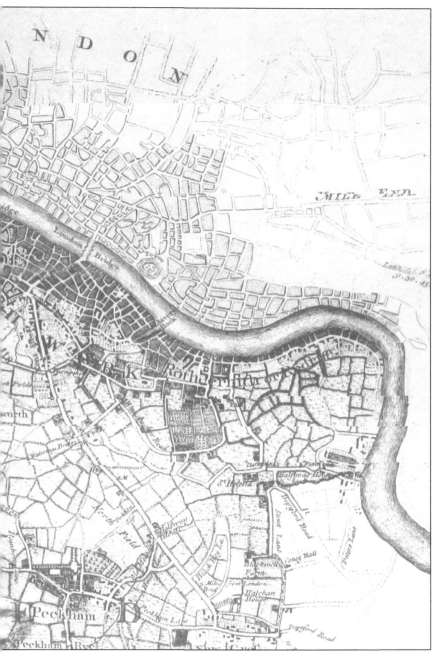

John Rocque, 'A Map of Surrey, 1768'

Prologue

I'm standing at the gates of Nunhead Cemetery, a place I've come to love throughout a very difficult period in my life. Over the past two years I have visited many times in search of the Cemetery's dead poets. This was the challenge I had set myself: to find a great lost poet in one of London's Magnificent Seven — the Victorian cemeteries opened between 1832 and 1841 — and that journey has continued here, into the lush and overgrown south London wilderness of Nunhead Cemetery.

On a late summer evening in 2014 I was at home in Liverpool, working through some inventories of London's cemeteries — looking for the known dead poets buried in Nunhead Cemetery — when my mobile rang. I answered to hear my sister's voice, trying to find a way to tell me that my mum had been diagnosed with breast cancer. Nick Cave's 'The Mercy Seat' was playing on the radio in the kitchen and I sat down on the edge of my bed to absorb the news. In the months that followed, my relationship with Nunhead Cemetery changed. At the start I was wary of being around so much death but then the dead poets I was becoming obsessed with began to appear, as if to offer me some of the peace that they know of the very strange and beautiful place they are buried in. As if in the land of death, they suggested, death could never find me.

I work in London as a Poetry Librarian and spend my weekday evenings in Dulwich, close to Peckham Rye where William Blake saw an angel when he was a boy — a short walk down the hill from Nunhead Cemetery. What began as an attempt to find

Blake's tree led to the mapping out of the poetic history surrounding Nunhead Cemetery. As well as getting to know the poets inside the Cemetery I also began visiting the sites made into mythic hollow-ways by the poets who have laid their tracks here before. By doing this something remarkable began to happen: a map emerged, in the shape of a casket, connecting the recognised poets who came to Dulwich and Peckham — Blake, Robert Browning, Barry MacSweeney, B.S. Johnson — with those buried in the Cemetery at the heart of my map. As if the celebrated poets surrounding Nunhead Cemetery had already forged a solid perimeter around the fragile reputations of the poets buried inside the Cemetery. As if they were offering their work as a way for me to reconsider what I had found of the poets who had been forgotten in the graveyard.

As my map became clearer, I began to see the place where I sleep in London as the centre of the casket, along with Blake's angel, and — higher up — the Cemetery itself. The larger geographical area, including Peckham and Dulwich, began to define Nunhead Cemetery: the living heart placed back in the corpus of south London. I became lost in the stress induced by my mum's illness and further lost in this obsessive journey into, and around, Nunhead Cemetery.

This morning I followed the local postman into the Cemetery, curious as to where the Cemetery's post is actually *delivered*. I watched as he walked towards the West Lodge, the deep Royal Mail flash of his jacket lighting up red in the early sun, the only colour against the dusty paths of the Cemetery. There was something about his build that seemed familiar, the way his shoulders rose in slow peaks towards the sloping tip of his balding head. Then I realised what it was: his shape was like the many headless figurines I'd seen in

Victorian cemeteries. If it was twilight his outline could easily have been confused with that other architectural death feature: the closed urn, half-covered with a shroud, which appears unexpectedly in the Cemetery like a bird of prey perched on its granite nest.

The postman drops the letters into a small black box. I think of all the postmen in the country, red blood cells carrying the white, walking along the streets of quiet towns and villages forgotten by WiFi. A long way from the God-like announcements that come from the hills of south-east London. The postman walks back out, under the huge upturned torches — symbols of extinguished life — which are painted deep red on the Cemetery walls. His right shoulder straining with the weight of the mail sack, he continues his delivery along Linden Grove.

I look around. A few hundred yards in front of me is the burned-out Anglican Chapel which was set alight in the 1970s by bored teenagers who will now be in their sixties with their own wills written and burial plans made.

There's a scaffold to my left, erected around the East Lodge. In front of me a man is leading a circuit-training session for teenage boys. The boys are lying down with their bodies horizontal to the ground, facing the floor, doing press ups. Then they group into pairs to press-up facing a partner. As their bodies rise they lift a hand to shake the hand of the person facing them, hovering for a second on one hand before lowering themselves down again. Then they rise again — with their whole lives ahead of them.

I think back to the moment when I couldn't face this Cemetery directly, with a parent recently diagnosed with cancer, just over a decade after my dad had died of the same disease. But then the poets rose up to occupy me, offering me the diversion of their work, allowing me to make connections between their lives and the landscape they haunt. They have fed my obsession. In the end it was as if the markings were already there, laid down for me, and I just had to walk to make them visible. Over the past two years I've walked the perimeter around the Cemetery, mapping out the woods, pubs, colleges and houses of south-east London's dead poets — the richest landscape of poetic activity in London. Most importantly I've discovered twelve forgotten poets whose stories and work have spoken to me across the centuries of silence which surrounds it. And it might just be that these dead poets have got me through the past two years, raising my pulse through poetry and — in endless steady inclines — attaching me, somehow, to earth.

Grounding me in this cenotaph south.

White Feather, New Hawthorn

From London Stone ... to Norwood south
William Blake, *Milton*

We've been preparing to get together since the start of the year. Ten years since my dad died: a decade of trying to make a fact out of his passing. Although the true anniversary was back in the winter, we have saved the moment of ritual until late summer and the day has arrived.

Since the news, this week, of my mum's cancer, we've decided not to visit my dad's grave after all but to plant a tree, instead, in the wood that runs alongside the Cemetery. There is something peculiar about planting a tree — a growing thing — at this time of knowing that unwanted cells are growing in my mum's body. As they had grown before in my dad's body. We worked through all possible trees and settled on a hawthorn. When my mum first met my dad, she told us, they were living on Hawthorne Road in Bootle, Merseyside. And the hawthorn proves perfect as a tree to remember my dad with: it is associated with lovesickness. There is also a personal link through the strong connection with a book that has obsessed me since my teens, and that I've been reading again — by chance or an intuitive sense of timing — Robert Graves' *The White Goddess*. The hawthorn, according to Graves, is one of the thirteen sacred trees of ancient Celtic poetic lore, the triple-leafed trefoil being 'celebrated by the Welsh bards with praise out of all proportion to its beauty. Homer called it "the lotus" and mentioned it as a rich fodder for horses.'

The family makes its way to the wood in two groups. My mum has gone up ahead with my sister Jackie, her husband and my nephews and niece. My son Pavel is with me, my wife Sarah and my two brothers, Ste and David. My older brother David drives us towards Fox's Bank Lane, towards the woodland, but the road turns out to be closed for works. A steamroller drives towards us carrying a dozen shirtless men — each of them wearing luminescent headbands — leaving no room for any other vehicle to pass. The driver of a Volkswagen is asked to reverse back the way they came. We pull up in a small car park next to a housing estate, into the parking bays laid out meticulously as tennis courts. We walk in the late August sun towards the wood, past the Cemetery we're avoiding today. Above the Cemetery a pair of kestrels are circling, their serrated flat wingspans like crafted planks of wood.

We walk in single file along what could easily be a country road, against the oncoming cars. We find the entrance opposite Dursley Drive when we hear my sister shouting to us. The rest of the family appear like revenants from the side road. Then, like an amoeba, the two parts of the family meet: we hug, become one unit. We walk into the wood with the conifers casting angular shadows as we approach them.

I'm carrying the potted tree. Hawthorn is part of the rose family, my herbalist friend Maria Vlotides told me, and has affinities with the heart. It has been used in treatments for those with heart failure and, by association, has become a rich symbol for loss. That staple of McCabe gatherings — the party — won't take place today. Not with the slow absorption of the news of my mum's diagnosis.

Two paths open in front of us. We take a vote on which way to go — drawing on the natural pull of the landscape — and opt for the left. An opening appears through the conifers and we follow in to a sunlit circle of coarse grassland. The ground is wet from the recent rain. Pavel leads the adults forward and we assemble the tools we've brought. We use whatever we can to get some purchase on the dry earth: undersized trowels, a toy spade, our bare hands. Ten years ago I helped lower my dad's coffin into the ground, 0.8 miles (according to Google Maps) from here. As we lowered the coffin I remember the grave attendant saying, 'don't wrap your hands around the rope, it will pull you down'; and I remember thinking — in the raw grief of my early twenties — 'What the fuck do you know?' The weltering, open wound of that grief has since closed a little, but the news of my mum's cancer is picking at the stitches. As we dig, the earth is reluctant at first but then starts to give, in cool grey-black slabs of loam. When we've made a big enough hole in the ground the hawthorn slides from its plastic and sits upright in its new burrow. We start to pack it into the ground, filling the gaps around the dried white roots which — like the barbels on some ancient river fish — are hungry for the earth's nutrients.

We stand around the tree looking at it — as if it's some God we've made together. As if the tree has the answers. Then Pavel has an idea: 'Let's sit around the tree and tell stories about Grandad McCabe.' There isn't an adult among us who has a better idea. Pavel starts us off with the story I've told him about the Grandfather he never met — I think of their non-meeting often: their bodies flung across misaligned time. His story is about when Grandad McCabe was a boy and had a misdemeanour with a bottle of ketchup — a story I've told to him. Inspired by his dad's war ration mentality of adding milk to any near-empty sauce bottle, my dad — twelve years old and struck by his initiative — took a fresh bottle of sauce and split the contents into two bottles. He then added milk to both of them before placing them back into the cupboard. What he hadn't considered was the short shelf-life of milk. When his father came home and worked out what the bottled pink — already turning to yoghurt — actually was, my dad got the birthright of all children of the fifties: a clip around the ear.

Pavel finishes the story then looks at me and asks: 'Did I get all the details right?' Yes, I tell him. I tell them the account of the Christmas morning when I'd received a new set of golf clubs and we set off in the fog to the local golf course — me, my dad, my brother and my brother-in-law — and halfway through the round we heard a shout: we turned around and my dad had climbed to the top of a tree and was waving at us. I wonder now if the tree was a hawthorn? Then everyone has a story and we sit around listening to them — the summation of the pilgrimage. My mum tells us how one time when she had stayed in a hotel with my dad — after too much to drink — he had sleepwalked into another room and urinated in the sink before getting into bed with a bearded man. Fortunately he woke up before the man did, and quietly tiptoed back to the right bedroom. Jackie then tells us about another time when my dad — also after some level of alcohol had been taken, a recurring theme — had thought that her pet rabbit had escaped and walked around the garden for an hour carrying the hutch, shouting the rabbit's name — 'Smoky! Smoky!' — until he realised that Smoky was in the hutch all along. The rabbit had been hiding in the corner. We hear about him camping as a boy and the time he climbed through the window of an expensive holiday home and kept lookout while his friend defecated into a vase, for a prank, and put it back on the shelf. There might be some class symbol involved in this. Mostly the stories revolve around his kindness — how he spent his weekends helping us to pursue our hobbies and

passions — and his wit, the sharp edge of his insight. I can distinctly remember him, on a holiday in Butlins, holding his own with the stand-up comic who'd decided to single him out from the crowd.

We talk ourselves into silence. For the quickest of moments time moves me into the future and I have this crashing, debilitating moment of picturing us here, telling stories about my mum. I know she must have felt that today too. We walk from the tree, leaving it to the elements to allow it to take root. Sarah finds a white feather besides the tree: a message from the dead, she says. Jackie shows us her tattoo of a white feather which she got for my dad. We leave the tree behind, to take root before bearing its first flowers next Spring, we hope, as a mayblossom. The path leads us back the way we came. Our only agenda now is to eat together, and drink. Not with the gusto of past family parties but we'll see in the early hours, holding tight to these precious moments — even under the pinch of stress — of being together.

As I'm lying in bed, after the Chinese restaurant and the drinks, I think about Nunhead Cemetery. When I get there the feeling will be one of connection with the physical world — the words of the poets will make it cohere. I remember a stand-in teacher in primary school who came in on Friday mornings and, on one occasion, read to us a poem about ivy growing up a wall. I realised later that the poem was really about time, or — more excitingly to my young mind — about two things *at the same time*. It struck me as a kind of magic that metaphor could work like that. It was the first occasion I can remember in which time made sense to me: the abstract made physical. My search for a lost dead poet might also be my search for that connection and discovery in language, the rush of that first grasp of what poetry can do: something I've spent my whole life thinking about — fixating on — as both a poet and poetry librarian. A handle — through language — attached to the vagaries and abstractions that so much of life is composed of. The rest of my class at school may have slept through that magical poem about time and ivy as many people seem to sleep through a life without poetry. Most of those who read it go for what's already known and available; few go underground to read the forgotten dead at first hand. But can I really face the Cemetery after what's happened this week?

I may be dreaming now as I picture the inside of the Cemetery that I'm yet to visit, flourishing with new life, each vine in a race for the light that breaks through the trees above. And there, at the end of a path of broken headstones — obelisks, roods and broken angels — will be a poet forgotten to time, one that gives me the words to live by. I will have a feeling then of finding poetry for the first time again, as on that Friday morning poetry class when moss and ivy collided through my mind and the world stood still for a moment. Perhaps all along I've been looking for that particular poem, that precise moment? I fall asleep thinking of a robin, landing on a headstone, tilting the wood knot of its head, listening: the word and the thing as one.

22ⁿᵈ August 2014

I let Pavel play with the old red garage. The one that my Grandad made for my dad in around 1956. PAUL'S GARAGE it says across the top in white paint. I remember why we called our son Pavel: Slavic for Paul. He said 'Will you one day give this to me, then I'll give it to my son?' Then he continues, in an exaggerated loop: 'then his son then his son then his son then his son then his son then his son then his son.' For the first time primogeniture hit him. There's a few seconds of silence and then he asked: 'Is that the way life works?'

23ʳᵈ August 2014

I think of all the things I love about my mum. They seem easier to see now. Her kindness, her humour, the way she thinks of our needs before hers. The way she loses words like some people lose keys. That time a few weeks ago when she was trying to describe her favourite lipstick, a pink — definitely something pink, she said, before describing an item of clothing that Mexicans wear: Sombrero? my sister Jackie said. No, she said: begins with P. Pon. Poncho. Poncho Pink! I love the way she bends titles and phrases into unexpected new meanings. Christmas lists crackle with mix-up potential. That time she went to a DVD shop and asked for Bend it with Beckham. When my younger brother Ste took a boyfriend home my mum asked if they'd like some 'bread and coumous', pronouncing the coumous with a distinct hard 'c'? Did she do it to make them laugh? Ste's never forgotten it. I told myself, again, her favourite joke — the one she's been telling to us for as long as I can remember. A little girl is at home, with no clothes on and asks her mother if she can play outside and the mother says:

No, it's raining. The girl says: Okay, but if I put on my hat can I look out the window?

24th August 2014
She was told today that she'll have to choose between a lumpectomy or a mastectomy. The removal of a breast or the removal of the isolated, cancerous flesh. The lump is six centimetres deep as well as wide. Think of it, she was told, as if it is a globe.

25th August 2014
A new world.

Angels Planted in Hawthorn Bowers: William Blake at Peckham Rye

Tarry no longer; for my soul lives at the gates of death.
I will arise and look forth for the morning of the grave.
I will go down to the sepulcher to see if morning breaks!
I will go down to self annihilation and eternal death...
  William Blake, *Milton*

I'm half a mile from Nunhead Cemetery, on Peckham Rye, when poetry — not for the first time — finds me out. Last week's news about my mum's cancer makes any cemetery the last place I want to be today. But I have a feeling that Nunhead Cemetery needs to be mapped within its social and geographical context. There is a strong series of poetic links surrounding it that comprise something of a mythology of their own. Today I'm looking for the tree in which the young William Blake saw an angel.

The first angel he saw attended his birth in a hosier's shop in Soho. No sooner was he swaddled, named and placed in the line of an ever-growing family, than he was out walking the streets of London. When he was around four he was beaten by his mother for claiming to have seen the Prophet Ezekiel under a bush. From then on he walked looking upwards, heading for the southern hills. When he was about eight he spotted an angel tangled in the boughs of a tree on Peckham Rye. This time it was his father who threatened to beat him though the myth tells us that his mother intervened to prevent it from happening — she seemed to be warming to this wayward child and had started to hang up examples of his drawings and poems in her chamber. Blake's road to the visionary was at first obstructed by his rational parenting though he persevered against their advice until they gave in and helped him on his artistic path.

It's down to Blake's nineteenth century biographer, Alexander Gilchrist, that we get the clearest picture of the walk Blake took to Peckham Rye on the day that the angel appeared to him:

> sauntering along, the boy looks up and sees a tree filled with angels, bright angelic wings bespangling every bough like stars. Returned home he relates the incident, and only through his mother's intercession escaped a thrashing from his honest father, for telling a lie.

Accusations that the poet is a liar go back to Plato's *Republic*, a work in which the philosopher banned poets from his ideal state for telling lies. But there are few poets whose mythology of being born into poetry — and the visionary confidence involved — could take on Plato from such an early age. As Blake matured as an artist his visions became wilder, leading to a unique creationist mythology that allowed him to see the world through the tension between elemental energies. His early visions of angels became grist to his creative mill — if he were scolded for seeing them this only served to prove that Albion was becoming nulled by rational forces, voided of imagination. Blake would later call on all citizens to use their imagination to invoke their own visions. As he wrote in 'Jerusalem':

> I must Create a System, or be enslav'd by another Man's.
> I will not Reason & Compare: my business is to Create.

Gilchrist had attended the Manchester Art Treasures exhibition in 1857 and had been drawn to a handful of Blake's images. They were tiny, just a few inches square, but there was more life in them than anything else that Gilchrist saw among the large scale paintings on the walls. I've seen these works myself at Tate Britain — even now, the casual, handwritten texts beneath the inked drawings are as modern as anything in the gallery, calling to mind iconic CD sleeves — but it took a brave Victorian to make the case. Blake had died in obscurity thirty years before Gilchrist's discovery of these; at that point his artworks were better known and more highly regarded than his poetry. Blake's poetry went against the metrical flow of the Victorians, creating a style which used long, ampersand-connected lines — laid down as quickly as frescoes — within an aesthetic which gave equivalence to text and visual elements. Thanks to the energies of Gilchrist, as the century slid towards the decadent, Blake the poet was at last finding an audience. When Anne Gilchrist, Alexander's wife — who had completed the Blake biography after her husband's death — had sent a copy to Tennyson, saying that she hoped it might 'win some share of your interest & sympathy', we know what a long shot that was. Tennyson would never fully grasp what Blake was driving towards, though a recent discovery does reveal that he owned a copy of Blake's *Book of Job*.

We also get a sense of how outside of the fold Blake was from a speech recorded at the reopening of his burial place, Bunhill Fields, in 1869. Bunhill Fields had been closed to the public since 1832 (five years after Blake's death) and in an address to the crowd the Chairman of the Bunhill Fields Preservation Committee, Charles Reed MP, made a point of mentioning the significant dead in the Cemetery — and Blake was not amongst those named:

> Not the 'rude forefathers' are buried here, but the founders of families, the pious and learned pastors and teachers of every religious community, not divines alone but men distinguished in literature, science and art, whose names are household words in every clime; John Bunyan, Daniel Defoe and Isaac Watts are the property not of any nation but of all mankind.

Blake had spent his artistic life encouraging the spiritual well-being and rights of mankind — 'Everything', he wrote, 'is an attempt to be human' — but he was far from embraced as the property of his nation.

There are, of course, many incarnations of Blake, and the tangled bracken of his poetic style would take decades to gain traction in readership. Gilchrist could only position him as a *visionary*, though we can see now that the mystical elements of Blake's work also contain a close engagement with the political crises of his time. The angel that presided over his birth also carried a Republican blade. In his work the major political figures of the time would thrash it out with Adam's split energies within the visionary city — a fictionalised London — that Blake called Golgonooza. The real world is intensified with the energy and drama with which Blake detailed his mythology.

I've reached the southern end of the park where the smell of dank running water wakes me from Blake's mythology to this landscape he knew. One of London's underground rivers, the River Peck, provides the pull to this part of Dulwich. The Peck was once a tributary of the Earl's Sluice which had drained into a basin separating Deptford from Camberwell and Bermondsey, thereby defining the boundaries of Southwark and giving Peckham its name: 'village on the river Peck'. Similarly to the River Effra, Victorian engineering rechanneled the Peck, which became part of the underground sewer. It now splutters into the park at the edge of Peckham Rye but soon disappears underground again before it even reaches the other side of the park. The Peck would have been here on the day that Blake saw his angel, and the poets — as he'd have known too — had followed the river before: Chaucer's pilgrims, travelling from the Tabard in Southwark, stopped at a point along the Earl's Sluice which ran under a bridge on what is now the Old Kent Road. It was here that they stopped to decide who would tell the first story on the pilgrimage:

> 'Lordinges, herkneth if yow leste!
> Ye woot youre forward, and it yow recorde.
> If evensong and morwe-song acorde,
> Lat se now who shal telle the firste tale.'

The Stanford's Library Map of 1862-71 shows an area en route called 'black ditch' and I think of a line from the start of Blake's 'Jerusalem' — remembering that Peckham was a part of Surrey until relatively recently:

> In all the dark Atlantic vale down from the hills of Surrey
> A black water accumulates, return, Albion! return!

You have to go through Dis to reach the Paradiso. Blake's gift is to make the real landscape of London appear as strange as Dante's visions of hell, purgatory and paradise. The real landscape that Blake knew is transformed through imagination; the closer we get to his creative world, the closer we come to tracking his relationship with London.

It's been argued that sightings of ghosts take place above

underground rivers, that spectres are the humidity-clouds of England's rising damp. Others have argued that underground rivers are the literal conduits for spirits that enter these channels. What could provide more draw for Blake than the underground drag of a hidden river, from which visions rise and where a clear line to past poets could be sensed?

And then there were the surrounding hills where the developing poet could captivate the city as audience. There would also have been more secular attractions for the young poet. There had been a market in Peckham up to the eighteenth century. Stephen Inwood, in his *A History of London*, talks of how the suburban fields of London were the playgrounds of children as there was so little in the way of entertainment in the city. From the medieval period places like Peckham drew the poor like iron filings to its magnetic core:

> William Fitzstephen's description of London in the 1170s offers us a glimpse of the lives of children and adolescents, taking fighting cocks to school on Carnival day, and then going out to play ball in the suburban fields. These fields were Londoners' main playgrounds, the scene of mock mounted combats on Sundays in Lent, and of 'archery, running, jumping, wrestling, slinging the stone, hurling the javelin beyond a mark and fighting with sword and buckler' in the summer.

Blake walked from Soho to Peckham: all lanes and paths led to the Surrey Hills. Peckham Rye was then at the base of Nunhead Hill, which would later become Nunhead Cemetery, built around seventy-five years after Blake's sighting here. Despite being buried in the north of the city, in Bunhill Fields, Blake's most satisfying walking route was always to the south. Ian Sinclair stated this at a lecture he gave at the Swedenborg Hall on 2nd November 2007 (and later published as *Blake's London: The Topographic Sublime*):

> The descriptions of Blake, from childhood, are of walking out, pushing out from the centre — because he is born at the centre, in Soho — moving into the folds of the surrounding hills. The hills to the south tend to be associated with visionary experience, trees of angels in Peckham Rye. The trips to the north were always painful.

Sinclair then quotes a letter from Blake to John Linnell, written towards the end of the poet's life:

> For I am again laid up by a cold in my stomach. The Hampstead air, as it always did … When I was young, Hampstead, Highgate, Hornsey, Muswell Hill, and even Islington, and all places north of London, always laid me up the day after, and sometimes two or three days, with precisely the same complaint, and the same torment of stomach.

It is pertinent that it is the location of one of these places that made Blake feel ill — Islington, near to Bunhill Fields — which has become his burial place. Blake had walked to the Surrey Hills as late as the 1820s, the last decade of his life. Blake read the hidden energies of the city — the underground pulls and anachronistic dead ends — better than any poet who came before and has laid down a personal map of the city that poets, walkers, spiritualists and readers have found useful since.

When Blake visited Peckham, the great era of cemetery building was yet to have begun south of the river with Nunhead,

West Norwood, Camberwell Old and New Cemeteries, Brockwell and Ladywell Cemeteries still to be built. It was only recently that the exact spot of Blake's grave in Bunhill Fields was rediscovered by Luis and Carol Garrido. Gravestones had been taken away in 1965 to make way for lawns — another act of charlatan revisionism of the dead that I've become used to while searching for buried poets — and the Blake Society is currently raising funds to mark the exact spot of the burial. Given Blake's strong feeling for the downwards pull of the compass, along with the mislocation of his headstone in Bunhill Fields and the endless threat of the digger and drill to the cemetery, his remains may have been better placed in Nunhead Cemetery, on this southern ground that he loved so much. However, and like so much else in Blake's time on earth, the timings were wrong: he would have had to have lived for another decade for the Cemetery to be built. There would have been a dissenter's corner waiting for him.

Blake's boyish instinct to walk towards the current site of Nunhead Cemetery — extending Chaucer's line from the sluice on Old Kent Road — marks the Peckham and East Dulwich area as a distinct feature in London's poetic folklore. Will the forgotten poets rise from the grounds of Nunhead, reach up for their fifteen minutes of readership? I need to level myself, be first of all ready to meet them: never enter a cemetery off-balance. Perhaps these dead poets should be pleased to be buried on the site of Blake's richest and most joyous path, even if it was one that nearly got him whipped when he returned home to Soho. Blake went out from his centre to miles of open fields and hills and reached the fringe — perhaps even walked across the open space — of what would become Nunhead Cemetery. In Blake's mythology, time exists in overlaps. The energies of the future dead would have been sensed by him; Nunhead's future dead poets were already here. The fields that the boy Blake walked through were divided into hyper-rationalist structures akin to the Enlightenment mind. No wonder the boy looked upwards from the fields that were divided into enclosures and farmers' private land. Blake skips the fences alongside the yet-to-be-built graveyard that would claim so many of London's children into its borders. Where the angel in the tree would soon become the symbol of memorials.

In 2011 the artist John Hartley worked with the support of the Blake Society and the Forestry Commission to plant a tree for Blake on Peckham Rye. Ian Whittlesea, another artist, created a piece called *Oak Tree on Peckham Rye (for William Blake)*. In a playground on Goose Green, just a few hundred yards from the north-west corner of Peckham Rye, there is a mural for Blake that has been vandalised over the years. These are all such lovely, spirited remembrances of Blake, but I want to get closer to the *exact* tree where Blake stood to watch his angel — and I have a lead that the others missed. A lead which was in Blake's poems all along.

I look out across this triangular, tapering hood of grass that connects East Dulwich with Nunhead, looking for a spot to pin the angel's wings to. A robin lands near my feet: a clockwork curio, waiting for me to make the first move.

I've done my research — at least the kind of research that Blake would have approved of — in sky-watching for tangential connections. When *The Guardian* reported on John Hartley's tree being planted in 2011 they talked of 'William Blake, who claimed to have seen an oak', but this isn't written in the only account we have of Blake's vision of the angel given to us by Alexander Gilchrist. Gilchrist had spoken to someone who had known Blake — albeit three decades after the poet's death. 'A *tree*', he reported, 'filled with angels'. The kind of tree wasn't specified. This has led me to mine Blake's poems, looking for all references to 'angels' and 'trees', taking the view that all the significant mythological aspects of Blake's life are somewhere here, in the work itself. There was, in the end, no gap between his life and work. And in the poems themselves he mentions angels and trees hundreds of times. I worked on this for weeks, even while watching Albion go by outside the window of a train, on a Good Friday, as I was diverted en route from Marylebone to Liverpool. I chased down each reference, pinning any clue for the exact spot of Blake's tree. A man across the table beat his smart phone with his fist as the football scores came in. A young couple lost themselves in the novels they'd brought with them, the genius José Saramego in the original Portugese. Bank Holiday England rattled inside a second class coach.

My contribution to England's rattling carriage of passions and impulses that day was to find that Blake uses angels and trees as symbols for very different purposes, depending on context. Angels can be guides, guardians, heralds, protectors of purity and innocence. Trees symbolise knowledge, peace, freedom, terror, decay, temptation, poison, barrenness, ageing, loneliness, separation, death. By the time the train had pulled in briefly at Lichfield Trent Valley I realised I'd made some gains, identifying four poems that reference both an angel *and* a tree. As I closed in on the clues the man in front of me slammed his phone into his forehead. I looked at the poems more closely, then found something solid: a link. In one of Blake's verse letters, written 'To Thomas Butts, 22 November 1802', he gives the only instance of an angel specifically *in* a tree.

With Angels planted in Hawthorn bowers
And God himself in the passing hours,
With Silver Angels across my way
And Golden Demons that none can stay
With my Father hovering upon the wind...

A hawthorn, not the oak attributed to Blake by Ian Whittlesea and John Hartley. An oak in bloom is a thick fuzz of dark green — it has none of the angel-inducing, limber, white-flecked movement of the hawthorn. Peter Ackroyd, in his book *Albion*, had come extremely close to making the connection between the species of Blake's tree and the angel the boy saw but perhaps due to the speed with which Ackroyd moves through history he couldn't see what was right in front of him when he wrote:

> The hawthorn was the home of fairies, and the hazel offered protection against enchantment; the great oak itself descended into the other world. It is Milton's "monumental Oke." As a child William Blake saw angels inhabiting the trees of Peckham Rye.

If Ackroyd would have paused for a moment here he would have realised Blake's tree could only have been a hawthorn: the home of the fairies. Young hawthorns often appear more as shrubs than trees, though they can grow to fifteen metres. I remind myself that Blake, not great in height in adulthood, would have been a small boy looking upwards: even a medium-sized hawthorn would have been easily big enough to house an angel. The white blossom in May — which provides its alternative name of *whitethorn* — could easily morph into a moving angel: a gauze of shimmering light. There is a further reason why Blake's father would have beaten him: it is written in folklore that bringing a hawthorn into the home was talismanic of death. I wonder if the young Blake dared to take some white blossom home with him? Blake's hawthorn also knits my past weeks of personal stress into the mythology of this tree. In Blake's worldview all time hurtled along in one synchronous channel: 'nor one Event of Space unpermanent but all remain' (*Milton*). Blake's hawthorn allows me to see the tree we planted for my dad as blossoming in parallel — even future time — to the house on Hawthorne Road that my mum had lived in when she first met him.

Further, in my reading around Nunhead Cemetery, I've discovered that the hawthorn tree has been a presence there too. The landscape of the Cemetery had deliberately included flora and foliage of all kinds, the hawthorn among them. Ackroyd, on the right lines this time, connects the hawthorn with language — another reason why Blake's angels would appear in 'hawthorn bowers': 'The mark or symbol of the hawthorn tree is to be found in the runic alphabet of the ancient British tribes, as if the landscape propelled them into speech.' Fresh leaves were printing in the burgeoning poet's consciousness.

An oak for Blake's vision is wrong in its lore. An oak is defined under medieval Brehon Law as a chieftain tree, with higher fines for felling than the hawthorn, which was a peasant tree. Blake was just a boy but in his nascent world of intuition he would have felt keenly this difference — he was always more akin to the original geniuses of the reprobates than the elect (to use the terms of his later mythology). Jesus, in Blake's mythology, was a transgressor, and it was the thorns of the hawthorn tree that many believed were used to knit the crown placed on Jesus' head. Blake's father, Gilchrist tells us, threatened to lash him with his belt when he returned home for telling lies. The precocious self-seer is beaten towards independence. This makes further sense of Butts' letter-poem, which not only presents an angel in a specific tree but is immediately followed with the line: 'With my Father hovering upon the wind.' Blake's fall from the heavenly vision, fulfilled by his father, is brought together in these lines.

I follow the Peck, looking for Blake's hawthorn. The chances of finding it are slim, maybe even impossible: I have a booklet called *Peckham Rye Park Tree Trail* by Christopher Howard. It lists forty-three trees and no hawthorn, though I have found one myself that is too small to be the one that Blake encountered. So I begin checking along the fringes of Rye Lane, following outside the lines of the park and into the wider expanses of the area as it was laid out in Blake's time. A hawthorn, I've found, can live for up to 400 years. Blake would have spotted the angel in the Peckham hawthorn around 1765, just 250 years ago — there's still lots of life left, potentially, in the tree he saw: years of further mayblossoming and bespangling of angels. I arrive at the Peck where it runs through an arched grill in the western corner. The rain has been coming down in gallons for what seems like months, changing the Peck's usual Bovril-like *jus* into something that can almost be called a stream.
 Peckham Rye Park was opened on farmland in 1894 and included a new landscape of enclosed garden areas. Since then there has been a fondness for Japanese design, ornamental bridges with wooden slats that lead joggers and dog-walkers over the sewer. The Peck weaves between the children's park and the communal outdoor gym. A sign attached to the rails of the children's play area pulls innocence and experience into reverse: ADULTS MUST BE

ACCOMPANIED BY A CHILD. Blake would have liked this: the child is father to the man when it comes to engendering visions.

I walk past the training area. A sallow-looking woman with green-tinged cheeks — suggesting that breakfast might be rising to meet the sunrise — lies next to her trainer. He wears a t-shirt declaring *trainer* — just in case the relationship might be misunderstood — and is counting down her crunches. A short man in a hoodie is doing dips with ecstatic heaves. Someone is kickboxing their own shadow. I look up at the trees: oaks all around. John Rocque's map of Surrey, created in 1768, shows the surrounding miles of Peckham Rye as a patchwork quilt of tree-enclosed fields. Occasional houses dot the landscape like infected pixels. By 1830 Georgian houses had begun to line the route from the Common up Rye Lane to Peckham. Blake would have walked from field to field, unfettered as the lapwings or hares that would have passed across his ardent strides through the long grass. His small room in Soho, the banging anvil of his father, was way back on another horizon — in another city.

A flattened can of Tennent's lies flat, bound by weed, at the base of the trickling Peck. Scotland's favourite pint has fans everywhere. In the trees across from a diminutive bridge, culled from some origami, two magpies are chasing a squirrel through the branches: cloned henchmen, clinical in the defence of their black and white flags. The squirrel, like a bulimic Friar Tuck, scrambles and dives into the air — clawing at a dipping branch to save it from plummeting down into the water. At the border of the park the river disappears underground, heading towards Telegraph Hill. Flotsam gathers around the grille: a red plastic comb with broken teeth, a plastic pack inhaling and exhaling pondweed like a detached lung in a frog pond. A football playing-card drifts across

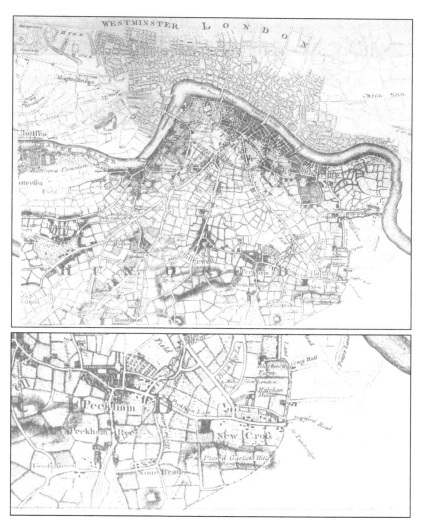

John Rocque, 'A Map of Surrey, 1768' (with 'None Head' area expanded)

the surface too quickly for me to detect the wage-slick face of the player. An actual football is stuck behind the rails of the grille: a severance behind portcullis. A bike flies past me over the bridge and I turn to look — a female cyclist wearing a shining gold helmet.

I follow the stream towards a dwarfed embankment covered with vine and bramble; the river disappears underneath, back through subterranean stone, above which a group of workmen are tipping out a truckload of woodchips. The river momentarily reappears — then disappears again — towards the Clock House, a pub which boasts (along with the delicious charred barley of its London Stout) a function suite called The Blake Room. Find your angel from the pub window.

I turn back on myself, facing in the direction of the higher ground of Linden Grove and Nunhead Cemetery. I follow the Peck past the dull gold medallion of the drowned Tennent's can and onto the very edge of the park, walking along the early morning commuter's congestion of Peckham Rye Road. A house has been scaffolded courtesy of SCAFFOLD AGENCY LTD. Commuters are hunched inside the anti-confessional of the bus stop. A murder of crows is taking exaggerated steps, as if wading through wet tarmac, towards a tree. One of them looks up into the branches and I check too. False alarm: oak. I carry on walking.

The diurnal joggers are doing the rounds, some with dogs in tow. Further afield is a young mum jogging with a three-wheeled pram, pumping the post-natal serotonin. Perhaps angels rise later in these days of social media? A tyre shop is just opening. A corvus shrieks. Curtains start to twitch. What was once Surrey is now firmly London: an arrow points me to the London Network. I think of how Blake laid down the route by foot, walking slowly as commuters now run for buses. I'm every nine-to-fiver's nightmare: a dawdling zombie locked into textland.

I cross over the road and suddenly stop at the drive of a semi-detached house: a hawthorn tree is there, though it's too young — too much of a sapling — to date from Blake's time. It's growing at a barely conceivable angle with just enough room for the Audi to roll in alongside. Vorsprung durch Technik takes ascendancy over the angels. The tree cranes its neck to reach the veranda. This is a new hawthorn for the professional classes — an adornment to the perfect middle class house — and not one established in myth by a pre-pubescent poet. I walk along Peckham Rye road again, towards the Peck-end of the Rye, past where the once open land between Waveney House and Rother House has been converted into car parks.

The blocks of flats opposite have reproduced themselves with symmetrical cloning, right down to the detail of the windows. Quaint English Bauhaus. There is a map of Peck Hill and Rye Hill Park Estate laid out in the colours of a Butlin's map: south London joyland. I check the Rocque map, completed almost to the date that Blake was here: this would have been open fields, the edge of an enclosure separating the Rye from what was most likely private fields. I weave through the outskirts of the estate. The land around Frome House is lined with what look to be ancient trees, bark knotted in folds. The trees grow within yards of the windows of the flats, past the patched light that breaks through the skeleton of a scaffold. The trees are trying to grow inwards, towards the sun. There is what looks like a hawthorn here — gnarled and ancient-looking, awesome in scale, towering over the flats. This is a hawthorn to take on the oaks. A hawthorn worthy of any angel. The sign on the scaffold next to it reads: CHILDREN STAY OFF.

In the flats around the tree people are using their balconies for drying clothes or growing flowers. One balcony houses a satellite dish and eight broken bike wheels. This could be it, I tell myself; the spot where Blake stood, watching the branches whir with the spangling spectre of the angel. On the highest edge of the common, along the route of the River Peck, within half a mile of Nunhead Cemetery. When angels hit the highpoint the poets follow, to witness and broadcast the news. And no poet forgets their moments of poetic becoming, as Blake wrote nearly forty years later:

> The White-thorn lovely May
> Opens her many lovely eyes...

26ᵗʰ August 2014
'Looks like grey thunder,' Pavel said today, looking out of the window.

30ᵗʰ August 2014
I know I'm in trouble: I booked tickets for a Beckett play to cheer myself up. A Purcell Room performance of three late plays. I sat in the dark, my friend Sophie next to me, waiting for the performance to begin. All of us are always too close to ourselves − Beckett knows this. I saw the three plays − Not I, Footfalls *and* Rockaby *− as a triptych of grief. The mouth in* Not I *as disembodied from decorum to the point where it flies by its own light towards the personal truth of hysteria − the hurled words of a troubled mind. 'Mother, mother,' it begins: 'were you asleep?' The mother replies: 'Deep asleep ... I heard you in my deep sleep ... There is no sleep so deep I would not hear you there.' The actress, Lisa Dwan, strode across the stage in raised shoes with a long white dress trailing from her hips. Mother and daughter have grown as one − make sense of themselves through themselves − with the fragments of the years passing through them. The daughter says that it's the sound of her mother's footsteps she needs to hear, to stay sane. They are the visible and invisible of the same mind, the duet of a single life.* Rockaby *is the strongest text of the three. Beckett's dramatic conceits − a mouth, footsteps, a rocking chair − are the barest essentials that are needed, the shadowplay of Plato's cave. At the end of the piece the rocking woman does not ask for 'more': she dies, nods off to sleep one more time − for all time − in the chair facing the window.*

Entering Nunhead Cemetery

> ... *all the Great*
> *Events of Time start forth & are concievd in such a Period*
> *Within a Moment: a Pulsation of the Artery.*
> William Blake, *Milton*

I'm walking towards Nunhead Cemetery, about to enter. The walk around Peckham Rye searching for Blake's tree has grounded this place in a larger mythology: if the trees were less dense in the Cemetery I could look down the old Nunhead Hill and see the boy Blake walking across the fields. Blake would have loved it here: birdsong, Gothic architecture, leafiness. Thriving woodland with quick access to the centre of London.

I've walked from Upland Road, the centre of the casket I've drawn on my map. I relish the names of the pubs as I walk: The Old Nun's Head and The Pyrotechnist's Arms. Developments along Nunhead Lane fit the same template as all London suburban high streets now: estate agency next to a fishmonger's, a bookmaker's next to a bakery. *Time Out* calls Nunhead a 'scrappy little no-man's land': all the more reason to love it.

I stand on the corner of Nunhead Grove for longer than I should, listening to the birdsong inside the Cemetery. I look towards the city to get a real sense of the height I'm at. Strata SE1 at Elephant & Castle stares back like a triple-eyed owl. An owl stripped of its curves and incarcerated inside a USB stick.

The outside walls of the Cemetery are yellow-green, flecked

with ashen black. Along the street a piece of old Christmas tinsel tumbles in figures of eight along the pavement. Trees grow over the top of the walls, out onto the road. The walls of the Cemetery seem to be buckling with the pressure of the nature inside seeking the light. No fortress holds forever.

I'm ready to go in, but nervous — nervous about the sheer volume of death inside, the accumulation of decades of buried bodies. There's one thing I have to do before going inside: call my mum. Am I holding her hand or is she holding mine? She started the course of radiotherapy this week and is still recovering from the effects of the chemo: hot flushes, aches, tiredness, loss of appetite — the hangover from the internal blasting of the medication. The radiowaves she'll receive have been tailored by mathematics to attack where the cancer was, seeking out lymph nodes, destroying any inadvertent growth. I'm listening, so glad to be able to stand here and simply talk with her — 'You don't ask questions', she says, then adds: 'You just trust that they know what they're doing'.

A green parakeet flies over me and into the Cemetery. Across the street a woman is shouting into her phone: 'Can you hear me?' My mum's telling me that she's found a new shortcut to the Clock Tower — the Victorian workhouse which overlooks her house — through a field and past the old union workhouse. Mostly she's getting taxis to where she needs to get to. She has an appointment at eleven today and needs to shower: ushering herself towards where her body doesn't want to go. I remember the hiatus in full living during my dad's treatment, the pause in everyday pleasures replaced with the immersion into a sickening medical agenda with the one aim of having to get to a place — later — where happiness might be. It didn't work for my dad but I feel hopeful and positive for my mum — and in those feelings grateful that chance might be dealing us a better hand this time. Before we hang up we arrange to meet on Monday. Pavel and I will meet her for dinner, then go with her for her treatment.

Then I do it: I walk into Nunhead Cemetery.

The Cemetery is a dogwalker's paradise. There are dogs everywhere I look — even the canines want to make the most of this landscape. Good Mornings and salutes pass between owners. Labradors sniff at the earth, slavering for bones. THERE'S NO SUCH THING AS THE DOG POO FAIRY a poster declares. I look at the first headstones I can see: moss has written itself into the glyphs of the text, cancelling out language. Urns have toppled and crucifixes broken. A stone dog has been placed back to rest on a gravestone. A vine has broken a gravestone in half. Roods rest against the memorials they've fallen from. A whole borough of broken boughs, vines and branches is in front of me, each element seemingly working to bring all attempts to remember the dead down to earth level. The clamour of nature here is unlike any other cemetery I've been inside: I instantly fall in love with the place.

My first impressions confirm a poem I've read by John Gibbens (1959-2015) called 'Nunhead', which perfectly captures its atmosphere:

> ... but there's fox-taint still
> mingled with the warm humus of English jungle
> and a feast of lairs where trees have toppled the tombs.

I recall that John had lived for a while in Deia, Mallorca, where he worked in a bar and met Robert Graves. Everything is starting to fit.

I have a choice between turning right along Dissenters Road or left along Catacomb Path. Both appeal but today I go with the Dissenters. A woman's voice wakes me from the trance.

— Can I borrow your eyes for a sec?

The woman puts her phone in front of me: she wants to know which of the two numbers on the screen begins with '07'. They're both in a tiny blue font but I pick one out: the top one, I tell her. 'Thanks,' she says. 'I shouldn't have come out with my glasses.' I should have brought mine too: birds I can't detect at distance are in full throat, landing on broken angels and urns covered in stone shrouds. An angel raises a hand to the sky on the family vault of someone called E. W. Williams. Another at ground level has lost an arm. A fly lands for a second on the angel's chest.

I notice how many deaths here seem to have happened in the 1880s, confirming what I'd read in Ron Woollacott's *Investors in Death*, that after the initial slow uptake for burial here the Cemetery became lucrative and thriving: 'By 1876 business was "booming" in every direction'. Buy earth, fill it, cash up: the London Cemetery Company, which established Nunhead Cemetery, was every inch a business — I remind myself — not the selfless auteurs of a beautiful Gothic paradiso. Woollacott writes about a custom people had at this time for buying fresh flowers to adorn the graves. Greenhouses were positioned behind the Anglican chapel. I walk past the headstone of William John Terry of Rye Terrace who 'fell asleep in Jesus' in 1876. His widow Matilda was buried with him in 1902: 'blessed are the dead who die in the lord' the text reads.

I arrive at the St Paul's view, the trees coppiced back to give a clear perspective of the cathedral which is just under five miles away to the north. The view from here gives more than the cathedral: the Shard flashlights the skyline. You get a different sense of the city here and I notice how the Shard's design seems to replicate the obelisks around me. Stone turned to glass: the suburbs made central. Robert Graves in *The White Goddess* says that obelisks in ancient cultures represented the 'upper pole', reaching from the king to the heights: the hottest point attained by the sun. 'It expresses dominion over the four quarters of the world and the zenith.' Looking down on the city from here I can believe in that dominion. A bench has been positioned to allow people to take in the view and a man in a pink shirt is sitting on it, cradling a sausage dog. 'Hell of a view' he says. I ask him if this is the highest point of the Cemetery? 'No,' he says, 'but hell of a view!'

A member of the ground staff briefly stops mowing and looks at me — I realise he is missing an eye. I wonder how it feels to be in here every day, growing accustomed to the contours and eccentricities of the landscape, allowing the changes of the seasons to become part of the intuition that you feel for the work that needs to be done — at exactly that point in the always changing seasons. I envy his work — at least on days like this. I'm beginning to look at the cemetery as a body: growing, decaying, in need of a plan to sustain it. I think of how 'cancer' got its name from the crab which grows sideways, like the growth of unwanted cells: there is a kind of beautiful cancer at work in Nunhead Cemetery, the whole drive of nature pushing against nature, against any manmade structure that gets in its way — its only purpose is to grow, whatever is in its path. But I check myself: I'm starting to see the world through cancer. Sometimes things grow without permission but sometimes those things can be controlled too.

Now I'm here, inside, I'm thinking about the poets — how I'll seek out the work of those who turned to words in life, as an antidote to death. I stand for a while at the war graves, a modernist wall of names, dappled with leaf light. I turn and stare back across the Cemetery and — through the trees — the imagined miles to the Thames, absorbing this cenotaph south.

My poets are here, I think, somewhere in the undergrowth: beyond the coppicing of any editor.

6th September 2014

Now that the August heatwave has reached its peak, Autumn has come early. I may have willed it on, buying new bookshelves and putting my poetry books in order — from Chaucer to Anne Carson. As I'm writing this, voices drift in from people in their gardens, poking the coals of barbecues with the last of the summer willow. A dog is rattling its larynx in the twilight; wasps with flaking wings buzz around the window's nets.

7th September 2014

Today I found the wasp caught dead in the net like a charred chrysalis, as if its wings were of the same fabric as the net.

8th September 2014

I spoke to my mum on the phone; she had sardines on toast in front of her just as I called. She's determined to eat more, she said, to get stronger: to be ready for the surgery. No vodka in the house, the occasional glass of red. I'd forgotten that her scan was today. I was only ringing to hear her voice, or to see how she's getting on, as I say to her. We talked about her garden, the new patio door, the pending flower border. I said: speak to you later in the week, get back to your sardines before they get cold. She said: they were already cold. They came straight from the can.

9th September 2014

I wake at 5am with a headache. In a dream I was back in my childhood home, my dad was there. In a grey storm, full of static, we were trying to stop spirits from making it into the house. We were trying to stop them. Outside the dream I knew the spirits were cancer — and that even in my dream my dad couldn't stop them.

The White Goddess

I have been fostered in the land of the Deity,
I have been teacher to all intelligences,
I am able to instruct the whole universe.

Taliesin, *Book of Taliesin*

The year grows stranger. I'm returning to a book that has meant a lot to me over the years, Robert Graves's *The White Goddess*, finding that it now seems like a guide to the poetic landscape I've entered: hawthorns, hills and mothers. It also argues with conviction for an idea of what the 'true' poet is. This will prove useful for me as I become acquainted with Nunhead's lost poets. I first read this book as an undergraduate and have returned to it like a crook in the slackly commercial world of contemporary poetry, a manifesto for poetic inspiration, rooted in Celtic lore.

Over the years I've probably heard every take on how poetic inspiration works: the rabbit in the hat, the heart in the head, the eye in the tongue. Graves subtitled his book *A Historical Grammar of Poetic Myth* — a brilliant ruse on his part to substantiate his eccentric interpretations of myth with historic fact. This has helped me as a poet and, curiously, as a librarian: although Graves said that he wrote the near-500 pages of this tiny-typed manifesto in twelve weeks, it contains whole worlds of lost poetry, and ideas on poetry. And Graves has an ace up his sleeve: his ultimate self-belief *as a poet* which allows him to find 'true' poetry as coming from a line of Bards from ancient Europe. His polemic is based on an argument that the White Goddess — a matriarchal muse figure in many myths and cultures — has been the source of all true poetry ever written. Graves leaves it open to those reading his book to understand what 'true' poetry might be, though he gives many examples of what *he* considers it to be. Graves returns us to the language of poetic myth used in the Mediterranean and Northern Europe, arguing that there was 'a magical language bound up with popular religious ceremonies in honour of the Moon-goddess, or Muse, some of them dating from the Old Stone Age, and that this remains the language of true poetry.' This was later tampered with, he proposes, when invaders from Central Asia began to substitute patrilinear for matrilinear institutions. Then came the Greeks, such as Socrates and Plato, who questioned the status of poetry. Graves returns us to these pre-Socratic times to resurrect the impetus of the master poets; those who have since become trivialised by gleemen and official court writers: those without licence to improvise or freely use imagination. Graves describes the figure of the White Goddess as:

> A lovely, slender woman with a hooked nose, deathly pale face, lips red as rowan-berries, startlingly blue eyes and long fair hair; she will slowly transform herself into sow, mare, bitch, vixen, she-ass, weasel, serpent, owl, she-wolf, tigress, mermaid or loathsome hag … I cannot think of any true poet from Homer onwards who has not independently recorded his experience of her. The test of the poet's vision, one might say, is the accuracy of his portrayal of the White Goddess and of the island over which she rules. The reason why the hairs stand on end, the eyes water, the throat is constricted, the skin crawls and a shiver runs down the spine when one writes or reads a true poem is necessarily an invocation of the White Goddess, or Muse, the Mother of All Living, the ancient power of fright and lust — the female spider or the queen-bee whose embrace is death.

I took up the call of the White Goddess as an undergraduate, establishing this version of poetic myth as a religion for a while. This served two functions: it replaced the orthodox God I'd given up on in my late teens — perhaps too quickly — and also gave me a way of looking at literature that was outside the official university curriculum. At that time I was winding a blind path led by James Joyce and Graves' esoteric theory. What I hadn't noticed before — had less need to notice — is that the White Goddess is a muse that combines many incarnations, one of which is mother: 'She is the mother of all things.' Am I reading it again now my mum has cancer, I wonder, looking for something I'd missed before — some kind of answer or solace?

Graves also talks about the importance of physical high points to all 'true' poets, a subject pertinent to the poets of Nunhead Cemetery, who rest at sixty one metres above sea level. Maybe Graves is the hook I need to climb up to them? In his chapter on 'The Triple Muse' Graves recalls the seat of the Muse on Mount Parnassus. The muses had to be called from Helicon where Hippocrene, a spring, rose up. The word Muse, we are told, comes from the root *mont*, meaning mountain. I think of the high points around Nunhead Cemetery, Telegraph Hill (where Robert Browning lived) and the higher neighbouring peaks of Sydenham Hill and Forest Hill. There is a pull to poets in these high points, an irresistible urge for the heights: light, perspective, space. Blake and Browning travelled to pay homage to their creative forces on the outskirts, where the peaks pulled the metropolis into view. The other poets of their time must have appeared as specular distortions in the distance. As the critic Peter Howarth suggests, the White Goddess scorns the lowland poets 'ruled by the God Apollo's golden mean'. Graves saw his own first true poem as being 'Rocky Acres', written in 1919 with four collections behind him: that's how long it took him to feel his poetic authority assert itself.

> He soars and he hovers, rocking on his wings,
> He scans his wide parish with a sharp eye,
> He catches the trembling of small things,
> He tears them in pieces, dropping them from the sky...

But as I read *The White Goddess* now, there's something else in the text which I'd missed before, something which — like Graves' test of the true poem — makes the hairs on my arm and neck stand on end: the White Goddess has strong associations with the hawthorn. She is, in fact, a hawthorn-goddess. Graves first cites this reference in relation to the ancient Welsh poem, the *Cad Goddeu*, in a version by Taliesin. Graves traces the use of the hawthorn as a sign of bad luck:

> *Strong chieftains were the blackthorn*
> *With his ill fruit,*
> *The unbeloved whitethorn*
> *Who wears the same suit.*

Graves finds resonances of the various instances of the White Goddess in relation to hawthorn, including in Ovid's *Fasti*:

> the White Goddess who destroyed children after disguising herself in bird or beast form, and the hawthorn which was sacred to her might not be introduced into a house lest she destroyed the children inside.

The hawthorn also bears the name whitethorn: the same colour as the

Goddess. The tree gets its negative associations from the month of May which is, in folklore, an unlucky time of the year. The hawthorn is a tree of 'enforced chastity'. The Greek Goddess Maia, Graves tells us, was an incarnation of the White Goddess who used the hawthorn to cast spells. I think of the tree we planted for my dad, and also of Blake's tree. It makes perfect sense that Blake saw an angel in a hawthorn; it could have been the Goddess herself, in hybridised bird or beast form. 'The destruction of an ancient hawthorn is in Ireland attended with the greatest peril,' Graves writes.

I have received some bad news about the hawthorn I'd found on Peckham Rye: the tree is not, in fact, a hawthorn. I made contact with the Woodland Trust and found that the tree is a decorative, probably non-native, white-flowering cherry-blossom Prunus that would have been planted since Blake's arrival at Peckham. Although its blossom is very similar, this is not Blake's hawthorn. London erases its history, its nature and architecture, and perhaps Blake's tree has gone with it. It is also possible that it's still out there, beyond the narrower fringes of today's Peckham Rye. Perhaps, too, this is how Blake would like things to be: in the realm of eternal time and the imagination. We can all picture his angel-filled tree for ourselves. But I am pleased to have pinned its species to hawthorn — perhaps I can plant one for Blake later.

My journey into Nunhead Cemetery is becoming part of a bigger poetic landscape, much richer — and more complicated — than I thought, but a journey that will allow me to make sense of the geographical context of the Cemetery and provide a measure against which to read the work of the poets I find there.

So I start to dig further into the poetic activity around

Nunhead, in the wake of Blake's angel, and am stunned by the richness of what has happened around these undulating heights. The trail opens before me. I discover that the greatest poet of the late twentieth century, Barry MacSweeney, gave his final reading just down the road at Dulwich College. And then I receive a tip-off about a long-running reading series at a pub in Dulwich Village nicknamed 'The Dog'. The poet and experimental novelist B.S. Johnson wrote a piece about this series which leads me to finding that hundreds of poets travelled and gave readings here in the 1960s and '70s. I start to realise that the finding of Blake's hawthorn isn't a diversion away from Nunhead Cemetery so much as the start of a larger mapping of the area that must — via some of the best poets who have written — lead me deeper into Nunhead Cemetery with a clearer sense of the kind of great work that I'm looking for.

10th September 2014
My throat's been sore and I'm reading **Lear** *again. I paused over this:*

> *Lear. O! how this mother swells up towards my heart;*
> *Hysterica passio! down, thou climbing sorrow!*

I read the note in the text to find out what 'hysterica passio' means: 'The symptoms of this malady are described by Drayton, Polyolbion ... Edward Jordan, A Brief Discourse of a Disease Called the Suffocation of the Mother, *1605, p.5, who writes: "This disease is called by diverse names against our authors, Passio Hysterica, Suffocatio, Priefocatio, and Strangulatus uteri, Caducus Matricis, i.e. in English, the Mother of the Suffocation of the Mother, because, most commonly, it takes them with choking in the throat; and it is an affect of the mother or the wombe, wherein the principal parts of the bodie by consent do suffer diversely according to the diversitie of causes and diseases wherewith the matrix is offended."*

I trace the word **Matrix** *back through etymology, the word that the novelist B.S. Johnson had chosen for his final unfinished trilogy, the one that he never completed due to his suicide. 'Matrix', I find, relates to the environment, is a mass of fine-grained rocks, a printing mould, Keanu Reeves, a computer-generated martial arts world. But there at its root is this: womb. Matrix is Latin for womb. I am lost.*

11th September 2014
My mum has always been happiest with a plan, a pathway: however forked. She will have the whole breast removed with a temporary reconstruction

there and then. Remove the cancer and start to build.

12ᵗʰ September 2014
When I met my mum today she was wearing a bright green suit jacket and thick black shades. I don't know what a woman about to have a mastectomy should look like — but this isn't it. The September sun renews endorphins: we sat in the front beer garden of the Wetherspoons on Whitechapel (Liverpool) sipping cold pints of shandy at midday. She's drinking less and eating fruit, nuts, vegetables. She attended a session at the hospital, she said, for those who have already been through the same operation she'll have.

She saw their reconstructions, the quick recoveries of their bodies.

The Fall and Rise of Nunhead Cemetery

Where we feed what kills us, the thrush expends his song.
John Gibbens, 'Nunhead'

The London Cemetery Company was set up in 1836 after an Act of Parliament was passed to establish 'cemeteries for the Internment of the Dead, Northward, Southward and Eastward of the Metropolis'. Highgate was opened first, in 1839, becoming the company's northernmost location. Nunhead followed a year later as the southernmost necropolis. The Company was founded by Stephen Geary, an architect who had also been responsible for opening London's first gin palace in Aldgate in 1830. Geary later became teetotal, possibly in response to the sight of the liquid combustion he'd caused on the streets of London.

This was typical of Geary's tumultuous career: often his successes were his losses. He is said to have lacked business sense and was smitten with bad luck. His commission to create a new police station with a monument at St Pancras — to be named St George's Cross — had to be renamed King's Cross due to the death of George IV. As Catharine Arnold describes, the monument not only became a hazard to traffic but was too small to function as a police station. The building of the monument had been stalled but Geary was bankrupt and could do nothing about it, eventually conjuring, as Arnold puts it, 'a pathetic, eleven foot high concrete echo of what might have been'. Not only did the police move out of the building but — in an ironic twist of Geary's intentions — the lower part of the building became a licensed premises for alcohol. The Dionysian and deranged flocked towards it and in 1845 the monument was torn down. Geary died in London's final cholera epidemic and his tombstone at Highgate was lost to view until it was refound in the 1970s.

After Geary's initial work at Nunhead Cemetery, James Bunstone Bunning became the chief architect. Bunning was another figure who has suffered subsequent misfortune through the destruction of many of his most highly celebrated buildings. Caledonian Market, Holloway Prison and the Coal Exchange have all been wiped from the London map.

Nunhead was one of three planned new cemeteries commissioned to be built by the company, to total 150 acres across Surrey, Kent and Middlesex. The great age of death was well under way in the suburbs. Thomas Miller wrote about these changes in death practices on central London life in his *Picturesque Sketches of London Past and Present*:

> The streets were no longer darkened with funerals; you no longer saw men running in every direction with coffins on their heads, knocking at doors, and delivering them with no more ceremony or feeling than the postman delivers his letters. The solemn hearse and the dark mourning-coach now moved slowly along, and the dead were borne away to green and peaceful cemeteries, far removed from the dwellings of the living. Nuisances were removed — sewers were cleansed — the abodes of the poor purified, and at last rendered habitable.

The first cemetery built by the company was London's most celebrated and the one Geary chose to be buried in: Highgate. Nunhead followed with land being bought in 1839 and a new road planned between Deptford Lane (now Queen's Road), Peckham and Nunhead Lane. It is tempting to see Nunhead Cemetery as drawing the poets to the area but the poets were already here, drinking at the Nun's Head Tavern, a favourite haunt of local artisans.

In the 1850s Camberwell Old Cemetery on Forest Hill Road, and Brookwood Cemetery in Surrey were built, along with over a dozen new suburban cemeteries in London. This competition put considerable pressure on Nunhead's finances. West Norwood had already been established just two miles away and thrived (not least for dead poets, as I've written about in my book *In the Catacombs: A Summer Among the Dead Poets of West Norwood Cemetery*). The cemetery competition around Nunhead was fierce: the Roman custom for burying in the east was moving south. As Nunhead itself had benefited from the new commercial drive to create outer-London cemeteries, so the 1852 Metropolitan Internment Act — which forbade further burials in the inner city churchyards — encouraged privately-funded cemeteries to emerge on the landscape. This allowed for a challenge from new cemeteries to the hegemony of the first buccaneers such as the London Cemetery Company who had built Nunhead. In addition to Camberwell Old Cemetery, Brockley and Ladywell was established in 1858 (this was originally two cemeteries, Deptford and Ladywell, which had opened within a month of each other) which also developed its own dead poet alumni glittering with possibility: artist and modernist David Jones and the tragic bohemian Ernest Dowson are both buried there. Dowson died of tuberculosis in 1900 as if to exactly validate his fin de siècle credentials.

The placing of these cemeteries on a map shows a ruthless sense of competition, not unlike the current trend for major supermarkets to pitch their 'local' and 'express stores' on the same high street to deter each other from taking complete control over an area's local market. The map of south-east London shows four roods rooted at odds with each other while all around is white space. The nearest cemeteries are Tower Hamlets, five miles north across the Thames; Greenwich Cemetery, five miles to the east; and, over six miles to the west, Battersea St Mary's. These new south London necropolises competed on an area of land no bigger than a football pitch.

The four cemeteries around Nunhead are within a few miles of each other: Brockley and Ladywell, Camberwell Old Cemetery and Camberwell New Cemetery are all — strangely — exactly 1.2 miles distant by foot, according to Google Maps, from Nunhead Cemetery. In addition, West Norwood is just 3.7 miles away. Brent Elliott describes how the rivalry between the cemeteries became apparent in the trade of the masons who established themselves in the area, who 'would set up offices either adjacent to the cemeteries or on the main roads leading to them.' Marble angels, Celtic crosses and Grecian-style urns do not fall from heaven — and money was to be made from them.

In addition to this competition for death, scandal also hit Nunhead Cemetery, causing further damage to its reputation (and security). Edward Buxton was the Secretary and Registrar of the London Cemetery Company who — after a sudden death in 1865 — was found to have embezzled the company through the keeping of a bogus set of books. After a drawn-out investigation it turned out that he'd helped himself to over £18,000 of the company's money. Hugh Meller and Brian Parsons point out in the grand bible of London Cemeteries — *London Cemeteries: An Illustrated Guide & Gazetteer* —

that this scandal was accompanied with another problem striking all cemeteries at this time: mortality rates were falling as sanitary improvements increased. As people began to live longer the undertaker's doorbell rang less.

In Nunhead's first years, uptake on burial — and down-payment on plots — was slow, with just 56 burials recorded for 1841. According to Ron Woollacott only nine burials took place at Nunhead in the first six months after its opening, though trade eventually picked up and the slow tick of death began to return investment.

There is tragedy at the fore of Nunhead's history too. On August 4th 1912, just four months after the sinking of the Titanic, a team of boy scouts became unstuck after their cutter had capsized after leaving Waterloo Bridge for the Isle of Sheppey. Eight boys aged between eleven and fourteen died. Winston Churchill, then First Lord of the Admiralty, arranged for the bodies to return along the Thames by destroyer, and hundreds of thousands of people watched the procession to Nunhead Cemetery.

Nunhead Cemetery lives with its history of tragedies, misdemeanours and shared collective guilt in a way I recognise from Liverpool's history. When I first arrived at university a lecturer said to me in a pub, over a pint: 'the thing with Liverpool is that people always know what to do in a tragedy.' Congregate, pay tribute, remember: the dead take their place in the living subconscious. I warm to Nunhead more for its realness: aren't we all, after all, coming to terms with aspects of our pasts? Nunhead Cemetery suffered increased vandalism between the Second World War and the 1960s; Meller and Parsons document 'wild stories of black magic rituals [which] appeared in newspapers and a white robed ghost [that] had been reported hovering among the graves.' The statue for the dead scouts — a bronze statue by Miss Lillie Read which stood on a monument designed by Giles Gilbert Scott — was damaged (or stolen, depending on source) in 1969. The Anglican Chapel was burned down and the cylindrical catacombs raided for jewellery, before being buried, their hollow shafts filled with earth.

In 1998, in a joint bid with the Borough, the Friends of Nunhead Cemetery applied for Heritage Lottery Funding and received over a million pounds to carry out urgent work, including the restoration of the view to St Paul's. The Cemetery is now listed as a Grade II* historic landscape.

The ghost in the white robe may well be a poet, I think — but will I be able to put a name to it?

13th September 2014

I had lunch with my mum in our favourite Indian restaurant on Renshaw Street — a few roads along, I realised, from Victorian poet Arthur Hugh Clough's Rodney Street. We drank raspberry cider: a late summer bouquet. One of our five-a-day she joked. She paid for the meal. She paid ... only my siblings know this dynamic, the codes of the Corleones are less severe than my Mum's insistence on paying. We walked to our bus stops and took our separate buses. Mine came first, then the bus I was on went past her sitting at the bus stop, a flash of green, her natural red hair dyed blonde: she saw me waving and, waving back, smiled. The city condenses to a glass orb, the bus turns the axis of the globe which is my eye — at the centre of the crisis — I'm smiling and crying as the bus turns the corner to the view of Lime Street, the Anglican Cathedral, the back-to-front colosseum of St George's Hall.

14th September 2014

We went to my mum's for dinner to mark, somehow, the day before the surgery. To take her mind off things. Everyone said she looked stunning: black lace blouse and trousers, purple eyeliner. She made a casserole in the slow cooker. She was keeping herself busy: cooking the meal, making a cup of tea, dessert, more tea. My younger brother said that it's not right for her to have a clear glass in front of her that's not vodka — we smelt it to make sure, laughing: water. She was struggling to set the alarm on her mobile and to make sure that she's up in time for the operation tomorrow so I helped her find the clock app and set the alarm for 4am. Pinned it to her desktop. 10 hours and 57 minutes. The proximity shocked me. As if sensing that, she started to prepare seven bowls of Neapolitan ice cream, a bowl for everyone, hacking at the surface of the frozen ice cream with a silver spoon. Like an explorer trying to get to somewhere and then back as quickly as possible. I took over the job, trying to balance physical gusto with dexterity to give everyone a balance of strawberry, vanilla and chocolate. She pointed into the garden at the new border she's been working on, planting heather plants that have been artificially spray-painted blue, orange and purple. We all sat with the ice cream bowls clinking, looking at the flowers.

The Prince of Sparty Lea at Dulwich College

'Can't you see it? It's printed on my forehead in blue ink, he told
me, shouting: "I AM THE NIGHTMARE."'
Jackie Litherland

The ghost of Barry MacSweeney, greatest poet of the late twentieth
century, could be said to remain just over two miles south of Peckham
Rye at Dulwich College. Continuing my mapping of the poetic history
surrounding Nunhead Cemetery, I find myself drawn to this place. I
walk from the room I've slept in, at the centre of my map, and down
the never-ending downhill of Upland Road, picturing myself as an
Eadweard Muybridge body photographed against the endless stop-
motion of Victorian terraces. It's early in the morning and the green
parakeets are out, shrieking like taxidermist's revenants against the
sheet-blue Autumn sky.

MacSweeney's final fling with a live audience — an
audience he'd come to greet with some level of resentment at their
collective inability to be any bigger — was on 20th April 2000. A
recording of the reading survives. The despair of the poet's voice
leaks like freezing, toxic gas through every syllable. A poet who'd
mastered the gift of making his private rages public. MacSweeney
died ten days later of a blocked airway — the poet of endlessly
syllabic lines, done-in from windpipe asphyxiation. An inglorious
choking on a pickle, it's been said.

Poet friends have told me about how MacSweeney would
call them late at night to read them his latest three or four poems —
if they couldn't answer then he'd leave a voice message: the words

like alcohol-saturated eucharists left floating in analogue. They'd lift the phone to the poet's opening mantra, flanelling himself back to consciousness after the latest visit from the muse: 'Barry. Mac. Sween. Ey. POET.' MacSweeney was the conduit for the muse's haywire faxing.

I arrive on Lordship Lane with Upland Road behind me. The map of Dulwich shows acres of green space like organs connected with ventricular roads. Lordship Lane on a midweek morning is like a funfair dodgem ride for prams: fathers skirt around recycle bins, mothers take over the pavements with Quinnies that look like cocoons encasing the wingless pink of triplets. This is a place to pleasantly multiply. I wonder what MacSweeney would have made of it, at the apex of his downfall, aware that his own destruction through drink was curtailing any last hopes he might have had for fatherhood? He had lived in London at various points of his life, leaving the North East for the first time in 1968 for the glamour of London's mod fashions. At that point he'd attended gigs at the Hampstead Country Club and bought crushed-velvet loons in Kensington Street Market. He'd also lived for a few years above a parade of shops in High Barnet, a journo amongst artsy, LSD-taking dropouts: another poet in the spindrift of the sixties. This was followed by spells in Barnet and Harlow. But it is here in Dulwich that his ghost remains and — I suspect — can still be heard: the bitter rattle of frustrated chains after a tense, awkward last fling with a live audience.

Blake's contrasting gradients of innocence and experience are at the centre of MacSweeney's late work. As Harriet Tarlo has pointed out, MacSweeney favours the oldest known name for Britain, Albion, as Blake had before him. Both poet's images are knitted together through the ampersand. The poet W.N. Herbert sees this

Blakean similarity in the later work: 'The two volumes of *Pearl* and *The Book of Demons* seem to exist for many readers in a Blakean pairing of early Innocence set against late and terrible Experience.' Yet Blake came here early in life for an angel and MacSweeney arrived late with a demon on his back. In fact, when he was withdrawing from alcohol in the mid-90s he claimed he saw a real demon standing over him with 'eyes / glinty like fresh poured Tizer' and blades in its mouth. His partner of the time, the poet S.J. Litherland, remembers him emerging from The Dark Room (the second bedroom where the deepest drinking happened, also called The Ravaged Corner) asking: '"Can't you see it? It's printed on my forehead in blue ink" ... I AM THE NIGHTMARE.'"

MacSweeney's account of his withdrawal from alcohol in his masterpiece *The Book of Demons* is written with long, ampersand-linked lines, redolent of Blake's long poems such as *Jerusalem* and *Milton*. Both poets stood by their visions — Blake with the steady eye of the sober seer-savant — MacSweeney with the ticking nerves of the addict. Like Blake, as Litherland writes, MacSweeney took his demons and 'wrote them into the script, he gave them starring roles'.

Although Northumberland was MacSweeney's cherished locale he wrote about London too, particularly in his long poem *Ranter*. Inspired by the seventeenth-century Ranters, this poem pans across landscapes at speed before focusing in on the Docklands area in the years following its regeneration. A few years before this redevelopment had begun the Tory politician Michael Heseltine had flown over the East End and the Thames, on a private flight and — looking down — had been struck by the development potential: 'vast tracts of dereliction spread out before me ... the abandoned docklands ran like open wounds east of the capital', he wrote in *Prospect* magazine. This is the kind of corrupt, hollowed-out language that MacSweeney loved to attack and thus reclaim in his work. As a trained journalist, and a union man, MacSweeney watched Murdoch's dismantling of the unions with despair and with anger. As in all of the best political poetry, MacSweeney retains control of his viewpoint — enough to conceal any political messaging — to allow rhythm, texture and image-making to propel the poem forward:

> Boats for pleasure
> Boats for war
> bobbing on the tide
>
> Isle of Dogs
> he ran with fangs
> barges for bridges
> across dry docks
>
> fipple bent
> in his creased beak
>
> singing:
> *make me a blackbird again*
> *not a groaning man*

I follow Lordship Lane to the South Circular and then walk alongside Dulwich Common towards the College. Today I've been asked to talk about poetry, and read poems, to a few hundred sixth formers. I'm wedged in the performance line-up between comedian Jo Brand and cartoonist Martin Rowson. The theme is Power. My role is to arrest the attention of the teenagers with metrical language and outsider-thinking. MacSweeney was here first, the graffiti would rightly say.

By the time MacSweeney arrived to read at Dulwich College in 2000 his work was no longer containable in standard print sizes. The long lines of his poems flowed to the edge of oversized trade editions. Image folded into image. The line between sentimentality and Punk-infused rage had collapsed into a unique poetic that leaves the reader somewhere between wanting to withdraw through discomfort and wanting to put their arm around the poet to comfort him. The highly stylized work shows the biographical facts of a man in trouble.

From the mid-90s until his death, the poems were arriving quicker than MacSweeney — or anyone who knew him — could handle. Nicholas Johnson estimates that he might have had thirty poems on the go, in different forms, at the time of his death. He had written a whole series of 'collaborations' with the dead Apollinaire which were published posthumously under the title *Horses in Boiling Blood*. This affinity with the great modernist poet of World War One speaks volumes for MacSweeney's self-confidence and — through association with the French poet's war experience — deepening personal crisis. The unselfconscious ease with which he allows the crisis of the First World War to provide the language, colour and tone of his poems is both compelling and unsettling. Through this technique he achieved some of his finest work and allowed his affiliation with one of the greatest poets of the century to add power and texture to his own poetic voice. The war within is bound and barbed with his war against the greys, the officials in suits churning out the 'Faberised' poetry he saw around him:

> I say: Fight the language which is nailed and then driven down!
> To let it go is a sign of complete lack of civilisation
> But reclaiming it   my dearest poets
> is a tremendous prize

('Victory Over Darkness & The Sunne')

It would be easy to embellish the Dick Whittington-in-reverse narrative line of MacSweeney's career: the poet who sold thousands of copies of *The Boy From the Green Cabaret Tells of His Mother* and who — embittered with his publisher's failed attempt to have him elected as Professor of Poetry at Oxford — then went underground with small presses like Fulcrum, Turret and Trigram. MacSweeney also set up his own imprint under the title Bluesuede Boot Press (all part of his fixation with stylish footwear). Like most of his own publications from here on, print runs reached just a few hundred copies. Such a quiet entrance to the artistic work can never lay the platform for a sensational Elvis-style come-back or a Going-Electric shocker.

As a seventeen-year-old MacSweeney had read at Bob Cobbing's Better Books on Charing Cross Road. The story goes that the leading modernist poet J.H. Prynne was in the audience and, afterwards, packed him into his car and drove him back to Cambridge. Prynne, who was working with the American Charles Olson and had been in contact with many of the American Objectivists, spotted MacSweeney's gift immediately. Despite Prynne's best intentions — to nurture the talent, to encourage dedication — Prynne was already driving MacSweeney away from his hopeless ambition to be bigger than Dylan, taking him towards a more closeted, coterie poetics. Towards the world of the small press and the enclosed symposium. The tension between his ambition and the large stage was gridlocked.

Dulwich College appears before me like an airbrushed workhouse. The clock tower has been restored and is in full working order, ascending between the buildings of the college. I walk through puddles of fallen leaves, bleeding their umber into rainwater. A student cycles past, weaving through the slowly creeping traffic. I follow his lead over the zebra crossing, a woman in a BMW allowing me to cross. In the field before me an army of Canada geese have ranked themselves along the old Alleynian sports ground. Opposite, the Queen Mary gates to Dulwich park are open, leading into Dulwich Common. At Hambledon Place, a private house, a security camera sits perched over a mock-Victorian lantern. This is as far away as MacSweeney's North East — and his London bedsit years — as can be imagined. A pied wagtail struts along the pavement before me, a teenage wag in a graduation gown. MacSweeney would have out-glammed it with his velvet loons.

Many novelists have emerged from Dulwich College — Graham Swift, P.G. Wodehouse and Raymond Chandler are alumni. Yet, over the centuries, poets have flocked to the school too. Through its Literary Society events, the College has attracted a whole rostrum of linguistically innovative poets from the 1960s onwards: Roger Langley, Lee Harwood, Peter Riley, Nick Totton and the Prince of Sparty Lea himself, MacSweeney. More recently, old boy of the school Tom Chivers has emerged as a luminous force in twenty-first-century poetry. Tom was also present at MacSweeney's last reading.

I enter the college and immediately find the poets waiting for me: up the staircase from the reception the walls are lined with framed portraits of London's early modern poets — Marlowe, Donne, Sidney — each one giving their name to one of the school's houses. I'm shown to the Great Hall and wait as the students arrive in clusters, bags across shoulders, fizzing with adrenalin. These pupils might represent the opposite of Nunhead Cemetery: bright faces above earth. A new morning with everything still to play for.

The headmaster steps up to the lectern to introduce the day. 'Without power,' he says in his introduction, 'there would be no resistance'. I see Jo Brand coming through the side doors, then she moves in beside me on a rickety bench before being welcomed to the lectern — a lectern that I later notice has the date 1875 etched into it. As she talks, the day's roving camera crew take a series of shots of her. She says: 'Why not take another seven, get the whole of me in?' When she comes back down to the bench she quietly asks if she has to leave. The assistant nods. Jo Brand leans across the wooden pews to me and apologises for missing my talk, explaining that she's working on *Bake Off Extra*. Poetry has to follow this. We shake hands and she disappears.

I walk up to the stage and take the roaming mic: positioned on a Victorian set that's connected to wireless technology. The hundreds of faces look back at me. I find myself talking about poetry as a place to find your own language and to thrive outside of controlled ways of thinking. I quote the American poet Charles Bernstein: 'Language control equals thought control equals reality control.' This is easy to say because I believe it. Why don't more poets use *style* this as their ultimate artistic goal — that thing that no one else can take from them? Whether they have a readership — either in this life and beyond — is a lottery anyway.

After the event, and in the absence of Brand, expectant boys come up to me to ask questions. The first boy has two of his fingers stuck together with plasters and asks if the situation in Iraq is really just about greed? He says he heard a businessman on the radio saying another war would be good as it drives the economy. The next boy, a pending doctor, confesses to writing poetry but says that he only likes poems that rhyme. Another pair of boys, alert to my accent, ask if I support Liverpool or Everton? Red, I say and they glow: they're both Liverpool fans.

Then Ian Brinton appears through the crowd. A former English teacher at Dulwich College and confidant of J.H. Prynne. Ian can say more through the raising of one eyebrow than most teachers do in a lifetime. He never speaks a word that isn't weighted for its full potential. We've recently been corresponding over MacSweeney's visit here and he has come armed with ephemera: a CD of the poet's last reading at the college and a pamphlet of poetry by Emma McGordon, who had come along with MacSweeney for that last event and was photographed with him before the event. She was seventeen at the time. Ian also has a postcard from Barry which thanks him for arranging a room in Cambridge when he'd visited for the launch of Prynne's *Collected Poems*. MacSweeney had orchestrated the live moment of Prynne's reading, arranging his own chair at the front of the gathering in order to take a directorial position over the mentor who had steered his own career.

Ian walks me to the Master's Library, the location of an earlier MacSweeney reading which took place in 1999. He hands me the McGordon pamphlet, *The Hanging Man and the Stars*. I read a few lines to myself, facing the fireplace where MacSweeney had once read, my eyes landing on the title poem:

> The hangman was playing in his noose,
> it had taken him a year to
> learn how to tie it.
> Stars were shooting at each other,
> they banged as they collided.

The short biography in the book tells me that McGordon was the same age then as Barry was in 1967, when he was nominated for the position of Professor of Poetry at Oxford. In the spirit of Chatterton and Rimbaud, MacSweeney cultivated a new movement in poetic precocity. The cover image on the pamphlet is a woodcut in blue ink of a man swinging from a gallows — his head is leaning to one side but his hat is still on his head. Behind him are shooting stars.

As Ian and I are talking I'm swept up and steered into a seminar by an enthusiastic Classics teacher. Ian heads outside for a cigarette. The teacher is ready, shirtsleeves rolled up, unshaven; he tells the class he put together his seminar between 9pm last night and 2am this morning. What he offers is worth listening to: a Marxist reading of the role of the poet in society. The poet, he argues, is a part of the economic 'base', an outsider who offers something valuable to culture which in turn adds to the superstructure of society. The poet is *of* the system *and* outside of it, he says. To illustrate this he provides a handout of salacious and outspoken quotes from history: Rochester, Catullus, Marvel. He shows the lines on a screen with images of the poets' faces. Ezra Pound appears on screen in two contrasting photographs. The first is the young dandy who had arrived in London in 1909 with the twirled moustache. The second, in contrast, shows the later eccentric: eyes brooding beneath unkempt eyebrows, potent with the optical precision of the scops owl. The teacher asks if anyone recognises who it is? A boy puts up his hand: 'Ezra Pound, sir'. Ian Brinton walks into the class, hair slick with rain — he must have heard Pound's name mentioned. The teacher reads a quote from Pound to the class:

Time, space,

> neither life nor death is the answer.
> And of man seeking good,
> > doing evil.
> In meiner Heimat
> > where the dead walked
> > > and the living were made of cardboard.

(Canto CXV)

Ian sits in the seat next to me. I move along the MacSweeney CD and the McGordon pamphlet to make space. The dead poets are in full voice today, as I'd hoped. The teacher says: 'Pound's legacy will be his Fascism, his association with Mussolini. No one can now forget or see past that to read his work.' I put up my hand — I have to speak — and say that, well, Pound's legacy amongst contemporary poets is much more than that. Pound continues to inspire and to be read. His politics were way-off, but due to the originality of his work he is the dead that walks amongst the cardboard living. Ian's nodding fiercely beside me and follows in: 'And wasn't Pound awarded the Bollingen Prize in 1949, long after this association with Fascism?' I start to feel bad for the teacher; his best intentions have found him walking into a headwind of modernist defendants. For the inner poetry circle, those who view the world through what they've read, Pound's legacy will always be his poetry. The teacher had earlier said that his favourite poet is Basil Bunting: without Pound, I suggest, there would be no Bunting. This is how the dead poets still speak — through the living.

While Pound frowns out from the screen, a camera crew enters the room: four men attached by wire and crane into a kind of roving velociraptor. The teacher rolls up his sleeves and moves forward with his polemic. He's a Latinist and comes into his own with the Catullus quotes, reading the lines about Catullus's penis with accentuated syllabic relish:

Mentual moechatur. Moechatur mentula? Certe.
hoc est quod dicunt: ipsa olera olla legit.

He then reads his English translation:

'The Prick is fucking around.' 'Fucking around? The Prick?' 'For sure!
It's like they say: the pot picks its own vegetables.'

Outside the window a man in a hooded anorak is walking up and down on a lawn, mowing the border around a World War One cenotaph. He removes the bed of auburn leaves before they begin to decay. A strong sideways wind bends a bed of roses like an alcoholics' jamboree. They look set to collapse, leaning against each other, and then — miraculously — spring back upright.

The next seminar is led by Ian himself: he weaves together a Shakespearean sonnet, Dickens' *Great Expectations* and Michel Foucault's *Discipline and Punish* to show how writers have explored how we remain haunted by our pasts. Through this powerful patchwork approach — raising his eyebrows as he waits for responses from the boys — he comes back time and again to a quote from American poet Charles Olson. More grist from the mill of dead poets, as if the Nunhead dead — just a few miles down the road — are imploring me to search them out:

As the dead prey upon us,
they are the dead in ourselves,

awake, my sleeping ones, I cry out to you,
disentangle the nets of being!

After the seminar Ian walks me to the site of MacSweeney's last reading which took place at the Salle, the cricket pavilion, which just happens to be where we're having lunch today. A shock of contrast: I imagine the poet of excess against the backdrop of the names who've featured in the cricketing XI since the 1880s. If only it was as simple as picking the canonical lists of poetry from those who had simply 'played'. Ian points to the boards in front of where MacSweeney performed on Saturday 29th April 2000, no doubt against a sky that MacSweeney would have described as *borage* blue. The most gifted poet of his generation taking his final bow.

Other poets were present that day: Iain Sinclair, Brian Catling and — reading alongside MacSweeeney — Lee Harwood. There was a small gathering of enthusiastic students, the young Tom Chivers amongst them. What the audience saw, and heard, was both astonishing and unsettling. A recording of the reading survives, released by Optic Nerve. There are signs that MacSweeney had been drinking that day and in his voice there is what Brinton has described as 'a sentimentality which may have been encouraged by alcohol.' The recording bears this out. MacSweeney's mood oscillates between forcing the audience to become intimate with the ravages of his experiences and delighting them with the lyricism of his yearned-for innocence. The ravages win out. Often it seems as if — in the electricity of his performed emotions — MacSweeney was being struck so hard by poetry to the point where he couldn't get out of the way of it. As if the weight of poetic language that he'd developed since writing his first poem, aged seven, had not only ruined any attempt to live a *normal* life but had failed to give him the fame that would make up for.

MacSweeney begins his reading with 'I Looked Down On a Child Today', which describes his witnessing a child being hit by a bus in Newcastle. MacSweeney foregrounds Blake in his introduction to the poem: 'it's a sad case of innocence and experience — which actually happened, quite recently.' MacSweeney walks away from the microphone as he reads the poem, as if the sound of his shoes, echoing to analogue, must have a moment in the recording — the hardened leather heels rapping from the wooden floor. He reads slowly, much more slowly than the speed of his language on the page, with languorous pauses between the lines.

In MacSweeney's poems every aspect of the unjust world is exaggerated: if the boy *might* have died by being hit by the bus then he did die ('He or she was dying or dead'); if MacSweeney might have been culpable in any way then he *was* culpable ('I stepped down from the steps of a 39 bus today with sudden blood on my shoes'); and — in a twist of reality possibly drawn from his own experience of not being a father and perhaps longing to be so — this child could well be the one that he might have fathered. *Might* have, though didn't: regret adumbrates all of MacSweeney's late work. This child that he never knew is somehow let down by the observing poet. Through MacSweeney's signature excess what *might have been* finds its fulcrum in a language that roots out the imagined possible so that the feeling of loss can be fully felt by the reader.

Despite the regret, MacSweeney can't leave himself — as the doomed rock star — out of the unfolding tragedy: 'which I can call mine in a very old-fashioned romantic Barry MacSweeney Elvis

Orbison Highway 61 way'. There is no sense with MacSweeney that the grey blocks of parental responsibility would have limited his rock 'n'roll lifestyle. We find out twice in the poem that this incident happened the day before St Valentine's Day. The poet, ten days before his own death, looks towards the saint of courtly love who might bring a child into the world. MacSweeney's excess is always propelled with a boyish impetuousness.

MacSweeney then reads from his magnum opus, the *Pearl* sequence. Iain Sinclair has talked about how MacSweeney was a great perpetuator of his own mythology, how he once listened to Barry tell him that he'd been on a train, late of an evening, with the England football coach of the time, Bobby Robson. They had ended up in an unnamed train station in the darkness — no doubt organising the best midfield for the perfect Albion. As Sinclair deduced: this was the poet's version of how England *should* be and the mythos of the *Pearl* poems are strident with poetic possibility. MacSweeney's first friend, and first love — in his mythology at least — was a girl with a cleft palette. He says that they were only five or six years old and they played together. All she could say was 'AH AH AH'. He taught her, he says, to read and write and years later he'd seen her again and she was married with 'two beautiful daughters'. In his introduction to the poem he describes his childhood self and the girl swimming naked, through the borage plants, practising the sounds of English: 'making our own laws, as all the best poets do', he says. As well as incredible beauty there is a great sadness in these poems.

MacSweeney's final reading in the cricket pavilion crackles with demonic glossolalia. At one point he shouts: 'SLAM DOWN THE BLACKBOARD — LET IT STAY BLACK'. And a table is slammed. He growls as if one of his demons — 'gargoyle head'

— is taking control of him. He is possessed with his own darkness: 'and I STAMP STAMP STAMP'. 'Please,' the poem ends, in the voice of Pearl, 'don't crush my heart'. MacSweeney's poem 'Pearl in the Silver Morning' is the most singular of his poems, leaving behind for a moment the narrative of lost possibility and pending hopelessness to contain what *might have been* in the glistening crucible of the text. As if a pure love like this might just cancel the poet's drive for self-destruction:

> Indeed the word you used was the word beautiful,
> pinning cowslips behind my ears,
> you patting and running fingers through our
> beckwashed hair.

Jackie Litherland, MacSweeney's partner in those final years, has written that when he first discovered alcohol in his mid-teens he had said it was 'like falling in love'. The *Pearl* poems describe a falling in love through nature, amidst the streams and wildflowers of Sparty Lea — way beyond any conception of the hangover.

At this final reading Blakean innocence ends when MacSweeney reads from his Mary Bell sonnets: a sequence which was deliberately withheld from inclusion in the *Collected Poems* but is proposed by MacSweeney here to be published under the title *Blood Money*. He describes his new focus in poetry as being driven towards experience:

> My concerns in writing poetry in the last three years are becoming increasingly concerned with innocence and experience, good and evil — whatever YOU wish to think that is. It usually concerns children and murderers and sometimes children who are murderers. So I decided to write a book called *Blood Money: the*

Marvellous Secret Sonnets of Mary Bell, Child Killer. And Mary Bell comes to me in the middle of the night, I hope one day literally, through the ether as it were, and I've written 300 sonnets under the general title *Blood Money* ... If any of this is distasteful to you, don't hesitate to leave.

There, in a single statement, is MacSweeney's complex relationship with his readership: a confessional opening — an invitation into his way of seeing things — followed by a suggestion that the audience might like to leave the room. This is a bold declaration for a reading at a boys' school, in the pavilion overlooking the cricket grounds.

At the age of eleven Mary Bell was convicted of killing two boys in Newcastle, one aged four and the other aged three. Later it was revealed that she'd been abused by her mother — a prostitute dominatrix — who had involved her daughter in sex acts with clients. There is in this horrific case the double tragedy of Bell's own upbringing and the murders she later committed. With typically convoluted mythmaking, MacSweeney ties up his own complicated emotional life with Bell's. He tells the audience that he had interviewed Bell, as a child, in her cell, when he was writing a piece about the case for a newspaper. Can we believe this? No. But it's essential to Barry's investment in the story that his emotional crisis is bound up with the young girl's crisis — as an artist, he knows that he can't write his best work without everything being at stake, including his own mental and emotional wellbeing. Critics of *The Book of Demons* often cite the demons as being the antithesis of Pearl's innocence but it's the Mary Bell sonnets that offset the poems of innocence most shockingly. Even in the structuring of his reading it's as if Pearl — representing innocence, freedom and good — is in the past tense and Mary Bell represents the final inner struggle that he can't win. The open space of Sparty Lea couldn't be further off from this imaginative cell housing a jaded journalist and abused child killer.

Cries Unheard: the Story of Mary Bell by Gitta Sereny was released in 1998, and MacSweeney, given the date of his sonnets, would very likely have read it. Sereny's book begins with a quote from Ben Jonson which would have made it all the more appealing to the living poet: 'Pray thee take care, that tak'st my book in hand, / To reade it well: that is to understand.' In MacSweeney's sequence, however, he is less concerned with giving Bell a fresh hearing than using her tragic life as the spur for propelling his poetic language. In MacSweeney's creative psyche an initially powerful reaction from an outside source — one laden with hopelessness, urgency, and, ideally, fame — provides the catalyst that kickstarts the new work into action:

> Bazza cash
> stinging fast into all night, alive with drink, single sussed
> towards death, no fatherhood, no blonde daughters
> or manchilds, there is no seek. Only slaughter.

('Sonnet 9: Still Justice With Her Shining Sword')

MacSweeney had written odes before — an open-ended form well-suited to his lyric flight — but this was the first time that he chose to constrain himself with the sonnet, setting a fourteen-line parameter to his buboes-tongued glossolalia. MacSweeney plays a swollen tongue-in-cheek game with this by adding numbers at the start of each line to show the sonnet unfolding line-by-line towards the summation of number 14:

1 There is no nothing but total terror in
2the night. Shall we forget each other, will
3we, sweetest?

('Sonnet 10: If You're Tired of Being Lonely')

The tension between excess and control here creates a tightwire for the reader. MacSweeney's tragedy fuels a language that is just about in control — in terms of pacing, imagery, tone (some of the lines in these poems even adopt a regular iambic pentameter) — but which is always in danger of collapse. In a sense it is the numbers at the start of the lines that allow the poems to retain a compactness that the reader might expect from a sonnet. The poems play out as a game, albeit a game that has the subject of abuse and murder at its core.

Perhaps the bringing to light, in print, of the Mary Bell sonnets will add to the recent swell of interest in MacSweeney's work. These poems show MacSweeney writing with the conviction that poetry is the only thing that might save him but, as always, this also spells danger for him: he's most safely attached to life when fully convinced of his purpose as a poet. What if the poetry stops or loses its purpose for him? In the Mary Bell sonnets he surprises his readers — and himself — with these hybrid mutations of the sonnet and at his final reading at Dulwich College he reads them as if they're evidence of the catastrophic brilliance of his failure. Listening to the recording is like walking down a darkened corridor in a house of murders — feeling the walls in order to make the right turn — being forced to wonder if your host might be toying with you all along:

Mary Bell wakes in the night and asks to look nowhere:
My name is Mary Patrick MacSweeney, my name is Barry Bell:
we may never meet again on a rocky country road to love.

Sell all of his poems and his murderers.

In the recording MacSweeney can be heard walking across the room, his voice and Cuban heels receding into the distance. There is no great announcement that MacSweeney is at the end of his career: his reading just ends. No thank you is given to the audience, there is no final round of applause. The phrase 'No fuss' is the last thing we hear. MacSweeney has transformed the room into an audience of witnesses, watching his collaboration — as if in a confined cell — with the teenage murderer Mary Bell. Miles — and years away — from Pearl, the borage plants and the running streams of Sparty Lea.

 After the reading MacSweeney walked the short distance to the bar, above which is written in gold *Detur Gloria Soli Deo*: Let glory be given to God alone. It's the kind of bar that's familiar to me from various social clubs over the years — only with football badges and beer logos in place of the Latin. MacSweeney, it's been reported, began fumbling for drinks and ice as Lee Harwood — in his naturally quiet manner — attempted to begin his own reading. Harwood glared at MacSweeney until he stopped — which he did, once he was equipped with a final drink.

MacSweeney died ten days later on 9th May 2000: the height of Spring in the opening year of a new millennium. I think of the other name for the hawthorn: mayflower.

It's time to leave Dulwich College and the trembling spectre of MacSweeney's legacy. The poetic layers surrounding Nunhead Cemetery are thickening. Outside the College it's raining. I walk down Lovers Walk under the driving sheets of rain, trying to find the nearest train station. For some reason Prynne's description of MacSweeney's ears as being 'bat-like' comes to mind now and then I remember the resonances of bats that Robert Graves highlights in *The White Goddess*: 'the two or three Biblical texts [which] refer to the queer bat-like voices in which demons, or familiars, speak through the prophets.' Blake and MacSweeney seem to be speaking to me in a shared symbolism, asking me to make sense of them through the landscape I'm traversing.

Three Dulwich College boys are standing under larches, trying to smoke, passing a match between them. The condensation has softened the tips of the matches to pink sludge. I ask the way

Barry MacSweeney and Emma McGordon on the day of
MacSweeney's Dulwich reading

to the station and they point me in the right direction. One of them shouts after me: 'I liked your talk!' Poetry, somehow, made it through. I realise then that I'm back at Belair Park, near to the rare surface flash of the River Effra, which might easily drag me back to West Norwood Cemetery where my project began — though there's a new map forming now and I have a strong, bat-like sense of where the next node point will lead me. Nunhead Cemetery is calling: I check my emails as I walk and find that a guide has appeared to introduce me to its poets.

15th September 2014

The house woke at 3.30am. Sympathy for my mum's pending alarm? It happened with that familiar knock-on effect: Sarah woke first, which woke Pavel, who shouted out that he needed water, which woke me. We tried to settle down, back to sleep. It didn't work for Sarah; Pavel tossed and turned, the springs of his bunk creaking in the next room. I lay in bed feeling a numbness through my bones — a numbness which ran along my arms and curled into the nerves in my fingers. I tried to lie as foetally still as I could: and breathe without moving.

When we got to the hospital we waited with my mum before she was taken to the ward, then to theatre. Wearing a pale green theatre gown. We spoke to the surgeon before going to the ward and then again before theatre, when the surgeon was also in her gown — strange how both the patient and surgeon wear the same clothes, like collaborator fencers. My mum joked: 'I bet you didn't recognise me without my make-up?'.

16th September 2014

She was wearing pink pyjamas with a blue courier bag around her shoulder which turned out to be draining a stent. There were nine of us around her bed, four children, three grandchildren and my mum's partner. She said how nice the anaesthetic was, the white swoosh of the blackout. One of us asked if she dreamt: no dreams, only silence. The white surgical socks are tighter than skin — she joked that she would have liked them in black. We set up the TV screen next to the bed, to give her something to focus on in the hours after we've left. I told her I had to go to London tomorrow but would be back Friday, earlier than usual, to see her. I waited in line to hug her at the end of visiting time, to tell her how proud of her I am.

17th September 2014
The drain draining fluid from her chest fell out in the night: a return to theatre, the local anaesthetic, the rugby-hold of a nurse positioning her body for the reinsertion. She didn't tell us because she didn't want to worry us, she says.

Into the Valley of Death

Cannon to right of them,
Cannon to left of them,
Cannon in front of them.

Alfred, Lord Tennyson, 'The Charge of the Light Brigade'

'There have been some DIY memorials here,' Tim Stevenson of the Friends of Nunhead Cemetery says. 'Recently a family were making their own memorial along the path there.' I look to where he's pointing but the portacabin has no windows. There's a packet of unopened digestives on a tea tray.

When I met Tim at the gates, standing underneath the upturned torches at the gates, we talked about where we'd walked from to get here. 'Upland Road,' I said, 'by The Clock House, the posh side of Peckham.' 'You?' I asked. 'Nunhead,' he replied. 'The posh side of Peckham.'

I've found a way in, a guide, an assured voice in the wilderness I'm trying to gain some traction in. Tim Stevenson is the man for the job — his twin loves are trees and poetry. He strikes me as someone who likes a challenge, and my search for the dead poets could be described as that. He's wearing walking shoes and the satchel over his arm might be filled with everything required for locating the dead. I tell him I've become a death addict, like a Victorian laudanum swallower. He's nodding as I talk, familiar with this kind of addiction: 'The culture has become so separate from death,' he says, 'but when you come to cemeteries like this all the time you become familiar with death. It's the same with people who read poetry. There it is: death, birth, love. What else is there?' I've not only found a guide into Nunhead Cemetery, I've also found someone who loves poetry. This is too good to be true.

Tim tells me about the plans someone he knows has for their funeral: 'One of the volunteers, quite a staid guy, wants to go via rocket lightshow from the top of the hill.' I think of Hunter S. Thompson, the cannon of dust, the news of his body's atoms exploding over the desert. Tim's view of death is so practical it flips into the intuitive and takes on an edge that Blake would have agreed with: 'Why pay thousands to the death trade, undertakers charging £3,000 to move a body a few hundred yards. Do it yourself: what more love could you show someone than fulfilling their last wishes?' This is so astonishingly true I wonder why I hadn't thought of it before.

In another life, the life of many lives, I'd be hanging out all day with eccentric guides to London's cemeteries, listening to their arcane talk of Victoriana, cutting at thorns and pushing aside vines to reach the graves of lost poets. Tim, never still for long, sets us to it and we start the walk along Catacomb Path towards the grave of Peter Marsh (1828-1909), survivor from the Charge of the Light Brigade. Death and poetry reside in the remains of this one man, his surname suggests Nunhead under rainfall. I've seen the footage: dogs running through metres of still water at the bottom of the hill at the Limesford Road end of the Cemetery. A marshland necropolis.

And there's something here I'd missed on previous visits: the filled-in catacombs are here, under this raised oval piece of land. These cylindrical versions of the catacomb, long cancelled for appointments, are beneath where I'm standing. Tim and I are now standing on Nunhead's higher class burial chambers: compartments for 144 coffins, along with eight ante-rooms and ten burial vaults. The Bank of England bought one of the ante-rooms when they transferred human remains from the churchyard of Christopher-le-Stocks in 1933. Death's equivalent of the wedding suite goes to the bankers. Family vaults weren't cheap either — you had to pay for the luxury of reunion.

'The catacombs were filled in after some serious vandalism,' Tim says. 'South-east London has always been poor and word got around that the Victorians were often buried with their jewellery.' Coffins were removed, broken, opened and human remains left along the paths. There's something of the fantastical about this, something hard to picture given the condition of the Cemetery today. Something Dickensian about it too: the poor who rifle through Scrooge's things, after his death, without a good word to say about him.

As we walk, Tim tells me how some of the graves were dug as much as twenty-six feet down, the clay pumped out with water and lined with wood to stop the walls from collapsing. We arrive at Peter Marsh's grave, a flat modernist slab of granite. I ask Tim if he includes this on his tour because of the link to the poem?

'Absolutely. I look at the audience for those with white or grey hair and see their reaction when I read this bit on the stone: *one of the 600*. Some of them start to quote it. Up until forty years ago this was known by everyone, taught in every school.'

Here's the last of the living poetry, language locked to memory via rhythm. The young on the tour are no doubt stunned by this trick of word conjuring. According to Tennyson's grandson the poet had written 'The Charge of the Light Brigade' in minutes, in response to a report of the Battle of Balaclava in which 600 men had been sent into 'the mouth of hell' on horseback.

I tell Tim this isn't seen as Tennyson's finest hour, but he knows that already and makes a case for the galloping repetitions of the poem: 'It's almost like a chant,' he says. 'No wonder it was popular with that clatter of horse hooves. Have you heard Tennyson's reading of it?'

I have, and can recall that Edison Wax Cylinder recording of Tennyson's reading, the poet's voice drowning far off in a gurgling parlour room. There is a clatter behind it which could be the ageing poet using a pair of clappers to add emphasis to the cadence of horses, but is more likely to be the cylinder clicking at each rotation. This is the advantage of the celebrated over the forgotten: the poet who is successful in life is canned for generational replay. The substance of material — words across media — builds by attrition to a state where the poet can't be forgotten. This recording was made thirty-six years after the poem was written showing how 'The Charge of the Light Brigade' was something of a party piece. The poet died less than two years later after reading this but here's the gift of his voice, the poet embodied in sound, bombastically pushing his words through wax. It's not Tennyson's best work — *The Princess* or *In Memoriam*, say — but due to the forces of popular demand and the poet's instinct for legacy it is this piece of Laureateship that has remained the greatest crowd-pleaser. It might have been a good choice of poem for the cylinder: a recording of *In Memoriam*, for example, would have found its subtleties scratched and muffled beyond comprehension. 'The Charge of the Light Brigade' is perhaps the only poem that could have been captured by this technology and remain listenable: the rhythm projected from Tennyson's lungs is trapped in the can, carrying his voice in the poem through to us.

Tim's defence of the poem forces me to reconsider it. Despite calling the 600 men 'heroes' there is an unswerving sense of the horror of war in the poem too: 'storm'd at with shot and shell'. It isn't the sentimental account that I thought it was. The 17th Lancers, whom Peter Marsh had joined in 1849, were sent to their deaths by strategic decision and by the whoosh of their horses. The man whose grave we are standing over was — through being part of so many — reduced to sound and the statistical body. Modern warfare was yet to materialise so it could be argued that the poem will never appear as modern — but it doesn't glamourise war either, or demean what Marsh went through:

> Flash'd all their sabres bare,
> Flash'd as they turn'd in air,
> Sabring the gunners there,
> Charging an army, while
>   All the world wonder'd:
> Plunged in the battery-smoke
> Right thro' the line they broke;
> Cossack and Russian
> Reel'd from the sabre-stroke
>   Shatter'd and sunder'd.
> Then they rode back, but not,
>   Not the six hundred.

There is great technical skill here: Tennyson undercuts the alternating six-syllable, three-stress lines with five-syllable lines to achieve the clipped patter of hooves. This creates a disconnect between the speed of war and the reality of what it left behind: rallying triumphalism followed with incomplete cadences to give a ponderous sense of doubt to any heroism. Tim's right: there's more to this poem than is commonly believed.

While I've been thinking about this, Tim's moved ahead — to Dylan Thomas. He's making the point that Thomas's shift from his difficult early poems to the later ones gave an audience what they wanted. The Second World War made Thomas the poet. His collection *The Map of Love* had bombed in 1939 but after the BBC had given him a public voice a new, more direct style solidified his popularity. I have a sudden realisation of how far I've come this year: I'm in Nunhead Cemetery, talking about poetry. I might be yet to find the dead poets buried here — but I'm getting nearer.

We look back at Marsh's headstone and Tim says: 'This is how to build a monument to last'. The headstone is very simple in fact: flat and made of granite. Nothing to fall, nothing that can collapse. Headstones like this last for centuries. And headstones that are simple and unadorned in form — like many of Thomas's later poems — are easier for successive generations to find.

Tim tells me that there are just 40,000 monuments for around 270,000 burials. How many poets might there be among Nunhead's unmarked graves? If there is a lost genius amidst the sheer avalanche of human cargo then there's work for me to do.

As we wind back to the portacabin I ask Tim about Nunhead Cemetery's hawthorns. He points out two kinds to me, the common and the midland. We stop in the Cemetery and he points out some hawthorns: I photograph their leaves, the distinctive pinch of the indented leaf edges. As Tim talks about maintaining the Cemetery, everything he says about that process also seems relevant to what I was led to believe about the poetic canon: trees need to be cut back to let others grow. By the time we arrive at the portacabin we're talking about the poet Ernest Dowson — part of the group Yeats later described as 'the tragic generation' — buried down the road in Brockley and Ladywell Cemetery. I recall some of the notoriety of Dowson; Tim agrees that Dowson made some bad decisions: falling in love with the twelve-year-old daughter of his landlord, alcohol, drug addiction. Dowson was found penniless in a rundown wine bar and was dead by the age of thirty-two. Tim quotes Dowson from memory: 'They are not long, the days of wine and roses.' The Cemetery inspires this call to *carpe diem*. There's something else about Dowson, he is another — like B.S. Johnson — whose attachment to the world was broken after the death of his mother. His mother was a consumptive who hung herself: ghosting her son in life. I wonder if any of Nunhead Cemetery's poets might still be quoted by memory?

As Tim quotes Dowson I notice the CEMETERY TOURS timetable swinging from a hook. Then a golden Labrador looks inside the cabin to see what's happening, sniffing out the decadent strain of poetry and making sure the hashish pipe is not being lit. Tim hands me a copy Ron Woollacott's *Nunhead Notables* and tips me off on a Nunhead Cemetery poet: Marian Richardson. A new path. The possibilities of the poet's work run ahead in my mind: is this the one I'm looking for?

Tim locks the cabin behind us. I ask him if — when the winter sets in, and the leaves fall from the trees — he might help me find Henry Mew's grave. Henry Mew, buried in Nunhead, was the insane brother of the poet Charlotte Mew, author of 'In Nunhead Cemetery'; a poem which might, in itself, be enough to place Nunhead Cemetery on the poetic map.

'That can be done,' he says, 'but we'll need tools.' I have a sudden feeling of being about to go deeper into the landscape of poetry and death — that feeling I had in West Norwood's catacombs of being beyond the point of coming back.

I shake hands with Tim and thank him. 'See you in a few months,' I say. 'I'll bring tools.' 'Don't do that,' he says after me, pointing to the portacabin with one hand and slinging the satchel over the shoulder with the other — as if he's ready to cut back the bushes towards the poets now: 'We've got plenty of tools.'

18th September 2014

We were originally told that chemotherapy was certain and there was a 50/50 chance of radiotherapy. Today we were due to find out. It's worse dealing with this 221 miles away from Liverpool, in London, where I can't go with her to the appointment. Autumn is settling across Dulwich. No answer to my calls; the phone rings out on silence. I decide to run around Peckham Rye before going for a drink at the Clock House, a pub facing the open grassland, well-positioned for the visions of angels that come after the fourth or fifth drink has lit up the heightened synapses with alcohol. I need to be careful not to try and cope with stress like Ernest Dowson. There's a broken sound to fin-de-siècle and we can all mark our end of millennium whenever we like. I ran the circuit once, twice, stopping to use the weight resistance machines that are hidden in a circle of hedges. Breathing, resisting, ventilating.

My mum called: she'd forgotten to take her phone out with her. I stopped alongside some wheelie bins, next to the pub, so we could talk. The doctor has given her the news that she'll need radiotherapy too. They found that the cancerous cells had passed through 13 of the 18 lymph nodes: enough to give a concern that the cancer's travelled further in her body. My mum is a planner, a forward-looking organiser of the new things that need to be done even after jumping through hoops of fire. She makes decisions before the smouldering has started. It's only an extra couple of weeks she said — and she wants to be sure her body's cleared. This isn't the news she wanted, or wants her children to hear, and we both know that — but what else can we do? We talked for a bit, silencing the cancer with news of other things.

After we said goodbye I stayed where I was for a while, standing as still as the wheelie bins around me. The pub sign swinging gently in the breeze broke me out of it — and gave me somewhere to walk towards. I ordered a pint and took it outside, sat at a table, under a heater, with the lights from the edge of the Rye, at Nunhead, coruscating through the tesserae of falling leaves. After three pints, the need to urinate steered me upstairs to the Blake Room where I could see the whole view over the Rye: the trees and the dark, empty spaces.

At Home with the BBC: Reconsidering the Canon

The morning you woke up and for a moment forgot
to call them "dead," it was the morning
of the poem.

   Peter Gizzi, 'Hard as Ash'

I've been at home all week, roving the house, picking out poetry
collections, reading half a poem, sliding the book back between the
hundreds of slim volumes. Reading again from *The White Goddess*.
Maybe a great lost poet will come to me? I'm 221 miles away from
Nunhead Cemetery. I want to be here, in Liverpool, near family. But
poetry never lets me go. I pick off more volumes, lay them out the
way a heron places its haul of dead fish in a circle on the bank: a
signal to the Sun god to send inspiration. To send healing and calm.
I am inside this process for as long as my mum is.

Reading poetry on the page doesn't hold me as it usually does. I put
the television on and flick through some programmes I've recorded,
stopping at *The Great Poets in Their Own Words*. These were shown on
BBC in the evenings, surreptitiously, without declamation. I knew
about them in advance as they'd used some of The Poetry Library's
books in the film: early letterpressed lines from Dylan Thomas's
Twenty Five Poems and the gold-foxed spine of an original *Four
Quartets*. I sit and watch, letting the known dead of poetry come to
me.

   The argument presented is that the BBC saved poetry:

'before the twentieth century poetry was stuck in a rut, poets wrote about nature in a language that was formal and ornate.' A visual montage follows: Pound raising his eyebrows; Auden wearing shades, driving a car; Larkin in a white mackintosh — the original whip-thin streaker in a church, looking up at the ceiling. The poets, I'm told, 'found words for the complexity, the upheaval and the doubt of the modern world.' Linton Kwesi Johnson appears with a crowd behind him at the Brixton Riots, closely followed by an image of an extremely well-fed Seamus Heaney, alone, in a field, wearing a turtleneck sweater and a leather jacket that looks like it's from the production wardrobe of *The Sweeney*.

The commentary goes on: 'And there was another revolution, in that twentieth century television brought poets into millions of living rooms. As the BBC cameras rolled, poets took the time to explain themselves to a mass audience for the first time.' The scene shifts to cameramen controlling camera mountains, technicians looking at a honeycomb of screens, Edith Sitwell wearing a peacock hat, Allen Ginsberg giving a perfect A-Okay to the crowd, John Betjeman raising both arms upwards in a dilapidated doorway.

Here, we're told, we'll meet the poets who set out to write for the new century: as if this was their purpose, to converge the twain of their work with the new possibilities provided by television. Eliot's face — a vamp-eared prefect — falls in sync with a statement about these new poets 'who dragged poetry into the modern age'. Here's Auden again — with the face of the chain-smoking pachyderm — 'witness to the chaos of the 1930s'. Next up is Dylan Thomas 'whose lyrical voice held audiences spellbound'. 'There were eccentrics too,' we're told — Stevie Smith, frail, bird-like, shies from the camera — and 'National treasures': John Betjeman sitting on a train, as nationalised in person as the transport he travels by. Juxtaposition is all: cue Hugh MacDiarmid — 'political rebel' — dressed for the office even as he walks through a field, hair like an enlightenment tailor, red eyes irritably deprived of sleep. We hear MacDiarmid in his own words: 'we must get rid of England somehow, completely.' The montage jumps to Robert Graves, the unwashed boxer, the Charterhouse troubadour, his face like a cast from a Roman centurion, inexplicably wearing a brown Del Boy leather jacket.

This pack of barely-functioning eccentrics is our celebrated poets: there's not one of them that you'd trust with your last pound to use a vending machine. These are the poets that the BBC are proud to have made famous, culled for the spotlight from the thousands of poets writing throughout the twentieth century. I pause the programme. Is this really the story of the poetry in the twentieth century? I write down the names of those who are missing from the BBC list, impulsively, from memory — the UK and American poets from the 1930s on, who have shaped and influenced the second half of the twentieth century and the beginnings of the twenty-first century: David Jones, e.e. cummings, Lynette Roberts, Basil Bunting, Marianne Moore, David Gascoyne, W.S. Graham, Roy Fisher, Rosemary Tonks, H.D., Charles Olson, to name a few. There are degrees of what a 'lost' poet might mean, but like the various prizes in the UK, and the exmaination syllabuses, there is always a drive to narrow poetry down to a handful of poets we can't live without. As Jeremy Noel-Tod writes in his short critical work *The Whitsun Wedding Video*: 'Poets can wait a long time for readers and recognition. Oeuvres can be lost and restored.' I'm starting to feel that this day indoors will, after all, further clarify the kind of poetry

I want to find in Nunhead Cemetery.

I press play again and here comes Pound through a whole range of haircuts: 'Ezra Pound rarely appeared on camera but in 1959 he appeared for the BBC in Italy demonstrating the qualities of Chinese writing.' Pound paints Chinese pictograms for the camera: a squared sun with a line underneath for the dawn. We are told that 'Pound read a controversial section of *The Cantos* for the BBC. In the poem ... [here Pound is walking down on an old staircase wearing a square hat, in shadow, his back to the camera] ... he attacks capitalist society for immoral money lending, or usury ... an evil for which he blames Jewish bankers.' There is no BBC footage of Pound before this 1959 film we are told: his biggest offence, before then, was presumably his obscurity. The puppy-eyes of Michael Rosen appear: 'I remember it was pretty controversial,' he says. 'The BBC went and dug him out and interviewed him.' Rosen is replaced with Professor Mullan, with the voice of a tourism salesman, hurtling the claim — as insult — that Pound is *studied* rather than read. (What kind of assault is that from a man whose career is *studying* poetry I think?) The screen cuts to 'the understudy that eclipsed him' and Eliot is back in front of us with the slicked hair of the Harvard tennis champion.

Eliot the poet was also Eliot the publisher who took over the Faber and Faber list in 1929, up until which point that very same publisher had been publishing — and would continue to publish — his own work. He was in the injudicious position of being the person who decided what to publish from his own work — as well as trying to play fair on the poetic enmities and alliances he'd developed up until that point in his career. Eliot had a background in banking, leaving the Foreign Accounts department of Lloyds Bank to join the firm. Although the screen is currently in colour, here come the greys: Blake Morrison making the claim that Eliot's city banker dress code is actually a huge breakthrough for poetry (he himself is wearing a brown sweater). The arc of the narrative is becoming clear: poetry was 'reflecting the turmoil and fragmentary state of the modern world,' while at the same time — the argument goes — the poet who is aloof from that world was most connected to it through his position within the media. Eliot, the day-owl, 'appeared tantalisingly rarely on television but he was filmed recording his poem *Four Quartets* for the BBC.' As he reads, Eliot looks up and down at the huge black BBC microphone, as if it's a rodent he might eat.

W.H. Auden walks down a carpeted stairwell, clawing the banister with one hand, the other in his overly-tight suit jacket, taking each step cautiously, as if concerned that his trousers might split. This is *The Parkinson Show*, 1972. Parky stands at the bottom of the stairs as the audience applauds, waiting to greet the ageing poet. Auden takes his seat and immediately lights a cigarette, flailing the lit match once the tobacco is smouldering, the flame momentarily refusing to go out. Parkinson questions him about his use of poetry as a tool for social reform. 'That it can't be,' Auden says with gravitas. 'At least not in the West'. The scene jump-cuts to the poet in his summer home in Austria. Auden pretends to be looking for a book on a shelf, over which we hear him reading his poem 'As I Walked Out One Evening'. He walks off, stiff-backed, across a field of chickens. His disembodied voice tells us how he serves his medium while everyone else is led to consume — 'like cans of soup'.

The master narrative returns: 'In 1950s Britain, poets turn away from the obscurity of modernism ... the cameras of the BBC brought their work into millions of living rooms.' The relationship between the twentieth century poet and the BBC is mutually contingent on a strange bond: the poet as outsider and the service of commercialisation. The BBC as a public corporation welcomes their selected poets, like under-employed stevedores, inside its white bricks. Clear communication takes over abstract compaction: those long clean lines of later Eliot are not unlike the architectural classicism of BBC Broadcasting House, which greets us now: a banked ship, rigged with antennae and aerials. Eliot stands in front of an oversized microphone with BBC emblazoned across the top; he looks down at the script of his *Four Quartets* like a sparrowhawk refusing to be fed petshop seed.

Larkin swings through the door of Hull Library as if the starched fabric of his stanzas has come at the expense of his joints and ligaments. 'In 1964 he allowed himself to be filmed for the BBC's flagship arts program *Monitor*,' we're told, as if any positive interest in his work was some kind of trap — the BBC as the groundsman that draws out the red fox with that sudden sharp stink of raw meat: audience. Larkin swings past the rolling stacks of the library in a kind of dance: 'Work and I get on pretty well,' he says, beaming inside but refusing to show it, like a blanketed Belisha beacon. The scene jumps to him cycling through a cemetery. Critics have talked about his powers of observation — on the human condition, post-war Britain, love and regret — but Larkin doesn't strike me as someone who wants to stop and read the names on the stones, to run his hand across the remaining Victorian heritage. In fact he's moving with the intention of getting through the cemetery as quickly as he can.

Larkin's genius was to capture the *surface mood* of the post-war state — 'a welfare state sub poetry' as he called it. 'What one writes is based upon the kind of poetry one can write,' he says cryptically. Larkin doesn't want to get down into the oozy grime of the real — like Birmingham poet Roy Fisher for example — to get too near to the surface where his work might reflect the floors people spend their working lives above. Larkin mops the spillage as it rises to viscous layers, granting his readers an experience of the floor without the threat of infection. Larkin is a cipher of dispirited times, to the point where he's almost not there himself: a hologram on a borrowed bike.

A cameraman sits on a swivelling high-rise camera lift with the unenviable job of pointing the lens at Kingsley Amis. Amis sits ferret-eyed in a tight suit and a chequered tie. He is being given an introduction by Spike Milligan. Then Amis himself reads a poem ('Should poets bicyle-pump the human heart?') which falls flat: no one laughs when they should and the profound moments in the poem skim like misshaped stones across a shallow lake. We *need* Amis to realise how good Larkin is.

Berryman is a relief. Berryman is always a relief — especially when making Al Alvarez uncomfortable. 'Alvarez went to meet him in 1967 for the BBC where he was writing his poems in a Dublin pub ... which is apparently where he did most of his writing and a lot of his drinking.' Alvarez, the suicide-sniffer, sits like the toad with the jewel-stone in his forehead, as the curling fumes of Guinness and whiskey chasers rise from Berryman like river mist. As Berryman talks he moves in his seat with a boxer's bob and weave. His bearded face is unnaturally large, the tang of his ennui and despair almost palatable across the decades. When he says 'but' — which he repeats — it sounds like a dog's bark. The body he is talking about, through his alter ego Henry, is that of Berryman's own father, who the eleven-year-old poet had found dead by suicide. The poet looks down the camera as if there's a sense — despite making this point to exhaustion — that his poetry can now reach himself, via his father, with some kind of solace. Berryman wants us to feel what he feels too, to know what he knows about grief: 'Life, friends, is boring: We must not say so.' Berryman *does* say so; tucked in this Irish snug he doesn't want to be Joyce, or even Beckett. It is Yeats and the Elizabethans with whom Berryman feels a kinship. Berryman's work bleeds into the energies of modernism with his fragmentary colloquialisms — whilst still retaining a deft Elizabethan lyricism and formalism: an incredible balancing act. The drop-shadowed title on the cover of the *77 Dream Songs* moves around the screen, and then pages from the first edition merge in to Berryman's face — as if canonical poets become their books, inseparable from the life and myth.

Alvarez, a cross between Errol Flynn and Sherlock Holmes, sits uncomfortably beside the ranting Berryman, sucking on a pipe in the way only an American in Ireland can do. This is the BBC's finest moment, here in this pub, where all staging has been lost: we're locked-in with Berryman the Broken. His relationships had failed, his therapy had failed, his poetry — whatever he thought the 385 *Dream Songs* could do for him — was failing, even as the art became unquestionably brilliant. It was failing for him as a survival tool: the meds of the sonnet were thinning as he approached the 400 mark. 'I conclude now,' he reads from a poem, 'that I have no inner resources.' He killed himself a few years later by jumping from the Washington Avenue Bridge in Minneapolis — the tides of alcohol replaced with the salt-foam of the Mississippi River.

The BBC, ever attuned to a tragic melodrama, take this as a cue to roll out a rostrum of American suicides: 'Sylvia Plath never appeared on television. In this radio recording in her final months she stressed her preference for intellectual rigour above a poetry of self-pity.' However — and here's the tangent — 'Her mother, Aurelia, was interviewed for the BBC.' I would have relished Plath on screen, a more original image-maker than any of her male counterparts. Her face in movement, which Ted Hughes described as making every camera its enemy, is lost to us. We get, instead — and inevitably — Ted Hughes reading *Crow*: pointlessly handsome, measuring each word between the earthly timbre of his voice and the sneering Elvis lip-curl of his clenched mouth. *Crow* isn't a nature poem; it's the poet's repressed, transformed and re-appropriated response to the death of two wives by suicide. It is not just about the savagery of the life-death cycle and the triumph of death over life, it's about the twisted, purposeless, perverse mystery which allows nature to make inexplicable decisions. The camera switches to a different scene, a more familiar register: it's Roger McGough, with his quickened and clipped Scouse quips, telling us he took up poetry for the women. It looks like he grew thin waiting for them. I pause the programme.

I write down a list of all of the poets whom the BBC filmed, followed by their publisher:

Ezra Pound (Faber)
T.S. Eliot (Faber)
Robert Graves (Faber)
Edith Sitwell (Faber)
W. H. Auden (Faber)
Hugh MacDiarmid (Various)
Stevie Smith (Faber)

John Betjeman (Macmillan and John Murray)
R.S. Thomas (Rupert Hart-Davis, Dent and Bloodaxe)
Dylan Thomas (Dent)
Philip Larkin (Faber)
Kingsley Amis (Cape)
John Berryman (Faber)
Sylvia Plath (Faber)
Ted Hughes (Faber)
Roger McGough (Penguin)
Seamus Heaney (Faber)

Seventeen poets, only three of them women. Eleven of the seventeen are published by Faber (the most notable exception being Dylan Thomas). Then I start to look at the number of poetry publishers in existence in the decades of these recordings and it's clear that the BBC coterie chosen here were a mere august wisp of hair on the well-follicled pate of the artform. I dig around, scratching away not at Nunhead earth but through various catalogues — the British Library, The Poetry Library — to find that the story of twentieth century poetry is much wider and more varied. I keep a track of what I find published within each year, decade by decade:

1920s: 58 collections from 28 publishers
1930s: 77 collections from 36 publishers.
1940s: 72 collections from 28 publishers
1950s: 105 collections from 53 publishers

This is an extensive list showing not only a much broader number of collections in any given year than ever made the BBC airwaves but also collections from quality publishers that don't make it on to the list of BBC poets: The Bodley Head, Chatto, MacMillan and André Deutsch, to name a few. Even within the Faber selected poets here there are only a handful of Faber's own poets, the giants making Lilliputians of names that we never hear and can barely pronounce. Who ever talks now of Ronald Bottrall, Clere Parsons and Marion Angus?

The BBC had been founded in 1922, became a public service shortly after and quickly developed a national audience. Soon after Faber and Gwyer became Faber and Faber in 1929 (there was no other Faber, the name was a ghost echo of the one man, masquerading under the ruse of a partnership) T.S. Eliot was promoted to have complete control of the poetry list. This was the year that saw Eliot's work with Faber and the BBC converging. Eliot was invited by Charles Siepmann, Director of Talks for the BBC to have the all-important 'voice test' in March 1929 for some talks he'd proposed on the Metaphysical Poets. In a letter sent to his mother on the 10th March 1929 we get a view of the century's most famous poet struggling to understand the new technology — though instinctively sensing its power to reach a new audience:

> I was taken into a little room, which seemed hermetically sealed, and was called a studio, and sat down at a desk and read a few paragraphs aloud in an ordinary voice. There was a little metal box hanging down over the desk, which is the microphone or receiver; and there is a red lamp on the desk which is supposed to go out when one's voice is inaudible. The official who was testing me sat at the other end of the room with 'headphone' over his ears. The test seemed to be satisfactory ... It is strange to think that anyone with a very powerful wireless set could hear me talking, I suppose, in Boston.

Despite his clear awkwardness with the equipment and terminology, Eliot very quickly grasped the potential of the medium to extend his voice much further than any live event. He wrote again to his mother a few months later:

> I have just had a very nice letter from the head of the Broadcasting Company expressing appreciation and a hope that I will give another series later. I should like to do that; once you get used to talking in that way, without seeing an audience, it becomes very easy; and there is a pleasure in thinking that people who listen really are listening, and not like so many people at a lecture who come merely to find out what you look like.

(Letter to his mother, 28th July 1929)

Siepmann was eager for Eliot to follow up with some lectures on contemporary poetry, but Eliot wasn't keen, saying it 'would be much too deep for your audience — if one is not cheap on the one hand or too technical on the other.' Siepmann gave in and Eliot delivered again on seventeenth century poetry. His biography for the programme said: 'T.S. Eliot is a Director of Faber & Faber and Editor of the *New Criterion*. It will be remembered that he gave a successful series in the summer session on Tudor Prose.' When it came to this audience Eliot was *the* new voice and not the mouthpiece for all of the other poets out there. He was presenting himself at the end of a successive line of poets: Donne, Milton, Dryden. To the new mass audience he *was* contemporary poetry.

In the same year, Eliot wrote to his brother Henry Eliot about his working relationship with Faber in which his business acumen and work as a poet became woven into a single, potentially prosperous strand:

> As you know, I am a director of Faber & Faber: I sold a bond to invest in shares in the new firm. Of course we have no expectations of dividends for the next three or four years; but I want to strengthen my position with them. If the firm goes on and prospers, I shall stay with them … It is a young firm, so that success is not certain. When it began as Faber & Gwyer it was very weak and inexperienced, and wasted money; since then it has been reorganised, and is much more promising … For a long time my own works were the best sellers of the firm, which gave a very dismal forecast; but latterly that is not the case, and the list, and prospects and prestige of the firm are rapidly improving.

(Letter to Henry Eliot, 19th October 1929)

Eliot was in the tenuous situation of writing books for his own firm, a prospect which he describes — like the city in *The Waste Land* — as 'unreal'. He was also having to subsidise his low income of £400 a year through reviews, writing and broadcasting. By 1930 the work on the lectures had yielded returns and Eliot was having his own poems broadcast, including 'The Hollow Men' and 'Journey of the Magi'. Eliot was in a position of double power. He was able to commission and publish books by the poets he admired and could then — if he chose — suggest them to the BBC. As poet and editor he was their go-to man for all poetry-related matters. Significantly, although radio play manuscripts were welcomed at the BBC (6,000 were received in 1929), they weren't open for poetry submissions: after all, Eliot was always available on the other end of the phone. Faber became the BBC's synonym for quality, the rioja-seal of full-bodied blood — and Eliot's nose was to be trusted.

The inference from all of this is that the BBC not only saved 'the best' of poetry but also gave it a larger audience. Eliot's preference for the erudite white male is presented as simply presenting quality rather than projecting taste. By following Eliot's decisions, the BBC took their poetry as cans of potted meat rather than finding it raw and bloodied in the abattoir — which is how it exists out in the world. Other poets of the time felt some frustration with this, including Basil Bunting, who made public his distaste for Eliot's controlling influence when he attacked the older poet in an issue of *Poetry*: 'I have nothing to say against his poetry, amongst the finest of the age; but against his influence on the poetry of others, the involuntary extinguisher he applies to every little light, while professing, maybe truly, to hate the dark.'

I walk back to my shelves and browse the hundreds of slim pamphlets I've bought over the past ten years. Poetry in 2016 is exactly the same as it would have been between 1930 and the 50s if the BBC-Faber pact hadn't existed: a gathering of talents that aren't household names. In the UK in 2012 there were 1024 adult collections published from 120 publishers: ten times as many collections from twice as many publishers than in 1950. This is aside from the hundreds of magazines, ezines, social media uploads, YouTube videos and — ever on the increase — live events, installations and exhibitions involving poets each year. I take down one of the most popular anthologies of previous decades, *Nine Modern Poets* edited by E.L. Black, and compare this presentation of nine poets to the range of modern anthologies we've had over the last five years: *Identity Parade: New British and Irish Poets* (Bloodaxe, 2010) has eighty-five contributors and *Dear World and Everyone in It: New Poetry in the UK*

(Bloodaxe, 2013) houses seventy-five. These days the green room isn't big enough for the contributors, elbows are raised to eye level and warm wine accidentally spilled on jostling poets' jackets. It might be hard for readers to find a way in to this but at least it's honest: poetry is broad and you have to dig about for the poets who speak to you. Don't ask: do you like poetry? Ask: what *kind* of poetry do you like?

The BBC no longer has the sway to bring poetry into our homes, at least not in a way that can bring a poet's name to the tongue-tip of everyone in the household. The organisation has developed from one radio station to over six, while the two stand-alone television channels they provided in the 1960s now compete with anything up to 300 other channels. There is more being published than ever before — more poets across more kinds of poetry — and, most importantly: there is no longer just one source of truth as to how we access it.

On the BBC's website *Poets Perform Their Own Work*, there is a spooky echo of the Faber-BBC pact. The site showcases nineteen poets, ten of whom are published by Faber. Given the 100-plus poetry publishers in the UK this is an obscene simplification of the textures and energies that exist in contemporary poetry. I've finished ranting, I tell myself, as I place my poetry books back on my shelf. The best thing about the dead poets of Victorian cemeteries is that they can be accessed for free. The history of Eliot, Faber and the BBC has shown me exactly why one of the forgotten poets could be the best writer of their age, overlooked by the mainstream eye. All I have to do now is find them.

23rd October 2014

Poets face this death inside them throughout their lives. They speak to it until it becomes their life's work. Today I read this from Dylan Thomas, written when he was nineteen:

> *And time cast forth my mortal creature*
> *To drift or drown upon the seas*
> *Acquainted with the salt adventure*
> *Of tides that never touch the shores.*
> *I who was rich was made the richer*
> *By sipping at the vine of days.*

This pending death inside of the poet speaks in their life's work: they must face it honestly and without compromise, but how would Dylan Thomas have dealt with his own cancer had it become real — would his lyrical waxing have been enough to forge him the wings to go over or at least around it? Thomas, like so many poets, hurled himself into excess before a natural process could kill him: his addiction to poetry exacerbated by alcohol.

Perhaps when poets start to play it safe with their bodily and life choices — striving to be on earth for the long term — then their work begins to die on the branch. But then I'm seeing death everywhere at the moment — and flying towards poetry somehow sure that it is the sustenance that will get me through.

Nunhead Poets: William Cox Bennett and Joshua Russell

Now I've found Tim Stevenson to walk me into the underworld of Nunhead Cemetery I'm reading everything I can about the dead poets, looking for links. He's sent me further information from Ron Woollacott, author of a series of books about those buried in Nunhead. Hugh Meller and Brian Parsons in *London Cemeteries* also detail some of Nunhead's poets.

The first image in the book, on the title page, is of a fallen angel — I read the caption: *taken at Nunhead Cemetery*. The intrigue and silence of the Cemetery are matched with its reputation for decay and squalor: 'Nunhead ranks among the best of London's large nineteenth century cemeteries, but its history has always been troubled and its condition is now critical.'

London Cemeteries is the *Yellow Pages* for the notable dead residing in London's 126 graveyards and cemeteries. I flick through the alphabetical contents of burials and find that there are three poets listed as buried here at Nunhead. The Old Nun's Head Tavern is mentioned again as a pre-Cemetery draw for the poets: a 'favourite resort of smoke dried London artisans', William Home wrote in 1827. Taverns of excess are well-positioned to give poets quick access to the afterlife. I write down the names of the three poets and am taken aback by how one of them, William Cox Bennett, has my mother's maiden name — the narratives and emotional concerns of the past year began to overlap a long time ago but this adds a new resonance.

In addition to the poets there is an incredible cast of eccentric dead in Nunhead Cemetery: a seven-foot clerk, a woman who died at 105 in 1911, a Gaelic lexicographer, a biblical scholar, a glass maker, a wigmaker, a surgeon and astronomer, the pioneer of horse-drawn bus routes, a bare-knuckle boxer. I also note the long list of song writers and comedians, such as The Great Vance (Alfred Vance, 1839-88) who had over 1,000 people at his funeral and Jenny Hill (1848-96), a Cockney music hall star who sang 'The Boy I Love is in the Gallery'. Augustus Durandeau (1848-93), another Nunhead burial, became famous for writing the song 'If you want to know the time ask a policeman' and then was buried in a pauper's grave.

But I've arrived at Nunhead today to find the poets and I've pinned their names and burial locations to a map of the Cemetery.

I start with the one that shares my mum's family name, William Cox Bennett, a name which could actually be a conflation from both sides of my family, 'William' being the male name passed down on my father's side (it's the middle name of my dad and younger brother). The emotional entanglements of the last year is made physical in the name of this poet — but is he any good?

The Upper Cross Path splits the section of land that Bennett is buried in: he could be on either side of the path I'm standing on. I look ahead to the undergrowth, urns buried beneath matted vegetation. Imagine a back garden unkempt for fifty years; add exotic plant species and a wood of sycamores: this is what's in front of me. This area is further complicated by the slope that runs through it. I think of my mum after her surgery, her arms tangled with wires and drips and move as far forward as I can into the thriving ivy, ragwort and vetches, pulling back the branches on the first grave

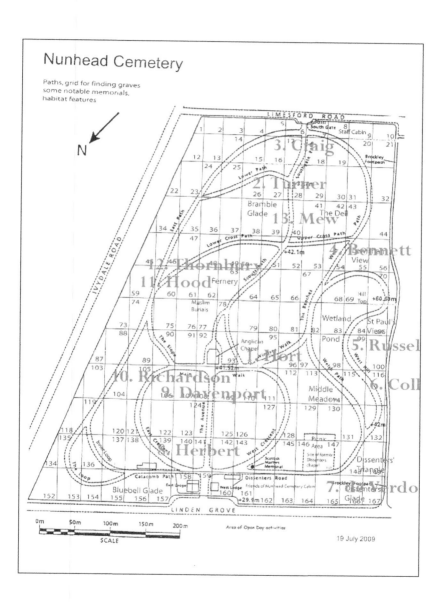

Nunhead Cemetery

Paths, grid for finding graves
some notable memorials,
habitat features

N

Area of Open Day activities

19 July 2009

I find: JOHN MAYOR WILSON. Wrong family. As I find all the time in the land of literature — when looking through books to find connections — words play games with sense, make the mind see what it wants to see. A grave with BENNEWORTH written on it makes my pulse rise. Then another: EDWIN BARNETT, who 'fell asleep in Jesus, June 10th 1880'. There's just one other word on his gravestone: PARADISE. This isn't my poet.

I regain a foothold, remind myself of the poet I'm looking for. William Cox Bennett was born in 1820. He began his life in Greenwich and, 74 years later, was buried in Nunhead. As a teenager he was forced to discontinue school due to his father's death — but self-made Victorians are resurrectionists and Bennett propelled himself into action on many fronts. His skills went across politics (he was influential in Gladstone becoming a Liberal candidate for Greenwich) and an effective campaigner for many changes in the borough, including the formation of a literary institute, reform of a charity school and the establishment of public baths and wash houses. He was also a writer and art critic for the *Weekly Dispatch* and, later, the *London Figaro*.

Bennett had ambitions for his poetry and Dickens — like a force-fed ostrich in his plumes and beard — was on the other end of Bennett's correspondence. Dickens wrote Bennett a note of thanks on 29th August 1848, addressing him as 'Dear Sir' (which makes clear that they had no relationship in the literary world or as friends):

> I beg to assure you, in reply to your obliging note, that I have felt from the first the liveliest interest in those verses which you have kindly sent me from time to time, and that I have very highly esteemed those marks of your remembrance. Believe me I feel indebted to you for giving me this opportunity of saying, that I

have been deeply moved and affected by some of your writings, and that I thank you with all my heart.

Dickens was never dishonest in his praise of other literature, though he was accomplished in telling writers what they wanted to hear: the clinch word here is 'some' — 'I have been deeply moved and affected by *some* of your writings'. Bennett reciprocated his praise for Dickens in a slightly more public way through the dedications he made to him in his poems. He wrote a sonnet about Gad's Hill, in which he refers to 'England's world-loved Dickens' and on Dickens' death he wrote an 'In Memoriam' poem, published in the *Penny Illustrated Paper*.

Bennett also provides a connection to Robert Browning, whose residence at Telegraph Hill forms the highest point of my map around the Cemetery. Bennett was unwittingly involved in a controversy many years after his death when the forger Thomas J. Wise named him as the person from whom he'd acquired a falsely signed copy of Elizabeth Browning's *Sonnets*, published in 1847. In 1934 Wise cleared Bennett by remembering that what he had actually acquired from Bennett was Bennett's own privately printed *My Sonnets* of 1843. Bennett was left to sleep soundly over the matter.

From 1843 Bennett published twelve collections of poetry to a mixed reception. According to Anne Lohrli one reviewer dubbed his poetry 'very sorry stuff' while he gained 'immense popularity' amongst another class of readers — though Lohrli doesn't say which class that was. In the preface to his 1862 *Poems* Bennett wrote that critics have said that some of his poems 'have been reprinted in almost every newspaper and popular periodical of England, America and our Colonies' but in the twenty years that I've been involved in poetry I haven't heard him mentioned once. Is he a poet for whom the case for a new readership should be made?

Of all of Bennett's poems it would be most likely that Dickens was impressed with Bennett's 'Baby May', his most popular poem. This poem is a joyous incantatory celebration of parenthood. Although the end rhymes are predictable, the poet displays a gift for metrical rhythm as he describes his young daughter and the new emotions she provokes in the father. The third line here is particularly skilful with the pause halfway through and the enjambment at the end, smoothly wrapping the line around to the next:

> CHEEKS as soft as July peaches,
> Lips whose dewy scarlet teaches
> Poppies paleness — round large eyes
> Ever great with new surprise,
> Minutes filled with shadeless gladness,
> Minutes just as brimmed with sadness,
> Happy smiles and wailing cries,
> Crows and laughs and tearful eyes,
> Lights and shadows swifter born
> Than on wind-swept Autumn corn
> Ever some tiny notion
> Making every limb all motion

Although the fatherly fervour slightly exasperates it's easy to see how the Victorian reader would be swept along with this unconcealed celebration of the newborn:

> Loveliness beyond completeness,
> Sweetness distancing all sweetness,
> Beauty all that beauty may be –
> That's May Bennett, that's my baby.

Bennett isn't always so compact and whatever stirrings of excitement were elicited by 'Baby May', they quickly dry up like unrefrigerated July peaches. The poem that follows 'Baby May' in *Poems* is perhaps the most disappointing sequel in poetic history, forming part of what Bennett called his 'Home Poems' and which gave him the very dubious title of the 'Laureate of the Babies':

O Those little, those little blue shoes!
Those shoes that no little feet use!
    O the price were high
    That those shoes would buy,
Those little blue unused shoes!

('Baby's Shoes')

Every parent knows the feeling of the expensive gift unused — there's humour in it — but as the basis for a poem, it falls short of the comic. Bennett plays straight to the middle-class audience for poetry in poems like this, confirming experiences, indulging their tastes. Given the extreme poverty across parts of London at this time — which Bennett would have known about as a councillor — there is clearly a disconnection between the unused blue shoes in the poem and the lives of those who couldn't afford a pair to walk in.

As I get further into the undergrowth the risk grows of tripping on a concealed piece of headstone or a broken piece of mausoleum. The ground is rich with dock leaves, ragwort, thistles and nettles, which thrive in the darkness above the earth where Nunhead's wealth of human additions have been buried. I kick a rusted watering can and regain my balance against a tree.

When reading Bennett's poems I was drawn to the appearance

of a hawthorn in his poem 'A Wife's Song' — which turns out to be one of his more successful poems:

> O WELL I love the Spring,
>   When the sweet, sweet hawthorn blows;
> And well I love the Summer,
>   And the coming of the rose;
> But dearer are the changing leaf,
>   And the year upon the wane,
> For O, they bring the blessed time
>   That brings him home again.

The conceit is simple: a wife looks forward to Autumn when her husband returns. In terms of style there is a flexibility in line length here which adds a naturalness to the poem's address. The poem is a straightforward lyric and — unlike Browning's monologues — makes no attempt to capture the psyche of the woman who is talking; perhaps Bennett was playing to his limits and was aware that if he tried to make his poems too complex they would begin to crack at the edges? Bennett is at his best within his comfort zone. A comparison between Bennett and Blake confirms the limits of the lesser known poet; Blake, for example, could clearly articulate a complex paradox. We see this when looking at Bennett's 'A Summer Thought' alongside Blake's 'The Sick Rose', both poems that deal with the decaying of natural life. Bennett attempts to cover the age-old terrain of human mortality through the image of decaying flora:

> IN thy circle, painted flower,
> What a world of wonder lies!
> Yet men pass thee, hour by hour,
> With no marvel in their eyes...

Blake deals with the same subject matter in his poem ('O Rose thou art sick') and, like Bennett, addresses the flower directly. Bennett, however, makes the mistake of overly personifying the flowering to the extent where he begins to ask it questions, asking if it is truly non-sentient and genuinely has no care for the praise of humans: 'When our tongues thy praises show, / Is no pride thy bright robes swelling?' As with the attempted evocation of emotion in 'Baby's Shoes' there is a slight inanity to Bennett's address; whereas Blake talks *to* the rose, Bennett asks the flower questions — highlighting the impossibility of the flower being able to make a response. There is also an arrogance to Bennett's posture here, a sense that the rest of the world doesn't appreciate the flower that only he — the poet — can:

> Ere decay hath crept unto thee,
> Did they dare, would pause delighted;
> Ah, that men, with noteless eyes,
> Thus to pass thee should have power

Re-reading Blake's poem highlights Bennett's awkwardness:

> O Rose, thou art sick.
> The invisible worm,
> That flies in the night
> In the howling storm:
>
> Has found out thy bed
> Of crimson joy:
> And his dark secret love
> Does thy life destroy.

I hover over that colon at the end of the fourth line and the enforced, dramatic pause it brings before the stanza break — as if the howling storm has reached a cliff edge. In just twenty-one syllables the reader is brought to a place of no turning back and whether they wish to face the end of Blake's image or not, it is very difficult to swerve away from this hinge in the poem. The propulsion of death is ever forward. Blake audaciously adds another colon into the same sentence, a colon which is followed by an 'And' which creates a double pause before the final two lines of the poem. 'The Sick Rose' works through enforced pause and quick reveal. The poet forces us to see what we didn't want to see — our own death inside the sick flower. Whilst holding back from us the image of decaying flesh, the full impact of the poem hits us after it's too late to be unread. Beginning with an address that is unequivocally *to* the flower, Blake takes just eight lines to collapse the distinction between its short insensate life and the human life of the reader. We can't get out of the way of the poem's eidetic images of decay that lie at the heart of pleasure. This is a great poem which reflects nature's processes in the flux of its very form.

What would an 'invisible worm' in a 'howling storm' look like? A foetal ghost shivering on a London hill. Adjective and noun coalesce into explosions of instamatic synaesthesia: all of death is captured in the flower's death. This poem that passes through the mind of most school children has been anthologised thousands of times and is known as a Blake original. Whereas Bennett's poem attempts a conceit which has the flower's death representing the entirety of mortality, Blake cuts his images so paradoxically sharp that it imprints itself in the reader's mind as a single image without stopping to draw out a moral. The reader is then forced to see, and taste the slow-worm-eaten petals for themselves.

I stop to wonder if I might be related to this poet that I'm looking for? If my DNA might be traced to the atomised remains that lie around here — somewhere — beneath my feet. I stop at a lacquered information board which tells me that the area I am in contains many eminent Victorians: drapers to nobility, type founders, shipbuilders, stonemasons, architects and a Romantic novelist: Sydney Carylon Grier. The novelists are written into the landscape while the poets are in silence. Perhaps there's a good reason for this? I continue to scratch around in the bushes amongst the rioting undergrowth. Stone-tangling brambles and decay: life and death in cahoots. It's in this field that Bennett is lost.

Bennett's in good company with Nunhead's music hall performers. It was through the writing of songs and ballads that he developed his literary interests. He writes in the preface to *Songs by a Song-Writer* (the tautological title is symptomatic of his habit of needlessly repeating himself:

> Ever since I could read Songs, I have loved them. The dearest shelf of my book-case is that where rank, shoulder to shoulder, in loving brotherhood, Burns and Beranger, Campbell and Herrick. There, too, are those best-loved of all book-companions, the volumes which bring together the quaint fancies and delicate music of the lyrics of our Elizabethan Dramatists and our Cavalier Singers, and treasure for ever, in the Songs of Scotland and of Ireland, the sobs and laughs of bygone generations, for the admiration and the love of all coming centuries. Chaucer, Spenser, and Milton, I reverence with awe.

The author's dedication to, and knowledge, of literary songs and ballads is impressive: he clearly didn't try to write his way to acclaim without a passion for reading. In addition to the names cited here he mentions Wordsworth, Coleridge, Byron and Petrarch. Bennett was so immersed in the ballad form that he wrote a diatribe for it entitled *Shall We Have a National Ballad-History for the English People: An Appeal to the Poets of England and America*.

His own writings in this genre, however, suffer from a problem: the melody often overpowers the sense. Like patting one's head while rubbing the stomach the best lyric poets have the ability to make sense crystallize into form; those with less talent sacrifice one for the other. Many of Bennett's conceits are glaringly ridiculous and despite their serious intent would work better as a pastiche of the form. In 'O Might I be the Happy Glove', how — it's tempting to ask — can a glove be happy? As with Bennett's questions addressed to the flower all sense is momentarily lost here:

> O Might I be the happy glove,
> The happy glove that clasps her hand!
>
> But, O more blest, how would I love
> To be her robe's glad girdling band,
>
> For ever press'd, in clasp how warm!
> What mighty raptures there to taste!

There is the further slip here in asking the reader to consider the band of her robe as something that can *taste*. This is an example of Victorian repression exploding into incoherence: the repressed emotion is more than the form can handle.

A further chattering to the birds rises on the air: schoolchildren, out on a day trip. One points to the tomb of a John Allen and says 'Wow, must be a rich person.' Another asks: 'Are there people in this cave?' I listen to the tour guide, hoping for news of a poet. Instead she asks them: 'What's the difference between a tomb and a grave?' but the children are distracted by two passing whippets. The teacher says 'Ignore the dog and it will pass,' and then adds, 'Your question for this tomb is: how many 3D shapes can you see on this?'

Bennett, at the end of his preface, asks the question which any poet who knows their worth and talent would never ask — least of all in the introduction to their own book:

> "Shall I publish them?" is the question which this volume puts to its critics and to its readers. Its reception will be the answer.

What, then, is Bennett's place in English literature? He was, at one point, on the edge of being canonised and was included in Alfred H. Miles' anthology *The Poets and the Poetry of the Century*, published twelve years before the poet's death. The period that embraced Bennett has since been re-evaulated through the lens of modernism; as a result readers look for different qualities than those Miles saw and appreciated in Bennett's work:

> His verse is characterised by hearty English sense and feeling. There is no obscurity of style to pass for profundity of thought, but all is written for the people in a manner easily to be understood. His work shows a clear eye for the beauty that surrounds common life, and a sympathetic heart for those who often miss it in the stress of toil and suffering … It is these songs and ballads which express the honest emotions of simple hearts, that give him his place in the literature of his time.

Time challenges the way we read and, as a result, Bennett is forgotten and in no danger of having his books republished, although poems of his have appeared in many modern anthologies. Every poet knows the feeling that comes with not being anthologised and the inner assuring voice that follows, convincing the hysterical ego that it doesn't matter. Poets should listen to that voice: it doesn't. Bennett is unknown by name despite his continuing inclusion in anthologies throughout the decades since his death. Here's a timeline of some of his appearances in anthologies, a kind of echocardiogram of the poet's afterlife pulse through the veins of readership:

1867: *Folk Songs*, Charles Scribner and Company
1886: *Through the Year with the Poets: July*, D. Lothrop and Company
1902: *Golden Numbers*, Doubleday
1953: *The Home Book of Verse*, Henry Holt and Company
1983: *The Book of a Thousand Poems: A Family Treasury*, Peter Bedrick Books

The problem with generation- or decade-defining anthologies, the ones that all poets want to be in, is that the included poets jostle for space as if they're crowded together in a small room with a shortage of spotlights. Grudges are borne over whose name appears on the blurb. What's forgotten is that the more general reader of poetry, those who might be looking for a poem to celebrate or commemorate an occasion, will look in themed anthologies (seasons, life events etc.) and read those books for *poems* rather than the names of poets. The kinds of anthologies that Bennett has appeared in aren't the movement and canon-defining anthologies that language artists would aspire to be in; nevertheless these books get more readers than many of the short-run edition anthologies that carry the kudos of being 'groundbreaking'. Bennett's poems will have been read thousands of times since his death although most readers couldn't possibly recall his name.

Anthologists look at old anthologies to create new ones: like the movie *The Human Centipede* the mouth of the lazy anthologist is stitched to the anus of the editor who recycled the previous anthology. What is clear from Bennett — seen in his proud quotes about being printed in newspapers and journals — was that he desperately wanted to be read: this was perhaps more important to him than any contribution he felt he could make to the art of poetry. In that he has at least got something of what he wanted. So Bennett lives on in anthologies, which are then added to databases such as Grangers, which are then made available to libraries in the UK and America and are used to allow patrons to search for suitable poems. Bennett's poems will appear hundreds of times each year to those looking for content on the theme of 'babies' and 'fatherhood'.

As I walk through the section that Bennett is in, by chance I find the headstone of another Bennett, Joan Rose, who died 18 years after husband Derek. Together again. Low stones appear over high grass like hiding children waiting to be caught out. Surnames that have failed to endure: Pook, Shotter, Keddell and Rumble. Names like typefaces sliding out of usage. The lid of a stone mausoleum has been lifted and — it seems — the contents removed. The text on the surface has been blasted by time. Beneath the ivy the headstone might as well read: MISSING POET, REWARD OFFERED.

The next poet I've found by name — Joshua Russell (1796-1870) — is buried just below the section where the trees have been coppiced to give a view of St Paul's Cathedral. Even now — when Nunhead is no longer the suburb it was — you can feel the remove. South London is not just distanced by a river but by hills: too many obstacles to quickly stride across. This distance invites introspection and melancholy: key shades to mix with words on a palette. Westminster Abbey couldn't be further away: any future readers of the work of Nunhead's dead poets will have to cross the channels of time with a Thermos and an incredible amount of patience to visit these poets. Unlike the elevated position of those buried in Westminster these are not monuments to be stared at on an indoor leisure trip.

Unlike Bennett, Joshua Russell has not been anthologised. His poetry has become quite literally inaccessible to the modern audience and can be found in neither the century-defining nor themed editions of the twentieth and twenty-first centuries. Russell also wrote prose about his Christian missionary work in India, a theme which often appears in his poetry. When I called up his collection *Poems* at the British Library — printed by F. Mason at the Borough in 1819 and sold at St Paul's Churchyard — I couldn't make out if the edition was mottled with blackened mould or if it was a deliberate mock marble effect. I like the titles of Russell's poems for their ability to name specifics — a relief after the vagaries of so much Victorian poetry. I've always admired the way poets such as Ted Hughes, Marianne Moore and Francis Ponge (and Blake) focus on individual objects in the world, allowing the reader to inhabit those things more fully. Russell's book focuses on a mix of abstractions and material entities — 'The Lunatic', 'The Rock', 'Moonlight' — as well as the usual vagaries found in poetry of this period, such as serenity and remorse.

Like Bennett, Russell wrote a preface which makes the

mistake of beginning with an apology — telling us that his poems were written 'in moments snatched between other occupations'. He uses a euphemism for self-publishing which is new to me: the book, he says, is 'a voluntary offering'. Russell, like many of the Victorians I've read, then goes on to talk about his distaste for war, 'its hatefulness, and practical evils'. He braces himself for further attack, taking on the public distaste for religious poetry 'that exists in the public mind [and] seems … to have no just foundation'. He calls upon previous poets William Cowper and John Milton to justify the genre of religious poetry and compares poetry not to the butterfly but to the spirit which 'may kindle a new glow, and wake sublime aspirations, even in the breast of a Christian'. He signs his preface 'Southwark 1819': the borough of his residency in death.

The first poem in the collection, 'The Morning Walk', wears the influence of Wordsworth heavily and is an exchange between a younger and elder brother. The language is archaic, infused with sentiment and the tropes of received poetic expression:

> Fresh sweetness from each little flow'ry cup,
> And now the pearly dew the sun sips up

'The Morning Walk' occupies the first fifty-two pages of the book after which is a poem called 'Pieces on War' in which a conversation takes place between a number of spirits describing a man:

> THERE was no moon but many twinkling stars
> Gave their faint light, when wandering by the verge
> Of an old forest, where, you well may think,
> Strange sights sometimes were seen

The adjectives here are lazy — 'twinkling', 'faint', 'old' — and make no attempt to present the world in a new way for the reader. Russell makes the mistake of using de-intensifying words and phrases such as: 'you may well think', 'strange sights sometimes'. I read on, in hope of the poet offering me a Faustian pact I can't refuse: it doesn't happen. Russell is rooted in the flattened vernacular of tepid language and declamation, a nauseous mix of registers:

> Poets will chaunt, and poor ballad singers
> Stretch their hoarse throats about to listening crowds.
> And all the world's for glory, and each one
> Feels that strong impulse, in particular,
> Of his own benefit, which war may serve.

There is an interesting connection made here between the career-mongering of poets before an audience, done 'for his own benefit', and war, yet it's clear that Russell isn't writing for the sake of artistic language: his religious polemics are infused with the drive of his missionary work. As with many poets of the period, the urge to convey the message overtakes nuance and originality of language. Worse is to come when Russell takes up end rhymes, such as in 'The Haunted Field':

> NAY, go not by that field, for there at night
> Strange sights, they say, are seen, and noises heard;
> Such as would chill the stoutest heart with fright,
> Many a heavy sigh, and painful word.

There are also poems about his *inability* to become enraptured, as in 'Sonnet', where he bemoans the falling short of 'nobler strains' in his work, which makes me wonder how much more loftily he could sit and look down on the world and his fellow poets:

> COULD I wake nobler strains, Oh! then I'd sing
> In Genius', Courage', and bright Wisdom's praise.

Despite the literal loftiness of Russell being buried on the West Hill, the path which leads down from the view of St Paul's is thriving with cornucopias of nettles. If I stepped into the undergrowth would I ever get back? I take a few steps — risking it — but there's nothing to step on, no traction between living and dead. I check the map and thank my instincts for not going in further: WETLAND POND it says. I've gone beyond the view of St Paul's. This is one of the wild places of south London.

Russell was acutely aware of his mortality and registered his fear of the grave in his poem 'The Tolling Bell':

> TOLL on, bell of death!
> Loosely this world we hold.
> How fleeting is our breath!
> The grave how still and cold!

As I looked through Russell's four published books — two of poetry and two written in prose — I found that his descriptive prose was far more interesting than his poetry. In his *Journal of a Tour in Ceylon and India, Undertaken at the Request of the Baptist Missionary Society ... With Observations and Remarks* (1852) he memorably describes arriving in Satberya:

> Travelled through a country, flat, watery, rich, and populous. Here and there our way was through slush and mud; then over green-sward; then a ploughed field. The clouds gathered in thick,

black masses; and just as we stopped near a shed for the bearers to rest, the thunder began to mutter, and a great storm followed; the hailstones were as large as pigeon's eggs.

The prose has speed, nuance, musicality and striking imagery: 'slush and mud', 'black masses', 'hailstones … as large as pigeon's eggs'. Here is a language that can be handled, that recalls the attentiveness of Gerard Manley Hopkins' journals. As he says in his preface: 'The following work is unofficial; being a narrative, such as any traveller might have made, composed from memoranda written at the places visited.' There is a sense here of the writer who isn't concerned with

Joshua Russell's headstone

listening to himself for 'mistakes' and — by freeing up in this way — gets closer to the objects he's looking at, capturing the *inscape* for the reader. In his poetry he tightens up, becomes conscious that he's writing a 'poetry' which should do particular things in a certain way. The world he occupied — and all the things in it — becomes distant.

His final collection of poems, *The Christian Sabbath,* was published a year later in 1853. This was the year after *Journal of a Tour* and two years after his other prose work, *Thoughts on Missionary Work in India.* Thirty-four years had passed since his first poetry book. Had his work developed in that time, I wondered? The title poem, 'The Christian Sabbath', is a long narrative piece in loose couplets which tells the story — with regularly inserted moral points — of a poor man called Campbell who sees the errors in his life and turn to Christ for solace. The poem is heavy in stock biblical imagery, propelling the vision of the world that Russell lives inside and doesn't want to question — least of all in his poetry. The purpose of his poetry, after all, is to teach the ways of Jesus. The suggestion of a fear of death which often surfaces in his poetry is absent from his tombstone: his huge pedestal monument dubiously claims TO DIE IS GAIN.

25ᵗʰ October 2014

Sometimes I forget who is supposed to be looking after whom. To remain well, well enough to be positive, she needs to remain enough of my mother. To look after her properly I need to let her keep doing things for me. I went with Pavel to visit her today and we gave her a bag of seeds, fruit and chocolate that we'd put together for her. She made me a cup of tea. She showed me an image of the wig she's bought. I made her a cup of tea. She showed me the pot of flowers that she's put together for us, a small circle of late-year bloomers. I ordered and paid for the pizza. She gave me a headboard that she's no longer using, one that belonged to her and my dad. I made another cup of tea. When I got home I put the headboard up, reading poetry, next to Sarah, in bed. I kept thinking of the scan my mum has next week, that will tell us if the cancer has travelled. I couldn't sleep, my head touching the same board my dad's head had touched. Eventually I gave in and reached for the Kindle, reading Dante's **Purgatorio** *in the gelid light from the device.*

26ᵗʰ October 2014

I read an account of a suicide called James William Trist. Trist had killed himself in the Cemetery in July 1864. He was found lying by the side of a grave: overdose of potassium cyanide. The verdict also confirmed he'd been mentally ill since the death of his mother five years before. From then on, as Ron Woollacott puts it, 'he had been acting rather strangely. He had been sacked for taking a holiday without leave, sold his furniture and turned his wife and young child out onto the street ... His head had been found resting on the side of his mother's grave.' Trist had left a letter to his wife: 'My dear wife, when you read these lines the individual who writes them will have taken the liberty of taking a view of the future state of society. I go to see my mother ... I believe now as Shakespeare says, that there is a method in madness. Farewell to this world. I am going to Nunhead.'

The Goose Pie at Telegraph Hill: Robert Browning after *Sordello*

Ghosts move about me
Patched with histories. You had your business:
To set out so much thought, so much emotion;
To paint, more real than any dead Sordello,
The half or third of your intensest life
And call that third Sordello;
And you'll say, "No, not your life,
He never showed himself."
    Ezra Pound, 'Cantos II' (1917 version)

Robert Browning hated Peckham. This might explain why, when his parents moved from Camberwell in 1840, they settled further south near Telegraph Hill. This was the most important creative period in Browning's life, and when he fell in love with Elizabeth Barrett Browning. What Browning achieved as a Victorian poet who went against the grain of taste of the time provides a way of looking at the work of the poets I'm finding in the Cemetery. Browning's Telegraph Hill is the next, and most northern point, on a map that is forming around Nunhead Cemetery.

From the age of nine to fourteen he'd attended the Elementary School of the Reverend and Misses Ready at 77 Queen's Road. Pamela Neville-Sington describes how he would turn 'an upturned cistern in the schoolyard into his private burial place where he would go after lessons to sigh aloud, "In memory of unhappy Browning"'. Luckily for Browning his cousin and best friend of the time James Silverthorne — also buried in Nunhead — lived nearby.

Silverthorne introduced Browning to Shelley. Browning later repaid the favour by dedicating his poem 'May and Death' to 'his dear cousin Jim'. As well as the cousin he loved — as I imagine with Blake before him — there was always the attraction of Peckham Fair.

Twenty years later, in 1840, Browning moved with his parents from the family home in Camberwell to Telegraph Hill, to a cottage which he described as resembling a 'goose pie'. He was in recoil from the poor reviews of his long poem *Sordello*. Five years later he would still be living there, in love with Elizabeth Barrett Browning and writing to her: 'I love your verses with all my heart, dear Miss Barrett'. This morning I'm on the search for the site of Browning's cottage, which is just a mile from Nunhead Cemetery and which was opened in July 1840, just five months before Browning moved here. A link between poetics and place: whilst *Sordello* strikes a unique and pivotal note in the Victorian poetic landscape, Nunhead Cemetery was part of the reconfiguring of the nineteenth century London topography. 1840 was a key year, pinning this enclave of south-east London to Browning's reshaping of the corpus of modern poetry.

Not long before Browning moved here Telegraph Hill had been known as Plow'd Garlick Hill. As David Cooper points out in his contribution to *Mount London: Ascents in the Vertical City*, Chaucer's pilgrims would have 'passed close to this mound as they walked'. The poetic line from Chaucer is becoming a holloway in my map of south-east London. To reach Browning's plaque I have to pass the Cemetery — the Cemetery that holds the remains of his half-uncle, the historical writer William Shergold Browning (1797-1874), the cousin he loved, James Silverthorne, and his mother. I've become so accustomed to thinking of Browning arriving in this area at the beginning of his success as a poet and his falling in love with Elizabeth — but history has since moved all the living people he loved into the Cemetery.

Browning had felt what it was to be on the outside of Nunhead Cemetery. When James Silverthorne died, the Brownings were living in Italy. Robert's impulse was to make the trip to Nunhead Cemetery for the funeral of his cousin. Elizabeth talked him out of it; Robert's mother had died just three years before and she was worried that a return visit might send him into a relapse of grief. Elizabeth also confessed her fear of 'the earth-side of death': a phrase which captures the essence of Nunhead Cemetery:

> in no paroxysm of anguish could I identify the dust there and the soul there ... I am horribly weak about such things — I can't look on the earth-side of death — I flinch from corpses and graves, and never meet a common funeral without a sort of horror. When I look deathwards I look over death, and upwards, or I can't look that way at all.

The news of Browning's mother's death had been delivered to him in a letter from an aunt which — along with breaking the unbearable news — congratulated the Browning's on the birth of their son. The strands of hair that Robert had cut from the baby's head and sent by post to his ailing mother had not reached her in time. Robert's grief was so extreme that despite turning to the baby to pull him out of the depression, he reached the edge — Elizabeth feared — of a nervous breakdown. His newborn son and the delicate health of his wife stopped him from making it here, to Nunhead, for his mother's funeral, but his thoughts turned constantly to the family home at Telegraph Hill. Elizabeth wrote in a letter: 'England looks terrible now. He says it would break his heart to see his mother's roses over the wall.'

Outside the locked gates of the Cemetery — I'm here early — the information board offers an overview of the Cemetery's history: architecture, trees, people, wildlife. 'At the time the Cemetery opened in 1840, Nunhead was a small hamlet surrounded by market gardens and open fields.' The hill that has now become part of the Cemetery would have been easily visible to Browning when he walked to the highest point of Telegraph Hill. I wonder if Browning, a self-declared child of nature, knew that the Cemetery was filled with so many rare natural elements: Italian alder, holm oak and gingko? He would have surely passed the endless lime trees that gave their name to the road below.

I look through the rails towards the graves. The signature symbol of Nunhead's gates are the upturned torches, which the information boards tells me are 'decorative devices which suggest life being snuffed out, cut flowers, weeping figures.' My thoughts turn to my own mother and her ongoing treatment — the word *cancer* hovering on the breeze that is passing through the Cemetery. Two squirrels are fighting in a tree above me, their tiny hare's fists jabbing with welterweight speed. A car goes past behind me playing Rihanna from the window. I walk away from the gates, past the rows of railings — bushes reaching out into the street — and a yellowing headstone catches my eye, foxing in the undergrowth. Extending out from the grounds and reaching up around a pillar are vines that have dried out after becoming attached to a stone column. The vines are like latte-coloured centipedes. I look inside the rails and see that the vines have actually been cut from their roots: dead tendrils frozen in mid-air.

I walk towards Telegraph Hill, pulling my thoughts back to Browning and the book he was in recoil from when he moved here

— *Sordello*. Thomas Carlyle's wife had always thought that Browning was a sham but when she'd finished reading *Sordello* she said that she had no idea if Sordello was a man, a city or a book. The playwright Douglas Jerrold (buried at West Norwood Cemetery) attempted to read the book after an illness and — failing to glean anything from it said — 'My God, I'm an idiot.' A reviewer for *The Spectator* described it as suffering from 'digression, affectation, obscurity, and all the faults that spring ... from crudity of plan and self-opinion which will neither cull thoughts nor revise composition.' Harriet Martineau, the English social theorist and Whig writer said that it made her feel physically ill. Tennyson said that he had only understood the first and last lines. It is unusual for a writer to go on to receive such critical praise and appreciation for later work after an early book had received such a public haranguing as Browning got for *Sordello*. Yet it's also worth remembering how restrained the poetry readership was at this time. Elizabeth Barrett Browning would visit an old, blind scholar and read poems to him; the man might be taken as an image of the Victorian reader that Browning's poems pushed against: he would sit in a chair all day quoting passages of Greek poetry. Elizabeth later wrote to Robert: 'As for you and Tennyson, he never heard of you ... he never guesses at the way of modern literature.' Most of the critics — and readers — that Browning challenged never guessed at the kind of modern poetry that Browning envisaged. As Donald Thomas observes in *Robert Browning: A Life Within*, the new literary scene of magazines meant that Browning's publication had entered into 'the trade of instant judgement'. A few years earlier *Sordello* would have been lost to silence, a position which would have pleased Browning but deprived modernism of one of its guiding texts.

It's the morning of a Tube strike. People — like silver damselflies — fly past the Cemetery on fold-out bikes. There is a mass walk downwards, towards the city — in the opposite direction to which I'm going. The Isle of Dogs looms like the Dark Tower in Browning's poem 'Childe Roland to the Dark Tower Came': 'a tall scalp'd mountain'. There is something of the day of the dead in this dawn exodus. I imagine that the river will come as a surprise as the commuters meet it, the embankment appearing like a final hurdle as they topple into the curdling whorls of the Thames. I walk along Ivydale Road against the flags of estate agent notices — including one from a company I've not seen before: NO FLIES. The *F* in *Flies* is presented in opaque letters so the viewer reads NO LIES. More magic eye than visual poetry.

Sordello is something of a knot — or perhaps a resistant gallstone — in the corpus of English literature. A knot after which the word 'obscurity' can be used as an *insult* to the author of the work. It would take the poets of modernism to challenge and reformulate the relationship between the reader and the poem; to present poetry as a form that can communicate without necessarily having to be understood; to ask the reader to become as much of a voyeur as an interpreter of incredible acts of language under pressure. Browning forces us to begin asking those questions which Ezra Pound would push further: What is meaning in poetry? What do we hope to extract from a poem? Isn't the act of capturing thought more important than offering simplified answers? Can't poetry simply be about language itself?

Narrative, character and poetic form were all important to Browning's approach, but also — and this perhaps complicates the other techniques — were the drive towards a cryptic, idiosyncratic use of language. *Sordello* is a difficult poem, but it is one that paved the way for later advances. Matthew Arnold characterised Browning's poetry as 'confused multitudinousness' but, later, Henry James described him as 'a tremendous and incomparable modern'. The Victorian critical hegemony struggled with Browning's excessive facility for jump-cuts across time and his probing representations of the human psyche — as well as the length of his poems. George Eliot wrote about his later masterpiece, *The Ring and the Book*: 'Who will read it all in these busy days?' *Sordello* too is not short, with its six sections running to nearly 200 pages. This isn't flash fiction for the commute.

It starts to rain, a cue for the smokers to light up. Somehow we're all walking together now, me amongst the commuters, all of us seemingly of the same purpose, heading the same way. I feel like a fraud amongst the striding purposes of these people, marching into the future moment. I'm walking backwards towards a long dead poet. I put my head down and walk. I look at the map on my phone which shows me moving as a blue dot, walking towards the site of Browning's cottage. I look up at a hovering piece of directional signage, the place I'm heading to. TELEGRAPH HILL >

Browning's work introduces something of an awkward double-helix into the Victorian canon; one strand hopes to engage the reader in elemental concerns in human nature but the other — wrapping around the first — is born of the Victorian urge for innovation and experiment. But why was *Sordello* so challenging, eliciting bewilderment, laughter and critical scorn from Browning's contemporaries? *Sordello* has too many individual problems to detail but the overriding one is that it attempts to do the impossible: to write an account of a poet's developing soul, in the form of rhyming couplets. The tension between the fluid and abstract inner life of the poet is weighed down by the endless slamming of the end rhymes. The subtle flex of James Joyce's prose in *A Portrait of the Artist as a Young Man* makes Browning's approach appear like a man trying to paint passing clouds with house bricks:

> A week he passed,
> Sucking the sweet out of each circumstance,
> From the bard's outbreak to the luscious trance
> Bounding his own achievement. Strange!

    (Book II)

All of Browning's poetry up to *Sordello* can be read as being about his own early poetic development as a poet, but he is yet to find his form — the monologue — through which he can shape the concern with writing into concerns that would more openly engage a readership. It is as if Browning has to declare his place as a poet before moving on to do the things that he's capable of doing: letting the spectrum of human society speak through his monologues.

A man in a luminescent orange jacket is shouting into his mobile, leaning against a vehicle that has the words FOOTPATH SPRAYING across its side. He's shouting into his mobile: 'But how can I do this?' Then I notice that all of the cars which are parked — and the ones driving towards me — are blue. I keep walking. When Browning moved here in 1840 the area just south of here went under the quaint Victorian name of Hatcham (recorded as far back as the *Domesday Book* as 'Hacheham'). Like Peckham and Dulwich this was part of the outer London county of Surrey. There is an etching from 1839, the year before Browning arrived, showing a train trundling under a billow of smoke, passing through the open grassland to Deptford, with the skyline of London behind it. I've occasionally seen the name Hatcham resurrected by canny estate agents to give an attractive sense of secluded village. They present Hatcham as a kind of succulent rind straddling the prime cuts of New Cross and Nunhead. Hatcham as a well located village for the uber-niche and vaporous emergent professional. Who wouldn't pay for such ethereal kudos?

Like Blake before him, Browning was drawn to the hills of Surrey, where the new music of poetry might be heard in broken white noise. To the outside places that offer the best vantage to make sense of the times that lived through him. Between 1795 and 1823 Telegraph Hill had been a semaphore station which, in 1815, had flash-lighted the news of Wellington's victory to London. Do poets rise to heights like these because they, too, sense a platform for their words? Poetry and semaphore as a kind of shared visual language, bringing the news of modernity to the blinded city? Browning would go on to see the strength of his work as being in making 'men and women speak' — but first he had to work through his disappointment over the public failure of *Sordello*.

One of Browning's biggest failings is his assumption that the reader will have a grasp of the politics of thirteenth-century Italy, the allegiances and manoeuvrings between the Guelfs (adherents of the Pope) and Ghibellines (supporters of the Emperor). Browning's text moves less forward than outwards, in increasingly confusing jump-cuts of location and narrative. As well as taking us on Sordello's journey as a poet, Browning wants us to understand the micro-machinations of the period. Sordello — who was a real troubadour poet who first comes to literary light in Dante's *Purgatorio* (though this Sordello is Browning's invention) — appears to flash his growing pains at the reader, then disappears into the shadows amongst the minor characters. It's easy to see why Victorian readers might describe themselves as feeling sick when reading this as Browning refuses to play the clarity-game with pronouns: it's hard to know if *he*, *she*, *who* or *him* refers to the Marquis we were with before or the Count we've just met.

Browning later agreed to rewrite *Sordello* for a new edition published in 1863 but this largely meant adding in speech marks and glossing the action with short notes which were placed alongside the lines in an attempt to elucidate meaning. These notes should be ranked up there with Eliot's *The Waste Land* for their cryptic tongue-in-cheek refusal to give much guidance to the reader — they read like a modern avant-garde poem in their own right:

> *or shame –*
> *which may*
> *the gods*
> *avert*
>
> —
>
> *and practised*
> *on till the real*
> *come.*
>
> —
>
> *how, poet no*
> *longer in unity*
> *with man,*
>
> —

and watching
his own life
sometimes,

—

finds in men
no machine
for his sake,

The notes engage in cryptic dialogue with the main text and, in a sense, come to reach poetic status on their own terms. They have an Emily Dickinson compaction and point towards the work of later American minimalists like Robert Creeley and Cid Corman. In Browning's introduction to the 1863 edition he precedes the modernist position of these later poets when he says: 'I wrote it twenty-five years ago for only a few, counting even in these on somewhat more care about its subject than they really had.' This push towards the arcane and elite paves the way for the razor-in-the-vellum techniques of later poets, particularly Ezra Pound, who was greatly influenced by Browning.

Between Telegraph Hill Park and Brockley Nature Reserve the universe is pinned by a traffic island, the centre of the sliding metropolis. The north of the city rises behind me. A lone red telephone box is angled into the world. This is the leisure land that London forgot. Far from the mayor and the tourist attractions, Telegraph Hill has disappeared into a fold in the map between Southwark and Lewisham. In Telegraph Hill Park the summer is embraced with balls and foaming dogs.

Sordello oddly foreshadows its own commercial failure through Sordello's distrust of the crowd's taste:

Lacks
The crowd perception? Painfully it tacks
Thought to thought, which Sordello, needing such,
Has rent perception into: it's to clutch
And reconstruct

(Book II)

Sordello's struggles to engage an audience with his experimental approach to poetry is curiously mirrored in the harsh critical feedback Browning would receive for his book. Browning's character experiences what his creator would later go through. The book seems in parts to be presciently about its own failure. The vocabulary he uses here — *clutch and reconstruct* — condenses the materials of language into the same kind of syllabic crunch, the same mulched texture that Pound would later develop in *The Cantos*. When it comes to the influence of Browning on Pound we don't need to surmise on this: Pound plays out the poem's influence in real time in an early version of 'Canto II', published in *Poetry* magazine in 1917. Pound kept the same opening line in his later book publications of *The Cantos* — 'Hang it all, there can be but one *Sordello!*' — which some Browning critics have misread as a slight against Browning's epic, but this couldn't be further from Pound's intentions. Pound had been under the sway of Browning's poetry from as early as 1906, writing in a letter that although Ovid was the first writer to investigate subjective psychology it was Browning who 'after 2000 years [was] about the first person to do anything more with it. I follow — humbly of course? doing by far the best job of any of them? not quite.'

Pound learned from Browning's genius for self-revelation and epiphany and — advancing his poems into the very essence of the moment and the image — sealed them in the iron ore of his consonants. Pound took forward Browning's technique of moving through time digressively, giving a pre-glimpse of how the mind would demand connections and speed in the GPS era. Pound extended the dramatic monologue towards the 'Luminous Detail' in which the moment could appear in a poem without unnecessary interference. The criticism that Browning received at the time for confusing readers became an appealing virtue in the creative mind of the American poet.

Still, Pound had to find a way to turn Browning into his own. Early reviewers could see the debt Pound had paid to Browning. F.S. Flint made the case that readers should look harder to see what was new in Pound's work:

> Mr Pound is a poet with a distinct personality. Essentially, he is a rebel against all conventions except sanity; there is something robustly impish and elfish about him ... Let us once and for all acknowledge what Mr Pound owes to Browning, his mediaeval poets, mystics and thinkers ... and take his poems as poetry, without references to source material.

('Verse', 1909)

What Flint was missing here was that for Pound, as with Eliot and Joyce, the source materials were inextricably linked to the new work he was making. For Pound, it was about finding the personal line in the tradition, and gutting out the living classic in order to have the entrails of the text thrash about on the decks of the ship. Pound discovered in Browning one of the few poets of the nineteenth century whom he felt had the materials to add to his wildly international and idiosyncratic rag-bag of influences. As he said elsewhere:

> The common verse in Britain from 1890 was a horrible agglomerate compost, not minted, most of it not even baked, all legato, a doughy mess of third-hand Keats, Wordsworth, heaven knows what, fourth-hand Elizabethan sonority blunted, half-melted, lumpy.

The important word here is 'baked': the contemporary poet has let the classic work assimilate and rise inside them in their own style, to come out bearing their signature. Pound shows us what the new poetry might look like by writing it live, capturing in poetic language his own thinking about it. And it is in this early, later revised and never printed in book form version of 'Cantos II' that we find the evidence of the significance of Browning's *Sordello* on the modernist mind. Pound oscillates between the text in front of him — the actual pages of *Sordello* — and the cobbled streets of Beaucaire that he's walking through[2]:

> Hang it all, there can be but one *Sordello*!
> But say I want to, say I take your whole bag of tricks,
> Let in your quirks and tweeks, and say the thing's an art-form,
> Your *Sordello*, and that the modern world
> Needs such a rag-bag to stuff all its thought in;
> Say that I dump my catch, shiny and silvery
> As fresh sardines flapping and slipping on the marginal cobbles?
> (I stand before the booth, the speech; but the truth
> Is inside this discourse—this booth is full of the marrow of
> wisdom.)

The synapses of Pound's mind are fired here by a number of possibilities suggested by Browning's *Sordello*: its eccentricities of style and diction, its rapacious greed for detail and conversation, the notion of the epic as the container for everything artists will have to grapple with in their working lives. Pound places *Sordello* on its pedestal as a unique thing and — fascinatingly for today's reader — he is skilled enough to show us the poetic influence *even as it happens*: 'say I want to, say I take'. The power generated in Pound's poem comes from his live reading of Browning — even as Pound walks and as he writes — showing how being influenced and writing new poetry are contingent on each other. The present tense epiphanies of the young poet's mind are fired like pistons as we read.

Yet we're also in a real place with Pound, as I'm in a real place here — walking to Telegraph Hill. His own catch (his cantos) comes in a language that interweaves the textual into the absolute reality of the things around him; images of sardines flap and slip in precise sibilants as he nets them in the 'marginal cobbles' of the poem's form. Pound's biggest epiphany is presented in parentheses: 'the truth is inside the discourse'. It is this tension that comes through the conversation between his own work and that of Browning that propels the poem forward — inspiration and influence are materials for poetry, captured in real time for future readers to understand. Perhaps Pound later thought that this poem was too revealing of his processes, which explains why he completely rewrote the poem for its inclusion in the book publication. For that reason this poem is buried alive in the archives, showing us Pound's mapping of a journey towards understanding what a great Victorian poet might look like — and how the creative psyche of the modern poet can develop in response to it. We should take the magazine version of 'Cantos II' as a gift.

I realise later that I'd hedged my bets on Browning's cottage being at the top of Telegraph Hill: it isn't. I spent fifteen minutes walking the grounds of Haberdasher's Aske's College. In the grounds a statue of a former rector towers over the wooden frame of the children's swings. The school motto, buckled over with two ramming goats, translates as *Serve and Obey*. Aske's College was built in 1875, thirty-nine years after Browning left for Italy with Elizabeth Barrett Browning. I walk into the grounds: the reception closed, the building ghosted by silence. Summer holidays. I walk around the back and through an entrance: a dark hall is fired with the sparks of working electricians.

Now I'm descending the furious decline of Jerningham Road. Victorian terraces built into the hill at a forty-five degree angle, surviving through deep stilts into London clay. Slanting but still standing. I turn left onto Musgrove Road. And it's there, in front me: Browning's plaque and the disappointment that comes with it: all that rich mythology reduced to a purple bin lid. A giant coin in the wrong currency. It's not the same feeling as standing at the grave of a poet you've found for yourself.

Browning walked in and out of London from here in a day, a starched green dandy rising from the choleric marsh of his muddy early career as a poet. If you listen closely enough you can still hear the creaking of his corduroy. Today, Musgrove Road is a brick orchard of butterflies and birds. When Browning moved into his new room he positioned two skulls on his desk, one of which became home to his pet spider. From his window he could see chestnut trees, a holly hedge and lambs in the fields. He soon began to write again, moving away from the cryptic style of *Sordello* towards poems such as 'Home Thoughts from Abroad', 'The Lost Leader', 'The Pied

Piper' and 'My Last Duchess', poems that would hold the public imagination and develop his readership. He was also here during the sultry summer in which his relationship with Elizabeth Barrett Browning intensified through their letters, committing their desire to crisp, blanched paper. Elizabeth wrote to him on 18th June 1846: 'If I am happy on any day it is through you wholly, whether you are absent or present, dearest and ever dearest.' The next day, the 19th, was reported as being ninety-six degrees in the shade. Elizabeth took her dog Flush to cool down in the Serpentine. The watermen on the Thames died of heatstroke. This was the day that Elizabeth agreed, by letter, to marry Robert and it was here that Robert received the letter. The cottage, like the beginnings of those early hopes is long gone.

There may be a connection between how Browning fell in love and how his poetic style began to simplify. He moved away from the claustrophobic internal wrangling of the fictional lives of poets and began to make characters of all kinds speak directly to the reader. The communication required to engage Elizabeth Barrett with him — in his life and work — was perhaps clarifying his verse too; after all she was a singular poet too and they were creating a world in which their poetics would have to be explained to each other. As he wrote to her in 1845:

> You *do* what I always wanted, hoped, to do, and only seem now likely to do for the first time — you speak out, *you* — I only make men and women speak — give you the truth broken into prismatic hues, and fear the pure white light, even if it is in me.

What is 'the pure light' that Browning fears? Is it the fear of writing himself into silence, outside of the reach of a wide audience? The fear of blinding his readers with words that don't speak to them as men and women? This could be the pure white light of death which hovers over every poet's attempt to write something that lasts. In the poet's mind, this light outshines death. It is the thing that radiates — long after their burial ashes have cooled.

31ˢᵗ October 2014

Thinking of the scan results kept me awake again. The night went so slowly as to barely move — dragging its shawls across the floors and hallways of the adjacent East Dulwich houses. Being in the wrong city didn't help. Then the morning brought sharp clear light across London. I could tell, as soon as I spoke to my mum, that the news was good: the right kind of tone — an energy behind her voice — even as she described — for too long — the domestics and delays before arriving at the hospital. The cancer hasn't travelled. It has passed through the lymph nodes but the doctors have caught it before it's settled anywhere else. This is news like the news that once came from the new world back to the landlocked: news that brought new scents, intoxicants, sugar-rushes. This is news that lives inside me, kick-starting endorphins and the synapse-triggers of optimism. This is news that feels like success.

Nunhead Poets: Cuthbert Collingwood and Kirwan de Verdon

Cuthbert Collingwood (1826-1908) was living in Paris until just two years before his death, in Lewisham Infirmary, aged 81. He was a man who seemed to defy any set expectations on how someone might apply themselves to just one discipline. He was trained in natural sciences and lectured in botany and biology but he was also a prominent Swedenborgian and, in addition to his books on naturalism, such as *Rambles of a Naturalist on the Shores and Waters of the China Seas* (1868), he wrote theological books — some in verse. Collingwood bridges the two cities I've been moving between, as he lived in Liverpool between 1858 and 1866, working as a Senior Physician at the Liverpool Northern Hospital.

Reading through Collingwood's publications I am astounded by how he makes the Victorian world that was very difficult to travel seem very small. One moment he is writing about a Kibalan village on the north-east coast of Formosa, describing the display of the natives like a scene from Conrad's *Heart of Darkness*:

> As soon as we landed, we were escorted into the village by the crowd, and, on reaching it, were received by sundry explosions, which we were fain to consider a small honour. Sundry warlike-looking personages, armed with matchlocks, had turned out to meet the suspicious-looking strangers; but seeing us walking unarmed and amicably among the citizens, they fired their weapons harmlessly in the air for effect.

The next moment Collingwood is addressing the Liverpool Royal

Infirmary School of Medicine, asking the students not to 'follow in the train of many, who, without having given the subject an independent thought, allow a prejudice to take possession of their minds.' Collingwood was never one to stick to anyone else's track and includes among his publications *On a Remarkable Phenomenon Observed at Rangoon* and a piece on the astronomy of the ancient Chaldeans. I was intrigued by what his poetry might include, not least for the Blake connection through Swedenborg.

Blake had been drawn to the writings of the philosopher Swedenborg on finding that, like him, Swedenborg had experienced visions and seen angels. Blake bought copies of Swedenborg's *A Treatise Concerning Heaven and Hell* and *The Wisdom of Angels* and although he didn't always agree with Swedenborg's views this didn't prevent him and Catherine joining the Swedenborgian New Jerusalem Church in 1789. This was a short lived pursuit; by 1790 Blake was mistrustful of the church's emphasis on the avoidance of sin and accused Swedenborg of 'lies and priestcraft', later mocking the spiritualist in his own *Marriage of Heaven and Hell*. As I prepared to look at Collingwood's epic poem *A Vision of Creation* I wondered whether he, too, could take the preaching of one man and transform it into his own poetic idiom, distilling Swedenborg into his own particular way of seeing — even questioning him?

Collingwood's intentions are sound: in this poem he attempts to bridge the Biblical view of the creation of the world with the geological facts that he is trained to comment upon. His preface and introduction to this epic poem are both calm, rational and inclusive — he wants both students of the Bible and of science to feel validated: 'I have strictly followed the brief and simple account of the first chapter of Genesis, and have endeavoured to show how each particular therein announced agrees with the recognised facts and sequences of modern Geology.' To this end his long introduction — 'Corroborative of Modern Geology' — is balanced and informative on how both visionary and literal readings of Genesis have missed out on their potential to do service to each other. Collingwood works through the seven days of creation to elucidate what was happening on earth at each moment — on day three, for example: 'Beds of mud, the necessary result of the constant pouring of heated waters upon the granitic effusions of the earliest solidified crust.'

Like Blake, Collingwood had been enamoured by the brilliance of Milton's *Paradise lost*, which he cites in his introduction. Collingwood's opening 'Proem' echoes the rhythm, tone and direct address to God of Milton's 'Invocation to Light' from Book II. Blake took Milton and — as he did with Swedenborg — questioned him, saying that Milton was 'of the Devils party without knowing it'. Blake created his own mythology to explain how the world was created and developed his own style in which to tell it. A quick comparison between the opening of Book II of *Paradise Lost* and Collingwood's poem shows that Collingwood has taken the essence of Milton's language but simplified both the syntax and the complexity of the creationism that Milton describes:

> HAIL, holy Light, offspring of Heaven first-born!
> Or of the Eternal coeternal beam
> May I express thee unblamed? since God is light,
> And never but in unapproachèd light
> Dwelt from eternity, dwelt then in thee,
> Bright effluence of bright essence increate!
>
> (Milton, *Paradise Lost*)

HAIL, great Creation! Wondrous mystery!
Divine expression of Omnipotence!
Stupendous plan! Whose all-embracing scheme,
Conceived within the unassisted mind
Of the great Self-Existent, found its vast
And most majestical accomplishment
In the eternal and almighty will
Of the Most High Jehovah, — thee I sing!

(Collingwood, *A Vision of Creation*)

Collingwood apes Milton's language — the exact opening capitalised with the declarative, 'HAIL'; the use of exclamations; the apostrophised address; the use of the iambic pentameter — the same rhythm and inflection and tone. The comparison also shows how rich, complex and sinuous Milton's language is in comparison: Milton moves his lines forward with the risk of contradicting himself, showing the essence of thought as it happens, creating short explosive images — 'Eternal coeternal beam', 'bright essence increate!' — and twists unexpectedly to ask a question amidst the praise: 'May I express thee unblamed?'

Reading *Paradise Lost* is a live event, an experience in which the reader is held buoyed by Milton's unconventional, rapid turns of thought and expression. Collingwood does himself a disservice by soliciting the comparison. His argument is already sterile in comparison to Milton's — after all, Milton is eulogising light here, and not the generic idea of 'Creation' itself. What's more, Milton never presents the fallen angels in anything but the true light of their complexity, but Collingwood's faith is unquestioning: 'majestical accomplishment.../ Of the Most High Jehovah'.

Milton's poem exists in the tension of how the fallen angels will deal with a world of free will — Milton lives every temptation with them — but Collingwood knows what his argument and position is before his poem has even begun: 'trust renewed ... / Undoubting, understanding': the tension in the poem is resolved from the start. As a literary world it is a flattening experience.

Collingwood goes on to retell the creation of the world through the character of a man and the visitation of an Archangel. Collingwood's argument, made first in his introduction, is then repeated in verse — in the mouth of the archangel. It is relentless: 'Nor shall thy soul prophetic overleap / The mighty lapse of thrice a thousand year.' The language here makes nothing new of the Biblical and Miltonesque, failing to add a new stylistic to the known poetry of the period.

There is, however, one image in the poem that I particularly like, which shows that perhaps Collingwood could work in his own metaphors — if he could just break from those of others — when he describes Jehovah whose 'throne is Heaven and Whose footstool, Earth'. The two hundred plus lines of limpid language that follows — as Collingwood expands on his argument — failed to reach this height again, ending with a laudatory celebration of order: 'HE HATH DONE ALL THINGS WELL!'

Collingwood is neighbour to Joshua Russell, who is buried on the east side of West Hill — Collingwood is on the west. The memorial is an impressive, modernist obelisk with a crucifix that morphs into an anchor, circled with text: SAFETY IN JESUS. A dead tree, lean and cracked, has grown up alongside the stone. This is a family vault for Frances and Samuel Collingwood — with Cuthbert later joining them here. The verb 'relict' is used to describe

Collingwood's mother who was made a widow after her husband's death — a description that she carried to the grave. What about the promised reuniting after, I wonder. Didn't she cease to be a widow then? BE YE READY ALSO is engraved onto a ledge in the base, a quote from St Luke. Behind me joggers pass with a collie on a lead, breathing heavily, as a plane moves across the sky above with that distinct sound of weight moving at height — rumbling and whistling — but no leaf moves around me in the Cemetery.

I walk down towards the Dissenter's Triangle with Brockley Footpath to my left, taking a wrong turn down a dead end of monuments

Cuthbert Collingnwood's headstone

made from wooden posts. I find the right curved path this time and hear a dog walker saying to her dog: 'Come on there's nothing to worry about.' Traffic fencing has been used to identify an unsafe tomb, its sides splitting under the weight of its slab: The Family Vault of John Wilson, of Lewisham, Kent. I wonder how many were in the family and if the weight of the remains has something to do with the sinking tomb?

Kirwan de Verdon (1800-1882) also determined his own spiritual path. After being educated at Trinity College, Dublin, he was preparing to join the Church of Ireland but instead became an Independent: which explains why he's buried in the Dissenters ground at Nunhead. De Verdon was a pastor in Southwark and, after the death of his wife in 1854, became a missionary in Turkey. De Verdon's poetry spanned the breadth of his life with his first publication — *Farewell, a Poem* — being published when he was just twenty-one, and later publications being released in the 1870s, in the final decade of his life. His first publication died without trace — not even the British Library has a copy. There is, however — and unfortunately — a copy of his *The Converted Jew: A Poem in Four Cantos* (1833) which was written with the intention 'to attract the attention of Jews to a consideration of the Old Testament proofs, that Jesus was the Christ, the Messiah sent from God.' As with Collingwood, de Verdon's poetry exists to tub-thump a pre-existing mantra, a poor position from which any poem should be hurled into the world. The polemic of de Verdon's long poem is asking Jews to admit that they've 'done wickedly, and departed from his [God's] precepts and judgements'.

I've entered the Dissenters' Triangle. Perhaps I mistakenly imagined the Dissenters here as glorious outsiders with their heads full of visions and a will — like Blake — to see things their own way? De Verdon negates that. Sometimes, when looking for the memorials of dead poets, I wonder why: do I want to single out de Verdon, to celebrate his life and work? Far from it, but I can't cut corners and need to attempt, at least, to find his headstone. This process requires the same care as finding his books. The headstone and publications are the facts — the material elements he left behind. Along with anecdotes of the life that was lived, this is all we have. Occasionally a clue or poetic addition can be found on the memorial too — it's always worth hunting these down.

This is the most beautiful corner of the Cemetery. The Brockley Footpath and another narrow, clear path, take me deeper in to the surrounding graves than it's often possible to go. The afternoon sunlight helps: I walk into the stillness and beyond the stillness there is something else: death and its saturation in quietness.

De Verdon's poem begins in a scene of apocalypse with the appearance of 'The Demon of the storm … / With his dread offspring, Death'. Perhaps because of the sheer invective behind the work de Verdon's polemic is more compact than Collingwood's: his lines are in four stress, eight syllable lines rather than ten. Collingwood had the advantage of working without end rhymes — de Verdon spurs his invective with rhymed couplets: 'perchance' rhymes with 'advance', 'God' with 'trod' and 'Pharisee' with 'enemy'. De Verdon is on far too quick a mission to consider cutting through the received expressions and clichéd imagery of his lines:

> Struck still beneath the clear blue skies.
> There the stupendous palace shines,
> On whose high towers dark night reclines.

There is little reprieve from the belligerent vision that de Verdon builds, layer-upon-layer, and the ineffectual imagery which he uses to paint it — the towers 'like armed giants' and dawn rising in 'radiant waves' — quickly becomes tiresome to read.

As I've found in the past, if you dig deep enough through a mired work with a critical scythe there might be something positive to take from it. I work hard with de Verdon and find these lines that I like:

> When dew-drops glisten o'er the bending flowers
> In brilliant multitudes, as if Night's car
> Had cast a glittering gem from every star

But it's hard to let the image linger with the bitter taste in the mouth that his polemic has flowered. Forty years after publishing this poem de Verdon published a prose work called *The Veil Lifted From All Nations: Discovery of the Lost Tribes of Isreal* in which his mission to convert the Jews has intensified into a plan to use the Israelites of the House of Joseph to gather all Jews and return them to Israel where they'll be converted to Christianity: 'Nations that are not only of Israelitish origin, but of the same tribe, must recognise the bond of brotherhood'. De Verdon claims that most of the English nation and America are 'of the house of Joseph, of the tribe of Ephraim'. Strangely, de Verdon published a poetry book in 1876 under the same title, albeit with a different subtitle: *The Veil Lifted from Israel: What Israel Ought to Do and Hymns and Hebrew Melodies for Israel.* Although de Verdon's views clearly hadn't changed in this time I was curious as to whether his poetry might have improved — though the commanding 'ought to do' in the title suggested not: it isn't poetry's job to tell anyone what *ought* to be done. After reading the poem I found that my suspicions were well placed.

The flies are thriving here; horseflies on the search for skin to pierce, bluebottles ploughing with bulging eyes towards any carrion they can find. De Verdon's headstone can't easily be found. I've walked to the northern wall of the Cemetery, as far as the path will take me into the undergrowth: beyond, cars carry the fierce missions of families through the summer holidays. Up against the wall I see something that breaks down the familiarity with death that I thought I'd re-established, but the feeling surprises me in stirring up anxieties I've experienced over the past two years: in the cracked earth, butting up to the brick wall, is a buried headstone with just the top of it visible. The stone is yellowed and green but some of the text is still visible — ants running across the legible letters:

IN LOVING MEMORY of MY DEAR MOTH
MARION DEA
WHO DIE

The rest of the stone is submerged in earth but the presence of MOTH is enough to show that this is a lost memorial for a dead MOTHER. The stone is too close to the wall for the coffin to be here too. Memorials slide. Intentions slide. The lives that grieve also — over time — slide. Like all of London's Victorian Cemeteries, Nunhead, and the attrition of death it's harvested, has been sliding for nearly two centuries.

3rd November 2014
She says it's flu. Hot and cold flushes, no appetite. Tiredness. All her life, she said, she's never picked up bugs: the symptoms come and they're gone by the next day. I can only remember one time when she was really ill, when I was a teenager. She had a throat infection. I can remember the pain I felt watching as it hurt her to swallow. I kissed her forehead before I left for wherever it was I felt I had to go — a friend's house, or a pub.

5th November 2014
It's not flu. The implant replacing her breast has become infected. I did what I always do at times like this — went out to run. I ran until my body realised that it was going in loops and not making it anywhere. I ran until my body told my body to stop.

6th November 2014
I identified something within me today. The word 'cancer' has always made me feel weak — made my bones go soft and my blood curdle. Made my tongue ache. Made me want to get out of the way of myself.

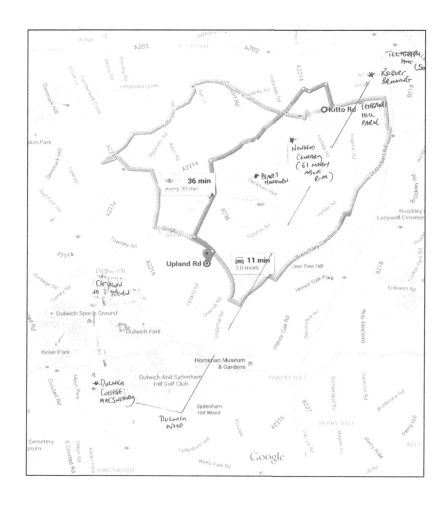

CFCs and English Bluebells: into Dulwich Woods

Thinketh, He made thereat the sun, this isle,
Trees and the fowls here, beast and creeping thing.
  Robert Browning, 'Caliban Upon Setebos'

I plot the sites of these active, restless poets around the Cemetery on a Google Map. At the centre I place a crude, childlike angel on Peckham Rye and then mark Nunhead Cemetery just above it. I also add in Upland Road, where I stay in London. Then I add an asterisk for Telegraph Hill, the home of Browning — the most central northern location — and at the southern end I mark MacSweeney at Dulwich College, an hour's walk from Browning's home at Telegraph Hill. When I draw on the next destination I'm heading to — Dulwich Wood — the map shows itself as two sides of a triangle.

If I were to close this off as a triangle I'd be engaging with the symbolism of three-sided forms and all the resonances of the number three that comes with that: the creation of the trinity, waxing, waning and full moons; spirit, mind and body; father, son and Holy Ghost; mother, father and child; past, present and future. Yet it's Graves' three Goddesses that come to mind now: maiden, mother and crone. If both sides are connected to create a third thing — as the connection of two hypotenuses together is said to do — then what, I wonder, am I creating by enclosing a triangle around an angel and a cemetery?

There are further Celtic inferences here, not least of which is that of birth, death and life. The chaos of the between-world I've been living through with my mother's illness but also, perhaps, the rebirth of a poet lost in Nunhead Cemetery. Another image connects with this: that of the Greek Delta glyph, which symbolises a doorway; balancing thought and wisdom, it has been said, can provide an opening towards a higher wisdom. Perhaps this feeling of being lost will resolve itself in the pure white light of discovery at Nunhead Cemetery?

But I'm not ready to close off this triangle or to infer a final hypotenuse: the poets are still out to lead me where they will. Which is why I'm walking to Dulwich Wood.

Dulwich Wood was initially part of the Great North Wood stretching from Camberwell to Croydon. The writers have been here before. The wood was known for its gypsy encampments and was most likely the one Pepys writes about in his diary on 11th August 1668: 'This afternoon my wife and Mercer and Deb went with Pelting to see the Gypsies at Lambeth and have their fortunes told; but what they did, I did not enquire'. The oracular symbolism is of death and augury: the lore of *The White Goddess* makes the place a natural draw. In 1722 Daniel Defoe wrote that many plague victims had walked as far as the woods to die in a place 'more open and woody than any other part so near London, especially about Norwood, the parishes of Camberwell, Dullege and Luseme'. But there is a more rooted link to the poets of the area: Browning had walked from Camberwell to Dulwich Wood many times as a child — it was a favourite haunt — and later, when he lived at Telegraph Hill, he went into the wood to write.

I walk there along Underhill Road, past Camberwell Old Cemetery, opened in 1856, fourteen years after the last of the

Magnificent Seven at Tower Hamlets. Compared to the view through the railings of Nunhead Cemetery, this is sparsely populated land, a conglomerate of ancient and new headstones in black marble with gold lettering. I don't stop. I walk past the houses for sale and TO LET, past a BMW for sale (£4k) and out onto the South Circular. The rush hour traffic is in gridlock, a grinding static above the cross weave of yellow paint on the road. I stop to read a sign on an electrics box for Forever Living Products: *Are you serious about maintaining good health?* it asks. I cross the road.

Dulwich Wood is a surprise in this now relatively central London location, a place that appears to observe the countryside code in Zone 2. A police siren swirls into a swazzle behind me as I enter the gate on Cox's Walk. The clouds overhead don't indicate visions born of rainbows, but Browning would have walked here in all weather. The cow parsley's tender, white-tipped broccoli dips across the path ahead of me. Through the netted fence and shrubs I can see the way to Dulwich College — this fringeland between the South Circular and southern expanses is MacSweeney territory to me now, one of Albion's city meadows.

Above me a magpie is clattering about, throwing its Newcastle flag around the delicately tiled away stadium of a tree. *Pips, curs* and *zees*: birdsong over the hum of traffic. Two green parakeets announce their glam night: the magpie watches, confused to see another male in such colour. To my right is a cricket ground; beyond that is a rugby pitch. The path towards Browning's inspiration narrows. The lamp-posts have been registered with specific numbers by the council: the trees wrap around them as if claiming them into their fold. A sign points the way above me: Crystal Palace three miles ahead.

The Crystal Palace was built to house the displays for the

Great Exhibition in Hyde Park in 1851 and it was moved here in 1852. This further split the Great North Wood in two. The city had done with its exhibitionism and after the effort of hauling this glass carcass to the suburbs it burned down in 1936. Arthur Rimbaud, on his return to London after his split-up with Verlaine, paid a visit from his digs near Waterloo Station: the dead beneath the city and its rejectamenta above it all figured in his work-in-progress of the time, the *Illuminations*. The Crystal Palace had once defined the city's leisure preoccupations as much as the O2 in Greenwich does now — though few contemporary poets are inspired to write about the O2.

Even as I've arrived at this most secluded part of south-east London it feels strange, like a bespoke oracle, to find a sign at a shadowy juncture read: NUNHEAD CEMETERY 3 ¼ m. Back in the direction I've just come from, on the trail of my lost poets. The green parakeets are shrieking hysterically above. I head towards the heart of the woods.

A wooden sign, not dissimilar to a headstone, lays down the law of the Dulwich Estate: all dogs to be kept on leads. No fires. I've come to a fork in two paths and follow my instinct. I keep walking straight ahead. A sniffer dog, tongue lolling, powers up the path next to me, chasing a blackbird. The path becomes tighter. I'm being led by a sloping ridge of upright oaks to my right, which slant away towards Dulwich Village. The blanket of cloud above the trees press down on the roof of the leaves beneath. It's only 5pm in May and it's nearly dark. The recent rains have blackened the path to mudflats. Wooden decking has been laid around an old black pond with ancient carp, I imagine, asleep at the bottom. They've been there so long they're oblivious to the building, moving and burning of the Crystal Palace.

An old railway bridge appears in front of me daubed with luminous graffiti. This is the high level line built in 1865 to service the relocated Crystal Palace. It ran from Nunhead to Crystal Palace, also stopping at Honor Oak, Lordship Lane and Upper Sydenham. I'm between connecting stations for Nunhead, looking at a line that has long been closed. You can't service a dying industry. There's no access through the tunnel: gates covered with artsy-graffiti including spray-painted bats block the way. The contrast between this urban art and the ancient woodland flora is disconcerting. CFCs rising over English bluebell and wood anemone.

And the wood itself is formidable, a place beneath the heights for poets to skulk with their introvert sides and addictions. A place to drop the chrysalis needed to face London's fury. As I walk I somehow incense a magpie with the scuff of my shoes — it clatters into branches, the sound echoing like a bed of oars. The path steepens: a sign pinned on a fence asks people to report any sighting of arson. Fencing around a heap of wooden posts have been removed and burned. The wood invites deep-rooted instincts within us to resurface — impulses to hide, to burn things — that are recursive in our genes.

It was here that Robert Browning wrote parts of his verse drama *Pippa Passes*, shortly after moving to Telegraph Hill and completing *Sordello*. 'Pippa Passes' sees a new clarity emerge in Browning's work and contains some of his most well known, if misrepresented lines:

> *The year's at the spring,*
> *And day's at the morn;*
> *Morning's at seven;*
> *The hill-side's dew-pearled;*
> *The lark's on the wing;*
> *The snail's on the thorn;*
> *God's in his heaven –*
> *All's right with the world!*

The first reviews of *Pippa Passes* were critical of its sexual openness and the suggestion it contained — through its characters — of regicide. It was also the text that led a character in a Walter Besant novel of 1875 to say: 'in fifty years' time, who will read Browning?' Nearly a century and a half later I am, following Browning's footsteps with his poems in my hand. *Pippa Passes*, in its initial sixteen page pamphlet form, was not a success — though time has been kinder to this poem than most poetry of this period. Donald Thomas, in *Robert Browning: A Life Within*, described the work as showing Browning entering the 'world of post-romantic modernism' and compared his authorial position to the 'camera in its loving description of objects'. On the original publication of *Pippa Passes* the biographical information said that this work was by the author of *Paracelsus*, a poem written five years before *Sordello* — *Sordello* itself was erased from the blurb.

After his move to Telegraph Hill Browning would have walked to the wood across open space — as if back to his younger self. I think about how far poetry has taken me in my life: twenty years ago I was studying Browning for A-level, walking home from school in Liverpool with chunks of his work sticking to memory, and now here I am in a dark wood, trying to trace his movements. For the rest of his life he retained the joy of immersion in nature that Dulwich Wood excited in him. Like Blake before him — and MacSweeney after — his experience of poetry became inextricable with being in nature: he would think of art whilst walking, allowing the chance encounters of the natural world to breeze in and out of the impulse to create in language. W. Sharp describes the effect of nature on Browning:

> It was from the Dulwich wood, that, one afternoon in March, he saw a storm glorified by a double rainbow of extraordinary beauty; a memorable vision, recorded in an utterance of Luigi to his mother: here too that, in autumnal dusks, he saw many a crescent moon with 'notched and burning rim.' He never forgot the 'sunsets and great stars' he saw in those days of his fervid youth. Browning remarked once that the romance of his life was in his soul; and on occasion I heard him smilingly add, to some one's vague assertion that in Italy only was there any romance left, 'Ah, well, I should like to include poor old Camberwell'.

In 1840, before the disaster of *Sordello*, he found himself on the other side of the wood, no longer making a start in life and finding his talents unappreciated, but also not revered amongst the highest ranks of poets where he wished to be. He had also not really begun his adult experience — despite approaching the age of thirty —

and as much as he pined for sexual experience he also lamented the loss of his boyhood self. He later described the walk he'd taken as a boy from Camberwell to Dulwich Wood to his future wife Elizabeth Barrett Browning as 'two miles of green half-hour's walk over the fields'. Browning loved the paintings in the Picture Gallery — particularly the Rembrandts — with their suggestions of stilled drama or reflective, psychological self-penetration.

There are clear similarities, I think, between Blake's and Browning's visions of the natural world. One of Browning's many biographers, Ian Finlayson, talks of how the visual works of Dulwich Picture Gallery had an influence on the developing poet: 'the critic ... was being formed, but the artist was still mostly whistling, ruddy by the hawthorn hedges, on the way to Dulwich.' The hawthorn again prickles its symbolism here. Browning's growing familiarity with the hawthorn, and of the area, all happened within Blake's lifetime — it is fascinating to think that Blake, if asked, would have been able to show the young poet the way to the angels. Browning was formed along the same adolescent paths as Blake. London was expanding at an accelerated pace, which Blake had experience from a decade of living near the Thames in Lambeth: circuses and leisure gardens provided the entertainment amidst the coagulating factories that made beer, vinegar and blacking products. Central London would have been even more congested by the miasma of industrial production for Browning than it had been for Blake, though the landscape of south-east London — despite its development, particularly in terms of housing — was still a great draw to poets in search of an idyll.

Blake and MacSweeney drew strength from living between the city and countryside and Browning too had the appetite for a life hybridised by contrasting landscapes. What he saw in nature allowed him to cast his eye more sharply on humanity: the latter no doubt taught him much about the former. Browning's relationship with nature was arguably even more animalistic than both Blake's and MacSweeney's. There is a remarkable moment in a letter that Browning wrote to Miss Euphrasia Fanny Howarth in 1838 in which he describes his instinct for tearing nature apart:

> I have, you are to know, such a love for flowers and leaves — some leaves — that I every now and then — in an impatience at being able to possess myself of them thoroughly, to see them quite, satiate myself with their scent — bite them to bits.

In a poem like 'Caliban upon Setebos' Browning climbs inside the mind of a freakish outcast of nature who views his God as being in the same savage mould as he is himself. The poem suggests a poet who has paid close attention to the cruelty in nature's selection processes:

> a certain badger brown
> He hath watched hunt with that slant white-wedge eye
> By moonlight; and the pie with the long tongue
> That pricks deep into oak warts for a worm ...
> Look, now, I melt a gourd-fruit into mash,
> Add honeycomb and pods, I have perceived,
> Which bite like finches when they bill and kiss, —
> Then, when froth rises bladdery, drink up all,
> Quick, quick, till maggots scamper through my brain...

Browning — as a biter of plants into bits — closes the gap between the instinctive animalistic drive and the possibility of capturing that in language. He employs all the techniques available within his resources to do this — taking the risk of alienating his readers — employing a slippery dissonance of syntax (noun and adjectives reversed such as in 'badger brown'); a use of odd phrasing, such as Caliban might have heard from man but reuses in the wrong context ('Add honeycombs and pods, I have perceived'); a relish for the physical ('gourd-fruit into mash') and the control of pace through enjambment and repetition ('Quick, quick') allowing the reader to move into Caliban's curious, difficult world more freely than it might seem possible at the beginning of the poem. What Browning creates is a language of *being* in nature, one that is infused with his own experience of submersion in the woods. He presents his version of Caliban as being able to destroy, inexplicably, for the sake of it. Caliban behaves just as he believes his God, Setebos, would do. Standing here, in Dulwich Wood, I understand what connects Browning the nature writer with the tooth-in-claw rawness of the wild and elemental aspects of this ancient land that he walked in.

I am, however, slightly lost. I look at a map on my phone trying to locate myself in this Land of Poesie. I can see that I've drifted through Dulwich Wood and into Sydenham Hill Wood. I must have left Cox's Walk miles back and landed, instead, on the well-named Lapse Wood Walk. Oak and hornbeam dominate here. I come to the edge of the woodland and the signs of civilisation move, shutter-like, through the railings: people, cars, a Domino's pizza courier. Above it all rises the tapering geometric rod of the Crystal Palace transmitting station. This marks the edge of the land once owned by Edward 'Ned' Alleyn (1566-1626) who had bought the land on the proceeds of the theatre. Browning, Blake and MacSweeney were here courtesy of genuine poetic real estate. At the centre of Alleyn's Estate is Dulwich Village and I look at the half-triangle on my map to see that it's there that I need to go next. Dulwich Village — the village that was paid for in theatre and poetry — is the missing node that will complete my map around Nunhead Cemetery.

8ᵗʰ November 2014

I watched a television programme showcasing new cures for cancer. Small tumours in lungs hard as marbles. A surgeon in blue applied purchase to one of the tumours with a knitting needle. A seventy-three-year-old man with blood cancer watched helplessly as the tumours manifested themselves on his neck in exposed, blackened boils. A fact: if a group of men over fifty years of age were gathered on the street and given a test for prostrate cancer one in three would have cancer, though most would never know it or die from that cause. What intrigues me is how we can say This *is a cancer,* This *Isn't a cancer, this is* That *kind of cancer,* The *cancer is* Here, *The cancer is* There, *when what we're talking about is something that has become a part of ourselves. But the language makes an alien of it. This thing in our body, born of our bodies, becomes other: an alien. The patient is made to go to war on themselves, to talk the language fight of survival.*

The programme showed a new treatment hitting lymphoma cells and creating new survival pathways. Can the lymphoma find another way to travel? The man's boil had nearly disappeared after just two weeks. The new treatment takes the lymphoma and twists it until it can't find a way back out. I wondered if my mum's watching this — this programme called Curing Cancer *— on the ward that she's in. The seventy-three year old man blew out the candles on his great grand-daughter's birthday cake. Then his wife was crying, describing how he used to sleep all morning: it's such a relief to see him better, she said. Another man with cancer says he knows his death is to come but now it seems closer. The human spirit that demands immortality now can't lie. Perhaps, he says, he can be more use for the time he has left?*

Then we moved forward in time. The seventy-three-year-old man is telling the doctor he has a new lump on his neck, next to the old one. The doctor checks and shares the concern. The lymphoma's broken through again. I watched the programme until the end, expecting something else, some positive news from science. Something confirmed to share with others. Not the man's wife, sobbing into her hands, the camera locked into the dark bubbling facts on her husband's neck.

I turned off the television.

Nunhead Poets: Colonel Richard Hort and Charles Godfrey Turner

The headstone of Colonel Richard Hort (d. 1857) might remain beyond me. The word from the Friends of Nunhead is that it was located years go — when access was easier — but is now lost in the depths. I make a start in looking, walking up The Avenue towards the Anglican Chapel. The Chapel sits at the top of the path — its double turrets and series of arches pulling me towards it. Through the arch is another arch, like a series of echo chambers. For a second I might be in another century, more so when two children run across the path before the chapel, a small blonde boy carrying a stick as if he's divining for water. The girl is slightly older, her dress the same colour as the chapel. I walk past the grave of Sarah Bagot, 'fifty seven years the good wife of Henry Vincent Bagot'. How far the female poet had to come to not just be the housewife. When I get to the chapel I see that huge steel rods have been placed crosswise from the main structure into the outer columns of the building: such grandeur is built on unstable ground. 'Charlie,' the child's mother shouts. 'Would you like a juice?'

Hort is the author of the best titled book of all the poets in Nunhead Cemetery: *The White Charger that cost me two hundred pounds; lost me seventy thousand pounds; drove me from society; eventually deprived me of my friends; and finally compelled me to quit the service.* The brilliance — and modernity — of this title for his novel raises expectations for Hort's poetry. There is something of Lawrence Sterne in the humour of this. Hort was way ahead of the Victorian middle way — there's also *Love a la Militaire, or 21! 22!! 23!!! A Farce in Two Acts*, the humour of which resides in one man being entrusted to find the wife for another man. This was performed at the Dublin Theatre and Hort writes in the introduction of 'the present popularity' of the play — I sense a strong ego with Hort but it seems that he was accustomed to some success with his writing.

As 'Colonel' suggests, Hort led a military life and having joined the army at fifteen he served with the Life Guards, the 8th Hussars and the 81st Regiment of Foot. Hort was also the editor of *The Royal Military Magazine*. This raises concerns: my experience of Victorian poetry by poets who support war campaigns — the queen and empire — has been far from good. *The Beauty of the Rhine: a Metrical Romance in Four Cantos* was published in Dublin in 1836. The first thing that strikes me about this book is the opening dedication, which follows the Elizabethan convention of being dedicated to a lady of the nobility — I notice that Hort works in longer lines than many of his Nunhead gravefellows:

> stout defiance hurled
> Against the oppressors, and the wished-for end
> Of plighted faith ...
> in defence of honour's laws,
> The gross injustice of the act laid bare.

There is a laid-back yet belligerent edge to this which numbs my excitement. Hort's poem is a story based on Richard I's disappearance after the Crusades, in 1193, and is set on the banks of the Rhine. 'The story I have endeavoured to portray,' he says, 'is supposed to occupy a period of two days and two nights.' The opening lines set out the poem that follows:

> The setting sunbeam stooped to lave,
> And o'er the water sent the while,
> To gild the scene, its golden smile.

This imagery here can only succeed if the reader's mind accepts that a sunbeam can smile or a rock can kiss the light. The four long cantos revels in a 'lingering o'er the scene' which quickly becomes tedious. Hort doesn't work as hard on making his poems as exciting as his titles.

It's in the introduction to a book called *The Embroidered Banner* that I realise what it is that rankles in Hort's work: snobbery. Here he writes about the age of restlessness and travel that he sees himself living in, saying 'it cannot be made a matter of surprise, that the inferior classes, always prompt to imitate the foibles of the aristocracy, follow in their wake.'

I take a look at the only other poem that can be found: *The Kilmainham Pensioner's Lament*, published in 1834. This is a satirical lament for the proposed closing of the Kilmainham Hospital, just outside Dublin, which housed war veterans. The poem is an extended squib of the kind still easily found in today's *Private Eye*:

> But who can tell what Fate may have in store?
>   Promise and Pension both appear a song,
> What *once* was sacred, now is so no more,
>   E'en our good Ministers may not hold long.

Hort's main problem as a poet is his desire to appear as both clever and entertaining — he is always conscious, with the uprightness of a military man and, as such, is incapable of limbering up in language or trying something new. If only Hort had written text for his headstone at the length of one of his titles it might have proved locatable above the families of Sprints, Cockrills and Bowdens that are all around him.

I continue up the Scouts Path towards the section where the New Zealander poet and journalist — Charles Godfrey Turner (c.1889-1922) — is buried, just up from the Bramble Glade. Turner had come to London in May 1914 when he was just twenty-five, as a journalist writing for the Christchurch *Sun*. According to the New Zealand press he had 'a shot at journalism in the big smoke'. The honeyed optimism of Turner's roving trip to London was cut short by the outbreak of the war; back home, he enrolled in the New Zealand Army. As with thousands of other soldiers Turner's worst experiences of war were brought about through natural means: the outbreak of the Spanish flu epidemic. On board the troopship *Tahiti* he watched his sick friends and fellow soldiers placed into what he described as a 'breathless hole' and the dead thrown overboard, mummified in blankets, cast to the ocean floor. Turner seems to have never recovered full strength after this — though it could be said that it was his love of London that killed him.

Turner is listed as a 'soldier poet' only it's clear that he never wanted to be a soldier and the description I have of his memorial doesn't mention his status as poet. His output was limited but — more than any of Nunhead's dead — he lived his life with the wanderlust and search for beauty that might be expected of a poet. His love of England fits well will the gorgeousness of his burial plot. Finding Turner's gravestone is going to be a challenge, Ron Woollacott has written to tell me that I'm looking for a small, rock-shaped memorial, but there's no ground to be seen through the jungle of ivy and bramble. If Turner wanted the depths and richness of England — this is it. Blackberries are bubbling into live firm fruit alongside the path I'm walking along. If Turner struggled to choose whether he preferred the city life of London to the rural aspects of England, then in Nunhead Cemetery he has both. Nearby I notice the more prominent headstone of William Clarence England, who died just six years after Turner. Next to him is the grave of Frederick Lewis which reads PEACE, PERFECT PEACE. Wasps skit in the shifting sunlight.

Turner had come to love London so much that, after the war, he went against medical advice to return to the city that he'd first visited as a journalist set for new discoveries. Perhaps it was that Edenic, pre-war innocence that he wanted to reclaim? Turner developed a nostalgia for the London he was always yet to find — a London of the mind in which it appeared as perpetually full of promises because he was never there long enough to exhaust it: 'By staying away two years at a time, a man may see a new London each time he goes back'. Anyone with a love for London who has been homesick for the city will recognise the smog-tinged lenses through which he wrote about it, shortly before the last trip which killed him:

> This is autumn. But, to make a mental picture of the seasons I must think back to England, to London and wind-blown, brown leaves. Imagine it late in the afternoon, and already the warmth has gone out of the day, and the wind holds a warning of winter at hand. Wide Holland Park Road, usually so silent, is full of the sound of little voices — the dry trees are whispering to each other of a summer gone, and of their own approach to a new dignity. For months they have had their strength hidden in green garments; now, they are about to stand revealed, and through all the grey hours of winter they will show a darker grey against the sky.

When Turner describes the trees here he is describing the possibility of the new self that London so often promises: the trees might be dying off for winter, but there is a promise of the 'new dignity' of restored health that the landscape of London promises to bring. It never happened: Turner was found dead on January 1922, aged thirty-three. He was in bed at home, just off Brook Drive, where the sewerised river Neckinger flows towards the gridlock of the Elephant & Castle.

Turner's small memorial, Ron Woollacott has written, simply reads: 'Soldier Journalist — He Loved England'. Where is the word 'Poet' on here? By December of the year he died, a book of his selected writings, *The Happy Wanderer*, had been published. It includes a photograph of Turner at the age of twenty-six, looking serene, slightly sleepy — and extremely happy. He must be in London. He's wearing a fedora hat and a skinny tie. The foreword to *The Happy Wanderer* tells us about Turner's concerns: 'Everything he wrote reveals his strong personality, his lively imagination, his intense love of beauty, and his whimsical touch. Based upon incident, he mingled fact with fiction, and used his craft as only an artist could.'

The book begins with Turner's poem 'A Ballade of Big Little Boys' which captures the discerning child-innocent in Turner, who can see through the world's intensities to the trees which are always sublime, if on the other side of the world:

> Nobody knows how the war began
> But the big little boy who is nearly eight.

Turner's life begins to appear to me as that of a man thrown into turmoils that were way outside his interests in beauty and romance. The book includes an epigraph from Kipling:

I had my horse, my shield, my banner,
    And a boy's heart, so whole and free;
But now I sing in another manner,
    But now England has taken me!

Turner was always trying to get back to his youth, before the outbreak of war. 'Childhood is a procession,' he wrote, 'and goes by.'

Turner wrote of the sadness of London in a prose piece called 'Lure of London':

Somehow it is easier to write lightly of London than to think back and know it as a city intolerably sad. Though every cobblestone stands for a broken heart, and each lamp-post is a station on the journey of the hopeless these things are not talked of too much. Failure must be picturesque to be noticed, and tragedy must be enacted on a suitable stage to attract attention.

In the 228 pages of *The Happy Wanderer* there are only four poems: this is all there is to get a sense of Turner the poet. All four poems are written in alternate end rhyme and in either eight- or ten-syllable lines — Turner was no innovator. The nostalgia that gives his prose a kind of searching, restless lustre works the opposite way for the poems — turning them to whimsy:

Yes, I had loved the laughter and the lights,
    And wine, and women, and their little feet;
Music and rhythm: and quiet English nights;
    Stained glass and ritual, incense slumber sweet

    ('Canto Et Oro')

This poem celebrates the things that Turner loved most in life — England, 'free moving horses', wine, women — and makes an interesting volta in the ninth line when the experience of war enters the poem: 'when they caught me in their far-flung wire'. It ends extremely strangely — perhaps going against Turner's own wishes for clarity — when the complexity of his feelings leads to an ambiguous syntax:

> Though I shrieked loud, some part of me would sing
> A prayer to those beyond the gates of gold,
> A word to those who know eternal fire,
> That one, the greatest, last largesse they fling –
> The dream I died for you might have and hold.

Turner writes of how 'the Lord your God' had given him such joy in the world — though curiously the God is not his own. The poem is addressed to another person, confessing that he would say a prayer for those who, perhaps, are in hell or damaged irreparably by war ('who know eternal fire') and yet who still give the gift of the dream that, Turner says, 'I died for'. Is this Turner speaking from beyond the death he knows is imminent? The lack of punctuation in the last line shows how any sense of stable meaning has slipped beyond Turner here and allows the poem to resonate in several ways. Was 'the dream' the peace that the person he loves can enjoy, although Turner will never know it? Is there a longing for a marriage that can no longer happen, with that final echo in the poem of 'to have and to hold'? This is a very interesting sonnet, one that performs a dramatic switch from peacetime experience to the damage of war, showing how language becomes fluid when put under duress, reflecting the poet's experiences in ways that he may have struggled to understand himself.

Turner wrote a prose piece called 'On the Road Again: Wandering, Watching and Writing', just before he made his final trip to London and to his death. He looks forward to the country he loves — London and rural Wiltshire — and recalls how the ship he'd nearly died on in the war had brought him to England:

> I lay panting like a weary dog, on a deck of the ship of the dead. When we saw England I knew it was going to be a new country to me. Already it had taken all I had, my hopes and my health. But it did not matter.

Turner describes being in a hospital in Staffordshire, reading aloud any poems he could remember by the London symbolist poet Arthur Symons. Knowing the work of Symons is a sign that Turner looked to modern, experimental poets for inspiration. There is an

awareness in Turner here that going back to England, especially in winter, will never be able to restore his health — every loved place looks different in illness. He is aware, in this piece, that he is going to London to die:

> My lungs may be black with the soot of housefires, and my eyes dulled for the reading of print by much staring at the sea. My road goes to London — there's heaven (or at least a change) at the end of my quiet life.

As I walk the Lower Path, the name Turner appears on the corner of a memorial, followed by 'Manor Park'. This isn't his memorial but the name of the company that made someone else's headstone: a flash of Victorian advertising from those that Ron Woollacott calls 'investors in death'.

10th December 2014

My mum's family history has always been incomplete. Her early life was full of disappearances and then silence. Her mother died when my mum was only twelve — she thinks. A woman blanched through memory, seen in the sick bed — then not seen at all. She remembers seeing her in a bed at her Aunty's house, after which she came home for a while. Then she was dead. Her dad never talked about it, laying down a silent expectation that — as the eldest daughter — she would be the one to take on the role of getting things done around the house. My mum had two sisters but the younger died following an accident when my mum was fifteen. Susan, her name was. I always remember being told as a child that her dead sister's name was Susan.

The Land Built on Poetry: Walking with Edward Alleyn and B.S. Johnson in Dulwich Village

And when thy state was to a better chang'd,
That thou enabled wast for doing goode,
To clothe the naked, give the hungrie food,
As one that was from avarice estrang'd:
  Then what was fit thou scorn'd to seeke for more.
  Whilst bent to doe what was design'd before.

William Alexander, 'To his deservedlie honoured frend Mr. Edward Allane, the first founder and Master of the Colleige of God's Gift.'

I'm standing on Alleynian land, the point which transforms the shape of my map from a potential triangle into a closed casket, the perfect shape to join up the poetic heritage of this area with the poets buried in Nunhead Cemetery. Standing on Alleynian land means two things. First of all, if I lived here I would have to pay ground rent to the Dulwich Estate; the estate would then distribute all income made above estate repair costs for the upkeep of its beneficiaries. Secondly — and more significantly for my journey — this is an estate created from poetry. Edward Alleyn was an actor who earned his first fortune performing the words of poets. His riches later increased with money amassed through his first marriage to Joan Woodward and through co-investing with his father-in-law, Philip Henslowe, in Bankside liberties: bear-baiting, stews and theatres. He was known as the 'master of the king's games, of bears, bulls and dogs'. Given the centrality of poetry in Elizabethan and Jacobean theatre — the poetic verse line as the flexible, fired substance of the plays — it could be said that Alleyn increased his riches through blank verse and metaphorical conceits. He was known for playing the villains in Christopher Marlowe's plays and then — as if to further demonstrate his commitment to the poetic word — John Donne's daughter became his second wife. The riches that Alleyn amassed from the theatre — along with ownership of various properties — was used to set up Dulwich College and, subsequently, Alleyn's School.

Since then the poets have congregated, arriving with purpose on this charged land — a land established by Alleyn in 1614 between Sydenham and the surrounding hills: Herne, Denmark and Champion. The poetry connection runs through the street names, I notice, as I walk: just before Dulwich Village, where suburban pastoral verges towards the chapel and gallery, runs Burbage Road. Richard Burbage (1567-1619) and Alleyn were the only two actors, it was said, who could handle roles over 800 lines. Burbage took plays by Shakespeare, Jonson and Webster and Alleyn took plays by Marlowe, Kyd, Greene and Peele. Alleyn performed at a time when bubonic plague would lead his company — the Lord Strange's Men — to tour outside London. In 1593 they visited Chester, Shrewsbury, Bristol and York. Behind them the bubonic plague was blowing like black gas through London. It is possible that the ill reception given by those in the provinces — calling caution on the dance of death in the bells and ditties of these roving players — made him pine for home. He wrote lovingly to his first wife Joan when he was travelling with his players:

> My good sweete mouse, I comend me hartely to you And to my father, my mother, and my sister bess, hopinge in god, though the sickness be round about you, yett by his mercy itt may escape your house, which by the grace of god it shall. therfor use this corse:-

kepe your house fayr and clean, which I knowe you will, and every evening throwe water before your dore and in your bake sid, and have in your windows good store of reue and herbe of grace, and with all the grace of god, which must be obtaynd by prayers; and so doing, no dout but the Lord will mercifully defend you. now, good mouse, I have no newse to send you but this, thatt we have all our helth, for which the Lord be praysed.

We can see here how attentive and loving Alleyn was in this firsthand account of how the Elizabethan home was prepared to fend off the plague. As Alleyn would no doubt have heard, the land he later bought in Dulwich had already been walked on by those who had staggered from London to save their families from infection, their lymph nodes breaking with buboes as they arrived at Surrey's freshening hills.

Alleyn immortalised himself in the founding of this land. As he wrote in response to a letter to Sir Francis Calton (from whom he bought the land at Dulwich and who had attacked his previous life as a player):

And where you tell me of my poore originall and of my quality as a Player. What is that? If I am richer than my auncestors, I hope I maye be able to doe more good with my riches than ever my auncestors did with their riches.

Alleyn's figure is illuminated with sunlight through glass in the windows of St Giles-without-Cripplegate church (he had established the nearby playhouse, The Fortune, which burned down in 1620) and in Ben Affleck's playing of him in *Shakespeare in Love* (1999).

There is so much pavement to walk on here but silence on this scale comes at a cost — there is the sound, on the wind, of barely concealed tension. In winter 2016 the Dulwich Estate came under attack from locals over the management of properties in the area. Residents — including contemporary actor James Nesbitt — marched through Herne Hill to protest against the Estate's treatment of a toyshop, *Just Williams*. The shop had been forced to close after the Dulwich Estate had increased its rent by 70%. *The Evening Standard* reported the furore caused by a school playing field being contracted under terms which allow it to be sold for residential housing at any time. Facts have surfaced from the controversies: out of the 1,500 acres of land, 85% percent of the Estate's revenue goes into three fee-paying schools: Dulwich College, Alleyn's and James Allen's Girls, which shared £5,815, 840 of the estate's money in 2014-15.

Out of sight, in a nearby road, is the sound of what could be an articulated lorry being squeezed. It could also be the sound of Edward Alleyn shuffling his ruff and moving the stones he's buried beneath in the old chapel at Dulwich. This was a man who dined with poor people and, as Thomas Heywood wrote in his *Apology for Actors* (first printed in 1612), 'when this college was finished this famous man was so equally mingled with humility and charity, that he became his own pensioner, humbly submitting himself to that proportion of diet and clothes which he had bestowed on others.'

Where are today's poets, standing up to take on corruption in a village made on poetry? Alleyn severed ties with the stage when he created the Dulwich Estate but still wrote accounts in the last years of his life which detail how 'Mr Myddleton browght me a book' and 'Goodman poet dined here.' Even the self-named Water Poet, John Taylor, who took subscriptions from people to fund his writing trips, was sponsored by Alleyn, who described giving 4d to 'Jo Taylor,

Edward Alleyn

the poet, for his journey into Scotland.' This was an age before Kickstarter and Taylor struggled to make those who sponsored him stay true to their word — but Alleyn was good for the money he had promised. Alleyn later became friends with the poet William Alexander. Alexander wrote a dedicatory poem to Alleyn, describing him as 'one that was from avarice estrang'd'. It's no wonder that the poets buried in Nunhead Cemetery are appearing thick and fast now: the wind blowing to them in a south-westerly direction is one infused with the earthy smell of seasoned poets.

Ian Brinton is currently writing his account of the visiting poets to Dulwich College and I recently came across another poetry connection to the area through Patricia Doubell's *At the Dog in Dulwich: Recollections of a Poet,* which details the poetry readings given at the Crown and Greyhound pub in the sixties and seventies. A pub known affectionately as 'the Dog', but which is currently closed. The Dulwich Estate might well want to limit the business of pubs in the area: it's where locals talk. The acerbic gutterspeak of the poets is never far away from a flowing tap.

I'm walking away from the Estate, further south. Maybe I've seen enough, but I know I can get closer to Alleyn than any other actor of the Elizabethan period — or indeed, poet — through his papers, which survive in the archives of Dulwich College. The Victorian writer J. Payne Collier later published them and used them as the basis for a biography of Alleyn. Collier describes the brilliance of his acting and his status among the poets who wrote for him — it's on their words that Alleyn takes his place amongst the immortals. Alleyn was praised for his role in Thomas Nash's *Pierce Pennyless, his Supplication the Divell*, drawing Nash to write 'If I ever write anything in Latine (as I hope one day I shall), not a man of any desert here amongst us but I will have up — Tarlton, Ned Allen, Knell, Bentley, shall be made known to Fraunce, Spayne and Italie.' Ben Jonson also realised that it is within the work of the poets that Alleyn should live on. What else could the poets give back in return for all the life he had breathed into their written words?

> How can so great example dye in mee,
> That, Allen, I should pause to publish thee?
> Who both their graces in thy selfe hast more
> Outstript, then they did all that went before;
> And present worth in all dost so contract,
> As others speake, but onely thou dost act.
> Weare this renowne: 'tis just, that who did give
> So many Poets life, by one should live.

Alleyn endlessly solicited dedications to his genius from poets. At the start of his career, in around 1590, he defeated someone called Peele (not the playwright) in a performance contest, a common pursuit amongst actors. Peele died three years later, broken by the defeat and the effects of 'the irregularity of his life'. From then on the door opened for Alleyn to choose from the best plays written for the playhouses he owned or had a connection with. Amongst the Alleyn papers an apocryphal poet lauds the actor's talents:

> The moneyes downe, the place the Hope,
> Phillippes shall hide his head and Pope.
> Feare not, the victorie is thyne;
> Thou still as macheles Ned shall shyne.
> If Rossius Richard foames and fumes,
> The globe shall have but emptie rooms,
> If thou doest act; and Willes newe playe
> Shall be rehearst some other daye.

The inference is clear: if Alleyn shines like everyone knows he can, then Burbage ('Rossius Richard') will be shown to fall short in Shakespeare's new play, which was being rehearsed down the road at The Globe. Dekker later wrote Alleyn a poem when the broken playwright was in the King's Bench prison; unfortunately the poem has been lost but the letter remains and makes it clear that Alleyn had continued to send money to the poet. Dekker was determined to struggle by with the milky earnings from the teat of his pen but Alleyn provided the rusk of benefaction when things got hard. The poets knew that Alleyn was rich on money acquired through services to poetry. Without their words he'd have had no plays to act.

Following Alleyn's marriage to Philip Henslowe's daughter his riches began to increase through new business ventures. The money Alleyn was buying into was a mix of old and new. Joan Woodward, Alleyn's first wife, was his new stepfather's stepdaughter by marriage. Henslowe had married her mother Agnes, after her husband died, and in doing so rose from the position of servant in her house. He came to money not through an inherited right but through social movement. According to Collier he was 'so illiterate, and kept his accounts ... so irregularly, that it is frequently impossible to make out at all exactly what they do, or do not establish.' From this low position he became a 'free inheritor' of playhouses, including the Rose. He also acted as pawnbroker 'and advanced money to any parties who were in want of it, upon plate, rings, jewels, and wearing apparel.' After Henslowe had been in the theatre business for nearly a decade he wrote to Alleyn to say that one of their players had been killed in a duel by 'bergeman Jonson, bricklayer', not realising that this was the Ben Jonson who'd written plays for their playhouses. As Jonson was already the famous author of *Every Man in His Humour* this shows scant regard from Henslowe in the art that was making him rich. The inference is that he had no interest in the theatre at all, beyond keeping a tally of earnings at the gate. It was this co-business of the theatre with Henslowe through which Alleyn would further build his fortunes.

Alleyn also owned the aptly named Fortune Theatre in Cripplegate which, as Collier states, 'ultimately formed part of the endowment of Dulwich College'. Alleyn may have connected the rise of Henslowe with the plot of *King Lear* and the comparable agitations of the bastard son Edmund up the buttery maypole of the social order. There are diaries in Dulwich College showing Henslowe's takings, night by night, of plays performed in the theatres he owned with Alleyn: he kept an accurate script of his growing wealth.

Alleyn was also embroiled in the machinations of these business deals, if with less relish than Henslowe. He owned a parsonage at Firle in Sussex, which he sold to someone called Langworth in 1596 and from the sale of which Henslowe was also paid. Alleyn wasn't always intent on looking towards heaven with the iambics of a great poetic line rising to his tongue; he was embroiled in the murky waters of real estate, witnessing an agreement written into Henslowe's diary between himself, Henslowe and Langworth:

> Mdm. that Mr. Arture Langworth hath promysed, the 16 daye of Maye 1595, to paye unto me Phillipe Henslow the some of j hundreth powndes for a howsse, and land, and goodwyll he bargened with me, with owt any condicion, but absolutely to paye me so muche mony, and to take such a surence as I have at this time. Witnesses to this promes of payment
> "E. Alleyn" Edwards + Allenes wiffes marke

What distinguishes Alleyn from Henslowe is the latter's relish for profiteering. When Henslowe writes to Alleyn during the plague there is some concern for an illness that Alleyn had picked up in Bath, but within these concerns — and relayed communications of his own family's health — Henslowe gushes into an ill-timed account of their Southwark tenants' inability to pay their rent:

> but your tenantes weax very power, for they cane paye no rent, nor will paye no rent while mychellmas next, and then we shall have yt yf we cane great yt; and lyckwisse your Joyner commended hime unto you and says he will prove himseallfe ane onest man

We never hear Alleyn's response to business priorities, He's often more set on describing what's in his wardrobe — 'clokes', 'gowns' and 'sutes' — and succouring his wife with affectionate cooing lover's language. Yet it was this money combined — that of poetry and that of property investment throughout the plague — that went into making the Dulwich Estate. Lump sums can blossom good works but, in the wrong hands, can swell into buboes. Collier points out that it was Alleyn's money from property which allowed him to later make his God's Gift to Dulwich:

> Independent of his interest in theatres, he was, at all events in 1596, and, perhaps, owing a considerable degree to his marriage, a man of property ... None of his biographers appear to have been acquainted with this remarkable fact, and all have speculated in what way he could have become possessed of sufficient money and land to enable him to build and endow Dulwich College.

After the deaths of Henslowe in 1615, Henslowe's wife in 1617, and his own wife, Agnes, in 1623, Alleyn seems to have taken ownership of all of Henslowe's property, which included a new Paris Garden and deals with local watermen. Alleyn had already begun building Dulwich but there was nothing in this ethics of acquiring money born of vice that held back his project — in fact, the more he made from these dealings, the more he could realise his new charitable venture.

Amongst his papers found at Dulwich College are some verses of Henry Wotton, written in Ben Jonson's hand, and a handwritten poem by Jonson himself. Both poems give instructions on how to live well and happily, to be healthy and free in the mind: Alleyn turned the tallysticks of business into a raft that would support his charity work. This was a man who later gave his wealth away — he didn't turn out toy shop owners for falling short of rent. The Wotton poem also appears in the papers, written in Alleyn's own hand, suggesting that this poem meant a lot to him. The poem ends:

> This man is free from servile bandes
> Of hope to rise or feare to fall;
> Lord of himself, though not of landes,
> And having nothing, yet hath all.

During Alleyn's last years in Southwark he split his interests in two, becoming a churchwarden as well as the owner of properties, thereby having to address the vices in the area from which he was also making his money. His sidesman as churchwarden, John Lee, would send notes to Alleyn with details of the people whose vices needed investigating, such as 'John Noble, for disorder in his bouling Ally'.

Alleyn, The Lord of the Manor of Dulwich, might have something else to say about the current running of the Dulwich Estate. As Collier writes, 'Though generous and charitable, [he] was careful and frugal'. Perhaps the myth that Alleyn turned to charity after seeing a demon whilst acting is true. MacSweeney, too, had seen a demon before arriving on this land. Blake's mythos ripples with the demons of his self-mythology.

It is in Patricia Doubell's book that I read of another writer, B.S. Johnson, whose demons had drawn him to Dulwich Village too — a writer whose creative life also held the White Goddess as a central creative force. Johnson brought this Alleynian land of poetry back to the fore in his 1966 article for *London Life* called 'A Hard

Glance at the Poetry Business'. Johnson focuses our attention away from the magazine scene towards that of the readings which took place at the Dog in Dulwich Village:

> The best of these in London is held not in Chelsea, or Soho, or Hampstead, but in SE22 by the Dulwich Group. The meetings take place in the upstairs room of an enormous, friendly pub, and audiences of over a hundred (on one sweltering occasion, three hundred) are common. It is no doubt the fact of being held in a pub, where the atmosphere is informal and where the audience can meet the poets down in the bar afterwards, that accounts for the successes of the Dulwich meetings compared with all other poetry readings in London.

Before Johnson turns his attention back to the print scene, hammering out the usual lines of argument around poetry's palpable invisibility, he puts his finger on the anomalous success of the Dulwich readings, writing that other venues draw 'nothing like the Dulwich crowds: and Dulwich is far from being the easiest place in London to reach by public transport.' The readings began before the Second World War and continued until the early eighties. As I'm finding, poets have been drawn to south-east London in such quantities — and qualities — that only theories of elevated landscape and *The White Goddess* can make sense of it.

If the Dog wasn't temporarily shut for refurbishment — an extended refurbishment which may well suit the Dulwich Estate — I'd be in there, trying to make contact with the tracks left by Johnson as I've done for Blake, MacSweeney and Browning. There is an extant photograph of Johnson at a reading in the Dog, looking slightly disenchanted, maybe even bored, as he listens: head back to the wall, quiff lilting, arms crossed and forehead ruffled. The readings here clearly weren't always clarion calls from Parnassus. But Johnson was right to identify this series as being significant: this is, after all, a land built on poetry.

B.S. Johnson (foreground, arms crossed) at the Dog in Dulwich

16th March 2015

An appointment has come through from the hospital for my mum to talk about hereditary illnesses, to help them learn more about her own illness. These questions about the past make the year more strange and difficult. All this and it was Mother's Day today. In the pub before the meal my mum said: 'I've got nothing to tell them, I don't know what my mum died of.' My mum thinks it might be stomach cancer. My mum's aunt — her mum's sister — died not long afterwards, but she doesn't know what caused it. Her other aunt lived until old age. It may have been the strengthening affects of the alcohol, but I offered to look into it for her.

Nunhead Poets: Albert Craig and William Herbert

Albert Craig (1850-1909), by his own admission, doesn't qualify as a poet, preferring to describe himself as 'cricket rhymester' (rhymester also being the description that Wiki gives to him). Yet he has gone down in the accolades as The Surrey Poet (quite some claim given that Henry Howard, Earl of Surrey, had developed the Shakespearian sonnet and wrote such beautiful lines as 'the nights car the stars about doth bring'). Like many poets before him Craig found that literary merit isn't necessarily the path towards prosperity. After selling thousands of copies of his verses about cricketers at Park Avenue he found that he could earn more by doing this than through his job as a Post Office clerk, so he quit the job and moved to London. I like the way Craig was under no illusions about what he was doing, and was reported as saying to members of the crowd: 'I know that any fool among you could write a better poem than this, but I defy anyone else, however intelligent, to sell it at 2d a copy.' His poems became the silent vehicle from which he could hold a live crowd. He enjoyed being heckled and living up to the pressure of taking on the audience as a current day comedian might.

Ronald Mason wrote about him: 'He had no authority but popularity, no recommendation but gaiety, no talent but wit.' There's only one Craig poem in the British Library: it's included in a personal scrapbook album of hymns and ephemera that spans from the 1850s to the 1890s. Looking at the printed page of Craig's poem it's easy to see where he went right. The poem is printed on thick card, making it both durable and appealing to the public, but it also includes an advert on the back which would have added to the income he sourced for selling the poems.

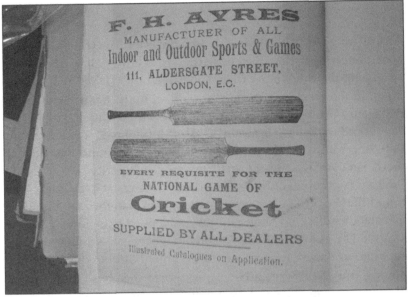

Back of a poem by Albert Craig showing cricket advert

Craig is buried in an unmarked private grave, not far from the Limesford Road entrance. Of all the poets here he's the one who reached furthest into popular culture and yet he is the only one to be buried without a memorial. He may have found that selling poems gave him as much cash in hand as his job at the Post Office but the security of a pension and savings were negligible; in that way he was living as a true poet. He is also the poet whose writings are most difficult to access: the only poem of his I could find is the one at the

British Library. The remaining solace, perhaps, is in that *had* he been given a memorial the chances of finding it in the section he's buried in would be slight, for the remaining headstones here are blanketed with ivy. The occasional crucifix has fared better, cutting with right-angles through the creepers and brambles.

It's hard to be too harsh on Craig — he was by his own admission, after all, a rhymester. The poem I found is called 'Oxford v Cambridge at Lords: June 30th 1892' and fits the Victorian spirit of playing up and playing the game which was the prevailing pre-First World War ethic, whether talking about war or sport. It's quite a relief after reading so many war-mongering poets to find that Craig really is just talking about sport:

> Never say die if the battle's worth fighting,
> Do what your hand finds to do with a will;
> If it be Cricket you take a delight in,
> Tread in the footsteps of Jardine and Hill.

'Do what your hand finds to do with a will' is a curiously off-putting expression yet Craig isn't lacking in his gusto for the cricketing legends of the day and lauds Jardine as 'a worthy exponent of genuine cricket'. The more excited Craig gets the more his roving, ever-lengthening lines hit the right margin until the final line extends outside of white space — and clumsily folds back to the line beneath:

> Which ever side wins boys, we'll give them their dues,
> They're the best of all Sportsmen, are the dark and light
> Blues. — A.C.

Craig signed off all his poems with his initials, presumably preferring the unsightliness of the proximity of his name to the text to the risk of being plagiarised. Unlike most of the poets in Nunhead, this was, after all, his livelihood.

I've again reached the opening avenue of the Cemetery and this time head straight across to the Catacombs Path. Just past the scaffolded East Lodge is the burial plot of William Herbert (1772-1851) yet I know in advance not to look for him: there's a note in Ron Woollacott's *Buried at Nunhead* which reads: 'Headstone believe to have been destroyed during the Second World War'. As Woollacott describes in *Investors in Death*:

> Several bombs fell in Nunhead Cemetery during the blitz on London in 1940 and 1941… A bomb fell in the East Crescent leaving a deep crater and damaging several substantial monuments, while another destroyed part of the boundary wall fronting Linden Grove causing much damage to graves and scattering human remains into the public road.

There is a reversal of the Blitz experience here: as civilians in London ran for underground cover the dead were exploded from their graves and projected back onto the earth. There's a surviving photograph showing gravediggers lined up facing a camera across an open grave. Two spades rise out of the grave, crossing each other, propped firmly in the London clay. The men wear hats and cravats as if they've plummeted downwards through the social stratosphere to land here in the mud. Riches to rags. They have the look of characters from Dickens, alert to any sliver of opportunity that might flash from the ground. The man at the front is a dead ringer for Finlay Currie as Magwitch in the David Lean film. When I look closely I could see that the photograph has been ripped and restored but with a part of the photograph missing so that half of one man is attached to half of a different man: the newly created face is distended by mismatch and an extended arm lags incongruously down to the left knee. As if this new man has been made from the scattered remains that were found on the road outside the Cemetery and the dead are now burying themselves.

William Herbert wrote just one book of poetry in collaboration with his friend and fellow antiquarian Edward Wedlake Brayley (1773-1854) called *Syr Reginalde or the Black Tower, A Romance of the Twelfth Century with Tales and Other Poems.* Herbert is another of those mercurial Victorians, his life an eccentric accrual of pursued passions. As Ron Woollacott describes in *Buried at Nunhead*, Herbert's early jobs of running errands for a bullying boss called Mr Bates and selling clothes for a tailor were replaced with a spell as a bookseller and then a time working for a London solicitors — but all of this was underpinned with a passion for the theatre. After meeting his future wife, Sarah Youens, at a drama school they joined the Royal Circus at St George's Fields and then travelled the country. Herbert returned to the day job of selling books but continued to keep an interest in the theatre until this was overtaken with his newly pursued interest of writing about London. He went from the circus to becoming a librarian and was then appointed as the first librarian of London's Guildhall Library in 1828, continuing until his retirement in 1845.

Herbert's only poetry book, his collaboration with Brayley, is now everywhere: search on Google Books and it's yours. None of that trawling through secondhand bookdealers or twitching like Wellsian Eloi in the British Library while the Morlocks clutter about in the bowels of the building for the request — though it is, in fact, the British Library that has digitised it for Google Books. In this collaborative work the two poets have helpfully inserted their initials after their contributions to make it easy for the reader to see who wrote what. I bear in mind before I start to read that this is the earliest work I've looked at amongst the Nunhead dead, being published in 1803 — the year that the third edition of Coleridge's *Poems* was published, and also the year before Blake wrote 'Jerusalem'. Herbert's book was written in the period of eccentric Romanticism and not that of the cloned stanzas of Victoriana — so I'm not sure what to expect.

The Blakean thought isn't wasted so far as the book's title page goes: it shows a picture of a man on a white horse being chased by a hovering black devil. The devil has a firework in one hand and what looks like a bone in the other. Biblical forces are unleashed. For reasons perhaps only known to the illustrator, a huge letter A seems to be floating in the backdrop of the picture and there's a short poem beneath the image called 'The Devil & the Lawyer' which ends: 'But ride this way, or that way, or which way he will / O'er his shoulder the Devil was peeping still'. The 'advertisement' to the book tells me quickly to hedge expectations — and my excitement for something in the Blakean mould vapourises:

> Engaged in pursuits far different to those of poetry, the authors of the following pages do not present them to the world as the brilliant coruscations of superior genius: most of them, indeed, were written with no higher aim than to amuse a circle of friends.

Are poets right to go against their better judgement and choose to publish because the opportunity is made available to them? I read on to find out.

The book is divided into 'Tales', 'Odes' and 'Miscellaneous', most of the tales being written by Brayley. I turn to a Herbert poem called 'The Traveller and Sexton'. The scene of the poem crackles with literary kindling as the presentation of the Gothic adventure unfolds:

> A traveller, at the close of day,
>   Just as the sun went down,
> With riding tir'd, pursu'd his way
> Towards where, involv'd in clouds so grey,
>   Dim gleam'd the ancient town

There's nothing firing the poetic here other than words chosen to keep the tale moving; the language is simplistic and worn ('sun went down','gleam'd', 'clouds so grey'). It's in the next stanza that Herbert's poetry moves from the simplistic and into the problematic with the line, 'The clouds look'd big with rain'. Not only is there a hesitation here with 'look'd' but the adjective 'big' is an extremely flat way to describe full clouds. As the character rides towards a village Herbert attempts to raise suspense in the reader: 'What shall he do? — where shelter seek, / To skreen him from the show'r?' I momentarily become excited by the word 'skreen' — an interesting verb — before realising that this is simply a variant spelling of 'screen'. In the action here there is none of the sheer Dante-esque strangeness of Browning's Arthurian poem 'Childe Roland', which includes an acutely described 'hoary cripple with malicious eye'. Unlike Browning, Herbert's poem lacks any attempt to remake the mythic tradition with individual weirdness. The suspense here is that the knight won't make it to the village and is worried about where he'll sleep. Whereas Browning's 'Childe Roland' is about a lifetime quest to make it to the tower — set in an oddly industrial and bleak landscape — Herbert's poem ends with an apparition appearing in the shape of his horse and the knight fleeing to hide in a church. The poem is so staid that I paused to wonder if it was meant as a parody of the Knights Templar or if it was written in the Arthurian ballad tradition: in either reading the poem fails.

I turn to the odes. Odes are traditionally lyric poems, usually about a person or abstraction, and, judging by their titles, Herbert's odes seem to fulfil this description. They are all about things — a storm in one instance, and in another superstition — but he approaches them with the same dramatic language and description of action as he uses for his tales. Whereas John Keats would remodel the ode as a form that can allow the poet to go beyond the constraints of known human perception in pursuit of the beautiful — an approach he called 'negative capability' — Herbert remains locked within an idea that he must project his subject with as much animation as possible in order to entertain the reader. His odes lack introspection:

> Hark! Heard ye that sigh? –
> Solemn and deep, it seem'd like Misery's tone
> 'Tis the grim tempest hov'ring in the sky,
> It louder swells, again — and hark — a groan!

('To Superstition')

Perhaps it's unfair to compare Herbert to a later poet who wrote some of the greatest odes. Keats was writing fifteen years later, in a world that had changed significantly. So I look to an earlier poet, Thomas Chatterton, and his poem 'February: an Elegy'. Although Chatterton defined this as an elegy it is, in fact, a true ode — lyrical and focused on a particular thing: the driving rain of February (and those who cavort through Bristol on floats of conspicuous consumption while the poet seeks inspiration from the Muse). Looking at the poem usefully reminds me of what was present in English poetry before this point and what Herbert is lacking in and Chatterton has in spades — style and attitude:

> Now rumbling coaches furious drive along,
> Full of the majesty of city dames,
> Whose jewels, sparkling in the gaudy throng,
> Raise strange emotions and invidious flames.

There is so much happening in these four lines: syntactic reversal and disjuncture, adjectives and adverbs layered on each other like coats of paint, additional half rhymes above the end rhymes and the surprise of the end rhymes themselves: 'along' with 'throng'. Herbert wasn't simply doing what all poets did in 1803: Chatterton had written this poem in 1770. Within the formulaic expectations of making 'verse' there was great scope for the individual poet to stretch language as a medium, to make poems sing with the distinct physicality of the individual's DNA. Chatterton did that.

The bombed section in which Herbert's destroyed memorial lies is split by the East Crescent, which swings south just before the filled-in catacombs. Cow parsley seems to nod towards the path, offering some kind of benediction to the poetasters. A friend of mine called my project of discovering unknown and lost poets 'doing a reverse Chatterton'. That seems about right today.

17th March 2015

I've started to look into my mum's family history. I've figured that if I can successfully dig into the histories of Victorian poets, tracing their records through musty receptions and records offices, then I must be able to find something out from my mum's past. I write down my grandmother's details — the few that my mum remembers:

Agnes Bennett (née Williams)
Date of birth unknown
Died around 1961 / 1962
Cause of death unknown

18th March 2015
I trawled through the details of dozens of 'Williams' at the Liverpool Records Office: microfiche misaligned and slowly scrolling as if it's analogue trawled across the floor of the sea. I couldn't find anyone with the name my mum's given, though I did find this:

Agnes Bennett
Born (about) 1927
Died June 1958
Aged 31
Liverpool, North Lancashire, England

The dates don't fit but when I spoke to my mum later she said, Well, Yes — I must have been younger than I thought when she died. It was different in those days, she said. You just got on with it.

   I asked her if I should look for the birth certificate of this Agnes Bennett? She said:

— What do you think? It could be interesting, couldn't it?

— It's up to you Mum, it's your history.

— Well we might as well, as the appointment's coming up.

— Are you sure? It's a lot to take in, along with your illness.

— Go on, ask them for it. It can't do any harm can it?

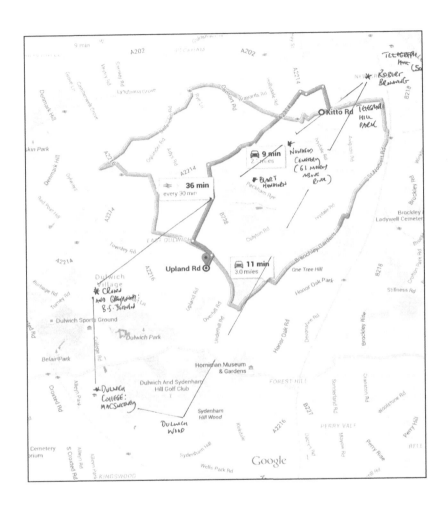

Drawing a Casket Around Myself

If a star were confin'd into a tomb,
Her captive flames must needs burn there;
But when the hand that lock'd her up, gives room,
She'll shine through all the sphere.
    Henry Vaughan, 'They are all Gone into the World of Light'

As I connect the sites of south-east London's poets to Dulwich Village there is something satisfying about how the incomplete map I had before has become a casket. I've carried myself into Alleyn's land in a self-made coffin. There is an echo here too of the shape of the upturned torches — symbols of life extinguished — on the gates of Nunhead Cemetery. Blake's boyhood rambles, Barry MacSweeney's last fling with an audience, the earth that's been nourished with plague victims, Browning's eating of flowers in Dulwich Wood and B.S. Johnson's abandonment of his muse all encircle Nunhead Cemetery in a powerful network of poetic activity.

The year is passing. I'm glad to be moving away from the crisis that the word 'cancer' spreads, crab-like, in the minds of those in health. Nunhead Cemetery has become the hypotenuse, that further thing made from joining together the sides of my map. Between Dulwich Wood, Dulwich College, Dulwich Village and Telegraph Hill I've discovered a history of poetic charge unrivalled in the metropolis. Where else can you find a village in London made from poetry? The boy Blake pinned his personal mythology to the centre of a field, following instinct and the draw of his creative psyche. The poets have followed. I've arrived behind them like a plague-fleeing bellman.

All time in Dulwich, as far as the poets go — and as Blake believed — takes place at once: in a great channel towards eternity. Poetry is the great dialogic art in which questions are asked and left hovering on the wind for others to respond to centuries later. Blake provides the call for later poets to step outside modes of thinking that hem them in, to map the world for themselves. The poetic force of the past was already here and will be so in the future — I just had to draw the plotlines to make them visible. No poet, or believer in poetic myth and the poetics of chance, will find this strange. In *The White Goddess* Graves describes his own process of discovering the answer to the *Hanes Taliesin* puzzle in his book as coming about through 'an arrangement of thought arrived at by unreason'. Like Blake, who wrote that 'the ruins of time build mansions in eternity', I can see how right Graves is to describe time in relation to poetry like this:

> In the poetic act, time is suspended and details of the future experience often become incorporated in the poem, as they do in dreams.

I start to look closely at another map now: the map of Nunhead Cemetery itself. The dream will break and the landscape will become clear to me, with its view back to the city where the known poets' names are hung on the walls of its once bohemian pubs, where the padded shoulders of bankers now meet.

Later that night I walk out from the Tulse Hill Hotel after drinks with a friend. It's freezing outside, I walk to keep warm — it's better than stopping to try and hail a taxi — and after a while I look up from the hoarfrost settling on the pavement to see that I'm passing the grounds of Dulwich College. A black cab is moving towards me, its orange light cut cleanly in the cold. I flag it down and climb into a moving cube of warmth, giving the driver directions towards Lordship Lane. He turns up the heating. Then I see that someone's left a bag on the back seat. I tell the driver. 'I'll take it back,' he says. 'The last guy was a security guard.' Cabs are ninety percent plasma these days: if it's not the panel of pixelated advertising on the roof, it's the screen in the back, like this, beaming *Sky News* across the seats. I'm warmed by news of global crises.

When I arrive back to my room three postcards have been left on my bed, a gift from my landlady, Vanessa, who knows about my journeys into the Cemetery. The pictures are in Victorian sepia, a kind of two-tone beigescale. One shows a vista of the Cemetery with a man digging a grave with a pickaxe, the handle of a spade next to him. Another shows the gates of the Cemetery with clusters of people entering: a couple and a child, a man with a walking stick, a lone dog looking in. The third is more recent, a vehicle with a man at the wheel. Along the side of the van are the words W. UDEN & SONS LTD. FUNERAL DIRECTORS, still in business with a shopfront on Lordship Lane. The black industry of death has proved sustainable when so many industries have collapsed and folded under. There is a parallel here with poetry in the sense that poets have relied so little on money that they too have continued to thrive in the cut and thrust of economics. And as I'm finding at Nunhead, wherever there's a cemetery there are poets.

19ᵗʰ March 2015

The three months of chemotherapy are catching up. The skin on her hands looks burned — the extremities nuked by medicine — and her body is aching. The will to leave the house, to do things, to keep busy — the energy's no longer there. She has a citizen's pass and enough weekly steroids in her system to fuel an underground gym instructor. The end of the treatment is coming — just two more weeks. And then a short strong dose of radiotherapy.

20ᵗʰ March 2015

The weight has been pressing from above — the way my depression has done before — forcing itself into everything. Like nature my depression hates a void and fills the vacuum — there's nowhere to go outside of it — it has to be faced. Except this feels like a different strain of my depression — more a suffering for lack of focus. I forgot about the eclipse — a sign that the Gods are angry — and walked along Lordship Lane last night, around midnight, looking behind me as I walked with this feeling — beneath the huge Victorian terraces — of being followed. Objects appeared strange: an old child's desk waiting to be removed, a recycling bin, a doll with no clothes. I woke up early and went for a run around Peckham Rye, the rest of the world — I realised later — was positioned behind lenses for the eclipse that I'd forgotten about. I ran, thinking about my mum: a world reduced to the size of a snowglobe. I interpreted the grey hood above me as cloud, a prognosticator of a pending storm, and carried on running under its weight. Later I realised that no eclipse came to London, not in the way the Cheshire cat grin had cut the sky over the North. Peckham Rye was untouched by it. Angels can appear where no eclipse comes.

Nunhead Poets: Richard Alfred Davenport and Marian Richardson

There is no doubting Richard Alfred Davenport's (died 1852) commitment to poetry — he was one of the contributors to the epic Victorian project *The British Poets: One Hundred Volumes*, which gathered together the works of poets from Chaucer onwards. His description in *More Nunhead Notables* lists him as being primarily a writer *about* poetry but, after digging, I've found that he is a poet in his own right and published a poem in 1851 called 'The Dying Druid'. This was a year in which expectations were set high in Victorian poetry. The year before had seen the death of Wordsworth; Tennyson had become laureate and his work was yet to be dulled by the ceremonial bells of public duty. The year before had seen the publication of Tennyson's *In Memoriam* and Elizabeth Barrett Browning's *Sonnets from the Portugese*. In 1851 Matthew Arnold published one of the great poems of the period, 'Dover Beach'. It is within this context that I looked at Davenport's poem.

The context of the publication of the poem is something of a mystery as it appears as the postscript to a long poem by another poet, Esther Le Hardy's *Agabus or The Last of the Druids: An Historical Poem*. Davenport's poem appears after the endnotes with the following introduction from Le Hardy: 'I know not how to end this little poem more appropriately than by closing it with the following beautiful lines, published some years ago in a periodical work.' Davenport's poem bemoans the wiping out of the Druids following the Roman invasion, offering an invented final monologue from the dying Arch-Druid:

'Oh! Most accurst, Oh! fatal day!
That bends us to tyrannic sway;
For ever fallen the British name,
Extinct for ever freedom's flame;
No more beneath the hallow'd shade
Shall to the gods our thanks be paid;
No more from us our youth shall learn
The unmanly fear of death to spurn;
Or when their country calls shall fly
Prompt in her glorious cause to die.'

'The British name', 'freedom's flame', 'country calls', 'her glorious calls': it's clear from Davenport's take on the Druids that I'm finding two of the weaknesses of so much Victorian poetry: a fall back to unquestionable patriotism and the use of the received patter of everyday expressions. The message flows with the emphasis that only rhymed couplets — with their assertive drilling of sound often a shorthand for artillery and the clarion call — can add. The verbs and adjectives used in the poem show that Davenport isn't out to conceive original imagery and fusions in language: 'groans of gasping' he writes and 'Rome's proud banner'. There are, I found, two nice lines in the poem which show an economy and the ability to create a verbal impact on the reader: 'Gash'd with wounds and red with gore / They lie extended on the shore.' There is something of Geoffrey Hill's 'For whom the possessed sea littered, on both shores / Ruinous arms' — but I wanted much more from Davenport like this. As far as his one extant poem goes this couplet would have made a more substantial offering in itself.

Davenport is a writer with an intoxicating mix of publications behind him, with titles including *The Life of Ali Pasha, of Tepeleni,*

Vizier of Epirus: Surnamed Aslan, or the Lion (1837); *The History of the Bastille: and of its Principal Captives* (1839); *Lives of Individuals Who Raised Themselves from Poverty to Eminence of Fortune* (1841); *Perilous Adventures, or Remarkable Instances of Courage, Perseverance and Suffering* (1846), *Sketches of Imposture, Deception and Credulity* (1861). He was a contributor to *A Dictionary of Biography, Comprising the Most Eminent Characters of all Ages, Nations and Professions* (1831). Davenport also offered a 'sketch' of the translator George Sale to an 1878 version of *The Koran*.

My favourite of his books is his *Sketches of Imposture, Deception and Credulity* which 'aspires only to give, under various heads, a sample of the manifold frauds which have, in all ages, been successfully employed to frighten and gull mankind.' He clearly enjoyed writing this, adding: 'If it should be found to afford to the Public only a quarter as much amusement and instruction as have been derived from those excellent works, his ambition will be amply gratified.' Davenport covers ground from the insurrection of Jack Cade to the disguise of Achilles; from Mary Tofts the Rabbit Breeder to the jargon of Dr Dee. 'Incredulity has been said', he says (echoing Aristotle), 'to be the foundation of all wisdom'. His account of vampires through history is written with the assurance of one who knows: 'Vampyres were not to be so easily got rid of as he imagined. Nothing short of burning would, at least in a majority of cases, put an end to their diabolical visitations. Some of them had the audacity to make a jest of driving a stake through them.' Davenport, I read in *More Nunhead Notables*, 'died from an overdose of opium at his residence … aged 75. When police discovered his body it was surrounded by piles of dust covered books and manuscripts. Headstone (no trace).' He disappeared into nowhere like a vampire scorched by daylight.

Davenport was the second of the poets to buried in the Cemetery, entering the earth here in 1852. His date of birth is unknown and there is no marker in place for his grave. The East Crescent is silent as I follow the path which is mirrored on the west path with the Avenue in between: this might be the only symmetry to be found in the Cemetery's looping, winding paths: there is no stake at the heart of this landscape.

If Marian Richardson (1830-72) is remembered for one thing — and it's not being a poet — it is for being the woman who brought Garibaldi to Peckham. The General visited her and her husband John Richardson in 1864. Marian Richardson only published one collection in her short life, *The Talk of the Household: Poems* (1865). In the book are seven poems about, or to, Garibaldi — the first making clear her view on the man's achievement with the title 'Italy and its Liberator'. There is a strong sense of hero-worship here which — on reading her poems — I soon realised brought out her declamatory worst (a trait which can also be seen in the royalist poems in the volume):

> Strong-nerved, thy Italy to fave,
> Thou GARIBALDI, rofe.

('A Welcome to Garibaldi')

Garibaldi is listed amongst the subscribers at the back of the book — the only Victorian collection of poetry I know to count an Italian revolutionary amongst its benefactors.

As in life so in death: looking at the map of Nunhead in front of me I find that so many of the poets are on the fringes, buried somewhere beyond the widest reaches of the Cemetery's paths. Richardson is in section 104 with the path I'm walking along splitting the section in two. As I think about her work I walk past a beautiful modernist headstone for someone called Walter Edward Oliphant — the surname being high German for 'elephant' — who died in 1934 aged sixty. Although his son is buried with him his son preceded him into death: killed in Arras in 1917. One of the lucky ones, it might be said, whose body was identified and brought back. The stone is pressed into the slender winding bough of a tree which has been slicked to umber in the rain.

The dedication to the book locates Richardson at two points within my poetic map of south-east London, here in Nunhead Cemetery, but also at a place called Lancaster House, Peckham Rye: within visual distance of Blake's angel. When her first and only collection was published Richardson had seven years of life left, making the dedication in her book a closer reality than she could have sensed:

> And ye, my Children, who in after years
> > May dearly prize these records of our day
> When they have sunk to silence in the Past,
> > And she who wrote them may have passed away.

In addition to the patriotism and fervour for Garibaldi I soon found that there was a further problem with the book, an unnecessary, jarring one. For some reason Richardson (or her publisher) decided on the Elizabethan conceit of presenting all letter 's's in the book as 'f's. This was strong period in the arts for returning to classical mythology and medieval literature but this physical reconstruction of an archaic style makes it difficult for the Victorian reader — and certainly the contemporary reader — to enter into the poem's meaning:

> Bright from the buried paft their deeds
> In undimmed luftre fhine,
> And fhining on, fhall ftill endure,
> Remembered thro' all Time.

('Heroes')

The kinds of words that Richardson chooses to apply the 'f' to increases the ludicrousness of trying to wade through to the meaning: the modern mind isn't trained to replace one letter with another as it reads. Robert Graves talks in *The White Goddess* of how Victorian poets often went in very strange directions to try and find originality, which often involved a 'mental squint' towards 'vulgar things': Richardson's resurrection of the dead 'f' is an example of that. Richardson could almost be applying a conceptual layer to her poems to create an effect very far from her intention. The list of words she applies this to becomes a sound piece of invented language: 'ftoried', 'ftar', fmall', 'forrow', 'fhed', 'filver', 'feize', 'fpirit', 'ftirring'. After a while it becomes possible to replace the 'f's with 's's, in the mind at least, but those placed within words are impossible to spot before the teeth have puckered the lower lip: 'lowlieft', 'moft', 'lifps', 'thoufand', 'Pleafure'. The double use within a line is particularly difficult to swerve smoothly around: 'lifps its fimple words'. This comes close to sounding like insult when used in 'fick'ning pang'. Other words are almost impossible to reconstruct back into English, such as 'fceptrelefs'. I try to see beyond this archaic style — after all hadn't Chatterton resurrected Chaucerian English for his Rowley poems? — but there is another issue here: there is a sentimentality to the verse. The poem quoted above ends by reminding youth that even if war doesn't give them fame, 'he a Hero too may be / Who nobly does his beft.'

I wish, now, that I'd brought my glasses: it's hard to spot the dead without them. I walk with my back long turned to the Bluebell Glade towards where the Inner Loop and The Loop meet to form a single path. Richardson's headstone is here somewhere. I stand facing a rising commune of ash, elder and low-lying rhododendrons. Stone mausolea slide into unstable loam. A woman is walking eight dogs, the Dalmatians bounding ahead. She talks to them like babies: 'Frank love, Frank, baby'. The walkers share handshakes and the secret language that only professional dog walkers know.

Richardson's poetic eye focuses also on 'Common Things, of Life's fmall duties nobly done, ... / Than ever Poet harped or fung.' This is a theme later picked up by international poets such as William Carlos Williams and Francis Ponge whose focus on a red wheelbarrow or a brief flash of rain enables the reader to see these things differently. But Richardson doesn't turn the gifted poet's trick of getting *inside* — or under the surface — of the common thing to allow us to see it fresh: the spirit of celebration of many common things is there, but there's no sense of occupying them for long enough for them to become strangely new to us.

Richardson's views on the place, and position of women — although not uncommon for their time — does nothing for the Feminist cause:

> WOMAN! Thou needeft no glory-wreaths
>   To glitter o'er thy name;
> 'Tis not for thee to hurry on
>   In mad purfuit of Fame;

> For lo! Thou haft a nobler fphere
> In that bright fpot called Home,
> Where thou may'ft reign, and hold fupreme
> A Queendom all thine own.

> ('Woman's Duties — Woman's Mission')

Added to this view of the woman's place being in the home — which also ran through much of the poetry written by male poets of the time, such as Coventry Patmore's *The Angel in the House* — is a strong message here of Britain's rightful place in Empire: 'The land that reigns in regal pride, / Crowned Empref of the Sea!'. At best Richardson's moralistic poetry confirms what people would have already known; at worst it comes across as a drum beat for the status quo. There is a section of the collection that is intent on addressing the big themes of the day head-on: cholera, prostitution, temperance and ragged schools. These are worthwhile themes but as Richardson's drive here is *message*, rather than the creation of poetic language for its own sake, there is none of the subtlety and poetic skill that I'm looking for in these lost poets.

There is one poem that I read with interest. Richardson's poem 'Charing Crofs' describes the familiar sense of travelling through a city that is in the midst of change, the iron weave of Victorian industry around her as she writes:

> The miles of ftreets, all canopied
> With interlacing wire,
> Where the trained lightning waits to work
> At mortal man's defire;
> And the broad river, bridged, and fpanned,

> Begirt, and overhung,
> With wondrous works of ftrength and fkill
> Acrofs its pathway flung.

Richardson is at her best when the short, racy measure of her lines is grounded by nouns. Materiality cuts through the verbiage of sentiment. There is a beautiful image in 'Charing Cross' which comes at the moment when she describes what must have been the extension of Brunel's Hungerford Bridge, opened in 1864: 'the trained lightning waits to work / At mortal man's defire'. Although literally describing the making of the bridge this image might also capture how the inventive, curious Victorians applied their imagination to the modern city. Electric lighting was a new phenomenon and although this wouldn't come to the embankment at Charing Cross until 1878 — the first street in England to be lit in this way — there had been displays of electric light in London before Richardson wrote this poem. In November 1848 a French inventor called M. Le Mott had demonstrated his new system for lighting up steam trains. The grime and soot of Paddington Station was illumined by this vision of the future. This phenomenon required new language for its description and a journalist for *The Spectator* was stirred into writing:

> A dazzling blaze of light filled the spacious station. The train started, and as it went down the line it was followed by a train of light more than a mile in length, and so bright that no engine could possibly approach it from the rear by mistake. The cone of light, seen from the carriage, was exceedingly beautiful; the borders of it being decomposed by refraction into a prismatic circle of rainbow tints, which rested on the steam clouds left by the engine. It is stated that bridges were visible at distance of two miles by the light; and that a gentleman read a newspaper by it at a distance of two hundred yards.

There is something of Richardson's 'trained lightning' in both the situation and the elevation of the writing. The 'interlacing wire' of Hungerford Bridge is still there today — passengers on the trains experience the views both ways across the river through a quick-fire crosshatch of broken light.

This is the high point of Richardson's collection, a poem that gives us a sense of Victorian London in change encased in the lasting gift of a memorable image: the condensed energy and restlessness of modern London is compacted with the resilience of original metaphor. When the dog walkers have passed I enter into the undergrowth, immersing in shade and foliage. This is the wrong time of year to be doing this: what seems like miles of dripping leaves and tangled traps of vines knit me into their territory. Within a few steps it's hard to know which way I came in, as if the environment thrives on a will to capture. Ivy and bracken swallow the headstones. The memorials that can be seen have had their inscriptions erased through time. I pull back a branch and another flings itself cane-like towards my face. There's a resistance to dead poets: I wonder if Richardson's brilliant image from 'Charing Cross' makes me try that bit harder to find her headstone? Some say that biography is a trespass. If so, then walking on these graves is an affront.

Through the undergrowth there's one headstone standing by itself, a gnarly green slab with an ornate design flowering from the top. I look closely at it: the words are closing over, fading into the constitution of the stone, on the border of erasure through rain and sunlight. Text like this has the look of wounds that won't heal over. I look closely, drawn to the almost illegible name:

MARIAN

HOLLY RICHARDSON

I try to read the rest of the words but am defeated by these flecked score marks which appear like unfinished cuts into peaty stone. A woodlouse crawls over the H in RICHARDSON. Perhaps Richardson wanted to be found after all. A thought I've had before comes to me now: is it best for dead poets to have their work critiqued but at least to be talked about? The simple relief of having their name breathed over a century and a half after their death? To hear the facts of their life brought back, in some way, to public memory? What, after all, can be worse than being forgotten? Of all the thousands of burials at Nunhead it's this specific person — this name — that I'm here to look for. As I prepare to leave I notice that the woodlouse wasn't alone: there's a party of them, like slow-moving dinghies, eating the moss from the stone. They stop to wave their antennae at each other as they pass, like poets at a public reading, pushing their latest pamphlets at each other.

Richardson's headstone

As I leave I think about the many graves mentioned in Richardson's poems, including a poem about city churchyards, a reminder that Nunhead — as with the rest of the Magnificent Seven cemeteries — was built to overcome overcrowding in the city's graveyards.

> Where peaceful reft 'mid London's ftrife
>> Her fons of want and toil;
> Yet are they fpots of hallowed ground,
>> By every tear-drop fhed

('City Graves')

This is a reminder of the significance of poetry as text: a form of documentation in language. Richardson doesn't write with the style of an original, but documentary poetry has its place. For that I'm glad to have found her headstone.

> It is the common lot
> To live, to love, and then to die,
>> And be at laft — forgot.

('Dead Flowers on a Grave')

23rd March 2015

My grandmother's death certificate arrived. Agnes Bennett died on 3rd April 1958, on Elstow Street. I rang my mum and read out the details to her. I get as far as deciphering 'Els' and my mum gets it — the name of the street opens the memory — the word connecting to the reality of visiting her sick mum in the house she was staying in, around the corner from Hawthorne Road. The memory of bedsheets and bedclothes and inside them, her mother — my grandmother. Cause of death: carcinoma of the colon. What my mum had remembered — and been told — was that it was stomach cancer. She also said that she had a fear that her father and mother weren't married: but this certificate confirms they were. Omnibus driver Ronald Bunting Bennett was widowed and signed to prove it. We have, now, some family history to give to the doctors: a date, location and a cause. A map, of sorts, which shows how my mum got here and the tracks of her DNA.

Nunhead Poet: Tom Hood

There are two poets left for me to find. As I'm walking southwards away from Richardson, I decide to leave Walter Thornbury until last and walk past the section that he's buried in. There is excitement to be found in Thornbury's work and I'll need that drive to keep me searching until the end of the day. That's not to say that Tom Hood (1838-74) is lacking in interest: here is a poet, novelist, writer of jokes and illustrator who died at his home near Peckham Rye.

Hood's father was the famous — and still more famous — Thomas Hood who had written a poem for Tom called 'A Parental Ode to My Son, Aged Three Years and Five Months' — a glorious and genuinely amusing poem describing the effects of a small child's unpredictability on its parents:

> Little epitome of man!
> (He'll climb upon the table, that's his plan!)
> Touched with the beauteous tints of dawning life –
> (He's got a knife!)

Being the son of poet Thomas Hood meant that Tom was destined for a literary life, although his legacy has been shadowed by the success of his father. There may be little for him to complain about in this; without the inspiration and encouragement of his father he might not have made it onto the list of Nunhead's poets at all. At an Open Day in Nunhead Cemetery I was standing over a table displaying examples of my research-in-process — including images of the poets I'd found, burials records and poems — when someone pointed at the name Tom Hood and said: 'He's buried at Kensal Green'. He had confused him with his father, as many have done since. Father and son are now buried in different Magnificent Seven cemeteries: Thomas Hood is in Kensal Green and Tom is somewhere here, in the dense foliage in front of me. Tom Hood deserves consideration in his own right. Although he died before he was forty, he had a part in over seventy publications.

Tom made no attempt to distance himself from his father's success and edited many of his father's editions, as well as adding illustrations to them, including the entertaining *The Headlong Career and Woful Ending of Precocious Piggy* (1859). In the short time he was alive he became a prolific author in his own right, publishing across fiction, plays, prose and poetry. He was also an illustrator of great skill and editor of *Fun* magazine.

'Fun' isn't a word usually associated with the Victorian era though Hood did his bit to alter that, particularly for children, setting up *Tom Hood's Comic Annual* in 1867. He set out to stimulate the young Victorian mind with riddles such as 'What English watering-place is like bees and nettles in grass that has been mown?' 'A: Hay-stings.' Along with visual charades, double acrostics and games of guessing the proverb he must have helped to while away many dull, wet afternoons for Victorian children. You only need to look at some of the titles of Hood's books to see that he helped set the Victorian mood of nonsense inspired by Edward Lear and continued by Lewis Carroll: *Excursions into Puzzledom* (1879), *Quips and Cranks* (1861), *Jingles and Jokes for the Little Folks* (1865), *Griset's Grotesques* (1867), *Vere Vereker's Vengeance: A Sensation in Several Paroxsyms* (1865), *A Bunch of Keys: Where They Were Found and What They Might Have Unlocked* (1865) and *Merry Songs for Little Voices* (1865). Four of these publications alone were published in 1865: Hood was incredibly prolific, illustrating many books by other authors and writing a three-volume novel under the imperious title *Love and Valour* (1871).

Hood was a compulsive collaborator. He wrote poems for a collaborative edition with the artist Gustave Doré called *Fairy Realm: A Collection of the Favourite Old Tales*. In his short introduction to this book Hood gives a clear indication of his poetics to readers, saying that he is concerned with presenting words plainly and clearly. Hood also mentions his ill health whilst writing the book and, like many Victorian writers, adds a touch of false modesty in relation to Doré's talents — as such, this might not be the most inspiring introduction to a book ever committed to print:

> The plan I have adopted is to give the tales in a simple metre and in the most unpretending manner, going, in short, little if anything beyond mere recital in easy verse. From performing even this plain task as I could have wished I have been prevented by ill health, and I fear that what I have written little deserves the honour of association with works of genius like M. GUSTAVE DORE'S pictures. But I have the single satisfaction of knowing that I have done the best I could.

Ill health and perseverance: two of the principal tenets of Victorian reality. What Hood's book actually shows us is that even while presenting the tales in 'simple metre' and 'in the most unpretending manner', Hood is highly skilled with poetic language. His account of *Sleeping Beauty* — particularly of a banquet — fizzes with sibilants and assonance to capture the luxriousness nature of Victorian delicacies:

If you want to find out
The amount, or about,
Of the salmon, beef, partridges, lobsters, sourcrout,
Macaroni, potatoes, cream, cutlets, ice, trout,
Lamb, blanc-mange, kippered herring, duck, broccoli sprout,
Sheep's trotters, real turtle, tripe, truffles, swine's snout,
Sole au gratin, snails, birds' nests, Dutch cheese, whiting-pout,
Jelly, plovers' eggs, bittres, liquers, ale, wine, stout,
Pease, cheese, fricassees, and ragout — (say rag*out*
For the sake of the rhyme)

Here is language that, like the list of foods, lives in the mouth — this is great children's literature to be read aloud. Some of Hood's best work of this kind is in *Griset's Grotesques* in which Hood provides the rhymes for 'one hundred quaint designs' by E. Griset. Poems include 'A Shocking Bear', 'The Dodo Discovered' and 'The Heron in Love'.

Hood was posthumously caught up in a controversy surrounding Lewis Carroll's *Alice in Wonderland* after the critic Edward Salmon suggested Carroll had plagiarised Hood's novel *From Nowhere to the Pole*. In 'Literature for the Little Ones', published in the magazine *The Nineteenth Century,* Salmon wrote: 'there is more than a suspicion of resemblance in some particulars ... Mr Carroll can hardly have been surprised if some people have believed he was inspired by Hood.' Carroll wrote to deny this, saying that his novel had been written in 1862 whilst Hood's novel wasn't published until 1875. In Hood's poems for *Griset's Grotesques* I come across a poem called 'Twixt Tweedledum and Tweedledee', characters who also appear four years later in Carroll's novel *Alice Through the Looking Glass* — though of course both took the source for this from the satire invented by John Byrom in the eighteenth century. Still, what both examples show is that Hood's creative imagination was pushing the literature of nonsense in directions that would later achieve a deeper legacy in Carroll. Hood's poem 'Daniel Dumkin's Nose' stretches the adenoids of the imagination at least as far as that of his more famous contemporary:

> OLD Daniel Dumkin
>   Had a nose so very long,
> He followed it where'er he went;
>   But it often led him wrong.
>
> He sometimes breaks folks' windows
>   Because his mighty nose
> Is such a distance from him,
>   He can't see where it goes.
>
> When he is fast asleep, his nose
>   Is snoring miles away:
> Says Daniel, waking, "Surely,
>   There's a thunderstorm to-day!"

Hood also wrote two books of prosody: I don't have to work out what he thought about poetry as he's done this himself. As I've gleaned from the introduction to the Doré edition these books tell me that his intentions were far from challenging the nineteenth century status quo regarding poetic style and technique. As he asserts in *A Practical Guide to Versification* (1877):

> It does not assume to be a handbook for poets, or a guide to poetry. The attempt to compile such a book as is implied by either of those titles would be as absurd as pretentious ... All, therefore, that this book aims to teach is the art of Versification ... versification is purely

Daniel Dumkin drawing

> a question of form … the writer of verse does not — and should not — pretend to give us diamonds. He offers paste-brilliants … The thoughts presented by the poet may be rough-hewn; the fancies of the versifier must be accurately finished … Poetry, therefore, bounds in licences, while Versification boasts only of laws.

Hood is right to distinguish between the artistic licences that are available to the poet and the rules and 'laws' by which those who are interested in constructing conventional verse are bound. This could be a useful distinction between the poets I've found in Nunhead and the poets I've mapped out over the last year: the diamonds of Blake,

MacSweeney and Johnson compared to the sugar-rush that comes from so many paste-brilliants. Why, then, does Hood write a book about verse when he can see the distinction between that craft and the art of the individual, unbounded poet? Hood believed that practising versification could help children at school to have an 'appreciation of their own tongue' and to help with both spelling and syllabics: 'Verse is but the ABC of Poetry, and the student must learn his alphabet correctly.' In order to do that which no one else can do, the poet has to learn the old tricks and tropes; to move effortlessly inside forms before twisting and reshaping them into unique expression.

Tom Hood's headstone is somewhere here, though it's proving to be impossible to locate. The sections of the Cemetery don't have a start and end-point: there are no markers, no laying out of gridlines which would mean something to the avifauna here. A blackcap passes: even the birds show their respects. There is none of the coruscating leaf patters of West Norwood here; instead the vegetation riots and the trees are absolute monarchs. Ahead of me is a fertile ecosystem for the scavenging and thriving.

Hood wrote poems for adults too though in these he suffers from a misguided sense that the joy and freedom in language that he uses in his children's poems might somehow not apply to his fully matured audience. This is so often a mistake. Instead of the fun and linguistic twists and surprises we get poems that posture. The playfulness of Hood's poems seizes up at the expense of their lyricism. Hood also uses the archaic 'f' (again, perhaps at the insistence of a publisher who had an old set of typefaces), a sign that he wants to attain a certain level of gravitas, as can be seen in his poem 'The Song of the Lark in the City':

Trill — trill — trill!
The fong of a lark
Scattered the vifions dreary and dark,
And woke my heart with a thrill.

The sound of the bird in the poem here fails to capture its distinct syrinx and its rhyming with 'thrill' is brazen compared to Hopkins' poem 'The Woodlark':

Teevo cheevo cheevio chee:
O where, what can that be?

Hood calls these poems — which come at the end of his collection *The Daughter of King Daher* — 'minor'. Perhaps Hood was comfortable in becoming a guide to verse-making as that description fits his work better than 'poet'? He never makes clear how his views on verse-making align with his own work. Hood developed a clear, simple style in his adult poems but one that doesn't include the unique textures that would make his work distinct within the Victorian trinket box of verse-making.

Like William Cox Bennett — and unlike his father whose poems 'I Remember, I Remember' and 'The Bridge of Sighs' are still known — Hood is very little read today, though he has appeared in more anthologies than Bennett. I track his contributions to anthologies through the years, many of which have been with high profile publishers. Despite his near-anonymity his work has stayed continuously in print, albeit in the subjective realm of themed anthologies:

1930: *A Nonsense Anthology*, Scribner's
1942: *Innocent Merriment: An Anthology of Light Verse*, McGraw-Hill
1953: *The Home Book of Verse*, Henry Holt and Company
1959: *A Century of Humorous Verse*, E.P. Dutton, Everyman's Library
1960: *Parodies: an Anthology from Chaucer to Beerbohm — and After*, Modern
        Library
1971: *Speak Roughly to Your Little Boy*, Harcourt Brace Jovanovich
1979: *The Faber Book of Nonsense Verse*, Faber and Faber
1981: *The Brand-X Anthology of Poetry*, Apple-Wood Books
1988: *The Chatto Book of Nonsense Poetry*, Chatto & Windus

Hood's attention from anthologists has been consistent since the 1930s and demonstrates how being read can come through having contributed to the right genre, at the right time. There has been a continuous and accelerating interest in the nonsense and light verse of the Victorian period and Hood — as a major contributor to this form — has been swept up in the mania and repackaged for new audiences. Whilst attempting not to care about anything but pigs and boats that fly — in a sense, *because* of this — Hood, the Victorian nonsense poet, has endured in the underworld of the populist anthology makers and the general audience that buys them. It is unlikely that there are many in that audience who could recognise a poem of Hood's by name but his endurance is a fact: money and ink have consistently been set to retype his name. I greatly admire his bringing of colour and fun to Victorian children and his advocacy for the power of the imagination in a period of intense rationality.

    I wonder if my afternoon of roving through the Nunhead undergrowth would have counted amongst Hood's ideas of fun? I've found so much of his work but his headstone eludes me. A headstone with the family name GIGGINS lies slightly crooked in the earth: I picture the family playing parlour games somewhere in south London, gently jibing each other as the fog swallows them into the past. I consider coming back for him in the winter, when the trees are bare, the best time of year for games and puzzles — and for spotting the gravestones of lost poets. But then it appears, beneath a caul of tightened ivy, a large granite pedestal that is stunning in its simplicity — the seven letters of his name declaring the legacy that perhaps he and the 'few friends and fellow workers' who paid for it felt assured of. When it comes to being remembered it pays to have been a good collaborator in life: his monument is in granite, the most lasting of materials.

There's one more poet to find today — the London writer Walter Thornbury — but I need to sit for a while and take the seat looking down on St Paul's, which appears as a pale bauble within the city. I watch it for a while through the small lens of light that appears between the coppiced trees. Looking down on London from such distance is a kind of narcotic, especially from inside the Cemetery: the blood pulse slows in response to a city that seems to be sleeping but is hurtling, as always, through channels of obsession and misplaced passion. When I wake from the trance I know where I'm going next: the burial site of a London chronologer.

Tom Hood's gravestone

26th March 2015

In the park today — the first real warm spring day of the year — Pavel and I lay down with our backs on the floor and threw a ball up to the sky, trying to catch it as it fell towards our faces. We called the game Spaceball. When we got home, the re-internment ceremony for Richard III was on the television. We listened to the running commentary and watched the panel discussion. A live link-up with David Starkey, who was by chance positioned in York for the Literature Festival, flashed on screen, his face pinched pink with bitchiness like a rubber devil forged from Jim Henson's workshop. He accused the nation of White Rose-ism.

As the ceremony took place on the screen we played Ludo. Pavel landed continually on my counters and sent them back to base. The television cut to Laurence Olivier playing Richard III in Shakespeare's play. Then, in a more recent performance, Robert Lindsay was playing the crippled king. Lindsay was then talking to the screen, saying that one critic had said he'd played Richard like he was playing Ken Dodd and that Lindsay was flattered by this because it was just what he had intended.

In the slowed-down double-narrative of the ceremony it was hard to know what we should be feeling for this king; who had lived over 500 years ago and is at last being buried; a man whom the panel couldn't agree was either good or bad. The BBC doesn't care about that: the spectacle for them is in capturing a moment in which the nation believes that history matters. Satisfying their quotas on ensuring history reaches the masses, as they believe they've done with poetry. A heated debate took place between Richard III's descendants — who had maintained all along that he was buried in a car park — and Oxbridge academics. The core of the argument was whether Richard had really had the true heirs to the throne — the child-princes — killed in the Tower of London in the summer of 1483. The children are the ghost figures in the narrative. They appear to us with heads like porcelain dolls, their bodies no more than fabric: doilies, rags made from their final bed linen. What the two sides want is to brand the dead children's bodies with a fact — half a millennium after those bodies began to disperse into atoms.

Pavel got bored with winning Ludo so we switched to Hangman. As the commentary on Richard ran in the background I selected the first word and Pavel guessed at the letters:

> — L?
> — Yes.
> — R?
> — No.

I hooked a cavernous plastic head onto the erected plastic frame made to hold the body.

> — P?
> — No.

I hooked a skeletal plastic ribcage to the head and it started to swing.

> — E?
> — Yes.
> — O?
> — Yes. Two 'Os'.

I reveal them both to him. The word now reads: -OO-LE

Pavel broke off to ask if Richard was a good king or a bad king. I gave him some of the basic facts that are known: the possibilities of both sides. Modern enlightened parenting: meat with dips and salad. I thought of the wedding of Charles and Diana, which happened when I was about the same age as Pavel and surfaces in my memory as a kind of joint crippled king. This time the moral quandary is discussed up-front rather than being dripped through a decade of tabloid psycho-drama. Here we have the ritual and the sensation at the same time: this is what happens when a King is buried 500 years after he has died. We know the future because it's half a millennium old. The books have thrashed it out without resolution, schoolrooms chalked with the elemental fabrications of bone and morality. The Tower. Bosworth. The end of the Plantagenet line. I told Pavel that the poets got here first, Shakespeare, then Geoffrey Hill. I go to the bookshelf and look again at the Hill poem, finding that there are pre-echoes of Richard's resurrection in a car park in Leicester:

> Under caved chantries, set in trust,
> With well-dressed alabaster and proved spurs
> They lie; they lie; secure in the decay
> Of blood, blood-marks, crowns hacked and coveted,
> Before the scouring fires of trial-day
> Alight on men; before sleeked groin, gored head,
> Budge through the clay and gravel
>
> ('Requiem for the Plantagenet Kings')

The poets always get there first, having crawled through the channels of time, between the fault lines, returning with history's true bone beneath their teeth.

As the entourage approached Leicester Cathedral the focus was on the two knights leading the procession, wearing the armour that Richard would have worn. Later, it's revealed that one of the knights was the curator of the mail armour holdings at the Wallace Collection. This isn't just pomp and ceremony; this is obsession, the archivist's heart beating fast against the regalia he conserves. He told his interviewer that the armour isn't as heavy as people think, that this is war-wear made to function on the battlefield.

At the gates of the cathedral the Dean of the University appeared to read out a statement to the Bishop; those who discovered through DNA research that this was Richard's body hand it over for safekeeping in the vaults of the cathedral. Antiquated language falls from a dry tongue like remains cremated into dust. We wait for a signal to tell us something. I wonder if Richard's bones are blackened through oil seepage from the car park?

The priest opened the ceremony talking of the 'God that giveth and taketh away'. I have trouble synching the phrase 'taketh away' in any time period: was he taken then, at Bosworth, or is he being taken now, as he's buried? And was he saying that God took away the last Plantagenet king rightfully, allowing the Tudor lines to thrive? A nation tries to grieve its heritage, new tears laid down in the grooves of ritual. The Queen was unavailable for comment.

— Google! Pavel shouted out. The word you've got is Google!

Haunted London: The Lost Chronologer Walter Thornbury

In the death-song lift the voice,
  Spread your gifts around;
So his spirit shall rejoice,
  In the hunting ground.
  Walter Thornbury, 'The Huron's Death-Song', from Schiller

I owe a debt to George Walter Thornbury (1828-1876); his work has appeared before in bibliographies of my own London writing. His co-written work, *Old and New London,* is a valuable London text written from the Victorian perspective. Thornbury had written the first two volumes of this before being incarcerated in the asylum he died in. The next four volumes were completed by his friend Edward Walford and published after Thornbury's death.

Like many Victorian works, *Old and New London* has reclaimed a new life on the internet, made available by British History Online. Thornbury and Walford's book is a thickly researched mapping of late nineteenth-century London, and attempt to 'consider the metropolis as a whole'. I realised quickly that Thornbury should be held up in the line of London writers: from the first chroniclers of the city, through John Stow to Iain Sinclair. Born in 1828 as the son of a London solicitor, perhaps the reality of the metropolis was brought to him from an early age? In one book Thornbury gives us an account of the Thames Embankment being laid, reinforcing a strong conviction I have that the best London writing always leaves room for the future to complete it. London writing should present the live moment with all its fractures and incompleteness in the view of the reader:

> On July 20, 1864, the first stone of the great Thames Embankment was unostentatiously laid. A couple of flags fluttered lazily over the stone as a straggling procession of the members of the Metropolitan Board of Works moved down to the wooden causeway leading to the river. About a thousand men are now at work on it night and day. Iron caissons have been sunk below the mud, deep in the gravel, and within ten feet of the clay which is the real foundation of London.

Thornbury contrasts the flaccid ephemeral flutters of flags and people — spectres on the wind — with the unmoving matter of London clay beneath the city. Thornbury also draws the reader to that other real foundation of London: the words and lives of the poets. His book *Art and Nature: At Home and Abroad* has a chapter called 'The Poetry of London' where he summons up the ghosts of the dead poets — the dead poets that I find myself still in dialogue with 160 years later:

> Are there no associations in these dull streets whose pavements grow transparent after rain and reflect the sky — no glimpses of Shakespeare, eyeing the river from Blackfriars or Southwark — of Milton, in Bread Street — of Lamb and Coleridge, at Christ's Hospital — of Charles I., at Whitehall — of Johnson, in Fleet Street — of Burke, at Westminster — of Hogarth, in Leicester Square? — and is this past world, the fact of its actual existence and the confusion of its fancies with our realities no poetry?

Thornbury writes with Blake's conviction that the dead and the living are continually in open dialogue as the layers of time hurtle them towards the one endpoint where all poetry is gathered together.

'There is poetry in the voice of London,' he writes. 'Shelley compares it to the roar of an insatiable monster; to me it comes like the thunder shout of a tremendous torrent.' Here's a writer who not only hears the great poets speak through time but has the confidence to rewrite their imagery. In Thornbury's vision of London he gives poetry its rightful, central character, as a kind of stream of water or light — or even a lens attached to a rat that captures the reality best through constant movement:

> Poetry scuttling away from the flood of cabs and the torrent of omnibuses, takes refuge in little nooks in the Temple, where a fountain waves its silver rod, which melts in the sun and dissolves into a torrent, as if in emulation of the shining river beyond; or in the brick archway of Christ-church, with its silence and repose; or nestles in the green tree in Cheapside, where, as in a cliff over an ocean, rooks build and clamour.

Thornbury has been a presence in my various pieces of London research but it was only on finding that he is buried here in Nunhead that I realised the scale and finesse of his prose works about the city. I've also found kinship with him in my exploration of Victorian cemeteries and my attempts to find the true language of London's maps in the language of poets.

Even Thornbury's introduction to his book *Haunted London* turns to poetry. *Haunted London* is the true masterpiece of Thornbury's prose writing. Although presented in its title as a book of haunting legends, Thornbury knows that walking above the sediment layers of old London with the dead poets in mind can lead to peculiar dialogues and connections between present and past that can enervate the waking moment and make sense of where we are.

Poets make the best ghosts as they work in open-ended questions. Ghosts that aren't poets are just vapours. Thornbury's introduction runs for a few pages before ghosts are even mentioned, preferring instead to take on those who were desecrating the Victorian city in the name of 'progress', assailing the ongoing rose-cankering, sold as renewal, that can still be seen in today's city:

> It took centuries to turn the bright, swift little rivulet of the Fleet into a fetid sewer, years to transform the palace at Bridewell into a prison; but events now move faster: the alliance of money with enterprise, and the absence of any organised resistance to needful though sometimes rather reckless improvements, all combine to hurry forward modern changes ... The tombs of great men, in the chinks of which the nettles have grown undisturbed ever since the Great Fire, are now being uprooted. Milton's house had become part of the "Punch" office. A printing machine clanks where Chatterton was buried. Almost every moment some building worthy of record is shattered by the pickaxes of ruthless labourers.

The dead poets are the true cipher to the city and Thornbury structures his book around these phantasms that he's come to know as bodily forces: 'Savage the poet', 'Lord Herbert's poetry', 'Donne's vision' and 'Ben Jonson the bricklayer'. This kind of correspondence is the only real way of speaking to past London, calling forth those who worked in paradox, whose active minds failed to cease after their deaths. Thornbury's book, I was delighted to find out, wasn't really about hauntings at all but — like all true London writing — is about the capacity that the city has to concentrate tides of human emotion into building, myth and lore. The word 'haunt' comes from the Middle English and simply means to frequent a place — and if you frequent a place with awareness of the dead, as I've found, then the conversation begins. There is another meaning to 'haunted' too, which is to show signs of stress and anxiety. These are the fracture lines over London's face that Thornbury recognised and which are still accelerating under reckless, greed-driven enterprises. If it wasn't for the Friends Groups in London the cemeteries I'm visiting would have long become silent voids, lost beneath the simulacra of high-rises.

Thornbury is buried somewhere in the intersection of what's known as the East Path and the curving Lower Cross Path leading to the War Graves. The land pushes downwards towards Ivydale Road, beyond the Cemetery wall; the road bears the name of this dense green undergrowth before me. Thornbury may have written across forms but he's emphatically grounded here, somewhere in section fifty-nine — somewhere beyond an arthritic black tree which is twisting against its natural upright growth to try and find the edges of the darkened cover, trying to reach the light.

In *Haunted London* Thornbury writes about the Coal Hole pub — still there on the Strand. Here he shows himself to be a remarkable Victorian in what he chooses to give the reader, including an account of Blake's presence on Fountain Court. Gilchrist's biography of Blake had only appeared in 1863, at which point Thornbury must have been well under way with his huge, 500-page *Haunted London,* which was eventually published in 1865.

This celebration of Blake makes Thornbury one of the few Victorians aware of his significance. Although Thornbury isn't fully attuned to the brilliance and originality of his poetry — describing Blake as 'the mystical painter' — the mere fact of his detecting Blake against the tide of Victorian reason is astounding. The proximity to the mythology of Blake's hawthorn on Peckham Rye is an association that Thornbury would have been pleased with:

> Blake, the mystical painter, died in 1828, at No.3, Fountain Court, after five years' residence there. In these dim rooms he believed he saw the ghost of a flea, Satan himself looking through the bars of the staircase window, Lais, the cruel task-master that Moses slew, besides hosts of saints, angels, evil spirits and fairies. Here he also wrote verse passionate as Shelley's and pure and simple-hearted as Wordsworth's. Here he engraved, tinted, railed at Woolett, and raved over his Dante illustrations; for though pure and unknown, he was yet regal in his exulting self-confidence. Here, just before his death, the old man sat up in bed painting, singing and rejoicing. He died without a struggle.

I'm grateful to Thornbury for this rare illuminated glow of Blake in the mind of a Victorian, confirming the modernity of Thornbury amidst his neighbours. Thornbury is the lost azure in the mosaic, the dead poet who evokes the ghosts of dead poets.

There is a cynical, weary edge to Thornbury's prose which is also strikingly modern in the context of nineteenth century literature and has something of B.S. Johnson's exasperation with the undervalued role of the writer-as-artist in an increasingly corporate world. Thornbury writes: 'There are materials for a dozen epics in the poetry of London, but I shall not write them, for they would not sell.' In addition to his London books Thornbury contributed nearly 200 pieces to Dickens's *Household Words* and *All the Year Round* and completed over twenty historical novels (with titles such as *The Vicar's Courtship*, *Greatheart* and *Wildfire*) as well as biographical works. He knew Grub Street as well as any of its hack and writers of 'temporary poems' — as Samuel Johnson defined all those forgotten poets — ever had. Thornbury was also an editor and worked on an anthology called *Two Centuries of Song*. The cause of Thornbury's death in the Camberwell House Lunatic Asylum, Peckham Road, was described as being due to 'overwork', the inference being that he wrote himself into madness.

Professional dog walkers in matching blue shirts are walking a tangled collection of canines along the path in front of me. The dogs bark at invisible nothings. Then what looks like a series of lit lanterns are moving through the branches. When I look more closely I see that the branches have split the beam of the headlights on a white Renault, creating the mirage of a broken plate of light. The city has moved to the necropolis.

But what about Thornbury the poet? He was not without acclaim in his lifetime, contributing to that central mainstay of Victorian literature, *The Athenaeum*. I've already been lucky to find that one of Nunhead's poets is also a great writer about London — but I remind myself that I'm here to find actual poets. One of the strangest books that Thornbury had a hand in was a translation of Pierre Dupont's *The Legend of the Wandering Jew*, which — like Hood's fairy tales — was illustrated by Gustave Doré. When I ordered it up from the underground bunkers at the British Library it arrived folio-sized, with its cover attached to the text block by a piece of white twine: the kind of tenuousness with which the average Victorian poet is attached to literary posterity. What the poet says about the work of others is always revealing and I find a way in here through Thornbury's introduction to *The Fables of La Fontaine* (again with illustrations by Doré). Thornbury discusses the importance of style and individual idiom — all of the things I've been thinking about when considering Nunhead's poets:

La Fontaine's originality does not consist solely in the particular bent of his imagination, but also in his language. It is true that his style bears the impress of the purity and elegance of the language of his age, and is characterised by that finish which is common to all the great writers of his time; but there is also a peculiar richness, suppleness, and naturalness about his idiom.

Thornbury's own poems were anthologised in the 1898 anthology *The Poets and the Poetry of the Century*, edited by Alfred H. Miles, sharing space with still much read and celebrated poets like Charles Kingsely, Matthew Arnold and Dante Gabriel Rossetti. Nunhead's William Cox Bennett is also featured, putting the dead poets of the Cemetery in a central place from the viewpoint of late nineteenth-century poetry. In his introduction to Thornbury's work Miles makes it clear that it wasn't on the strength of his early collections that he was included — 'the miscellaneous pieces do not exhibit any signs of marked originality' — but the work including, and following, his 1857 collection *Songs of the Cavaliers and Roundheads*.

Thornbury is an accomplished balladeer. The ballad form relies on a well-maintained metrical pace which allows narrative to unfold effortlessly and Thornbury excels in this, writing with clear imagery, witty asides and evocative colour — all serving to add atmosphere to the stories that he tells. He holds the reader inside his worlds. One of Thornbury's main passions was the Elizabethan period and the Jacobite uprisings, which he conjures evocatively in poems such as 'The Three Troopers':

> THE old men sat with hats pulled down
>   Their claret cups before them:
> Broad shadows hid their sullen eyes,

The tavern lamps shone o'er them,
As a brimming bowl, with crystal fill'd,
Came borne by the landlord's daughter,
Who wore in her bosom the fair white rose,
That grew best over the water.

('Jacobite Ballads III — The White Rose Over the Water')

As with his prose Thornbury excels in description, but he is also adept at controlling couplets and enjambment:

Over clover wet with dew,
Whence the sky-lark, startled, flew,
Through brown fallows, where the hare
Leapt up from its subtle lair,
Past the mill-stream and the reeds
Where the stately heron feeds,
By the warren's sunny wall,
Where the dry leaves shake and fall
By the hall's ancestral trees,
Bent and writhing in the breeze,
Rode we all with one intent,
Gaily to the Tournament.

('Historical and Legendary Ballads I — The Old Grenadier's
Story')

These lines brings to mind Browning's lyrics from *Pippa Passes,* as well as the lush green landscape of the Cemetery he's buried in. Thornbury maintains the same pace of four stresses per line and effortless end rhymes for the whole of the thirteen stanzas of the poem. These lines contain an immense amount of atmospheric detail but Thornbury doesn't allow this to slow the pace: the story is always in service to his poetic techniques and not the other way around. Thornbury falls short of conjuring stark and arresting new images for what he discusses — 'sunny wall', 'shake and fall' and 'writhing in the breeze' border on stock. These images should be judged by his balladeering intentions: his aim is to keep his story moving forward without asking the reader to pause to clarify sense.

On occasion Thornbury can push the language within his ballads towards a more sprung and surprising melody — such as in 'Rupert's March', the first poem in *Songs of the Cavaliers*:

> Carabine slung, stirrup well hung,
> Flagon at saddle-bow merrily swung
>
> ('Rupert's March')

Thornbury has a section in this book called 'Dramatic Monologues'. This shows a clear indebtedness to Browning, who came to modernise the form with his skill for acute psychological subtlety. The contrast with Browning begins to show some shortcomings in Thornbury. In 'The Suicide in Drury Lane' his end rhymes obstruct the natural idiom of the thinking mind and spoken vernacular, making the poem less convincing for the reader who is being asked to believe that the character speaking to them might well be real:

> 'O Lord! This rheumatiz! damn suicides!
> Don't they know wrong from right? Bah! Cutting throats –
> And costs the parish something, too, besides.'
>
> ('The Suicide in Drury-Lane')

The over-influence of Browning is never clearer than in the use of the colloquial 'rheumatiz!' here with one of Browning's characters, Fra Lippo Lippi, famously declaring in a poem 'Zooks'. Thornbury takes the essence of the dramatic monologue but doesn't take the risks that Browning takes — perhaps for fear of losing the reader in his character's mind. Thornbury doesn't do what Browning does in asking the reader to complete the poem for themselves, through their own intuition. His monologues fall back time and again on expressions such as 'Oh, ah!' and 'Ah, ah!' to the point where they could be parodying Browning's invented inflections of the mad and despairing. Browning is often difficult to read because he knows that it's natural for the human mind to skirt around the thing that they might find difficult — and need time — to say. Thornbury cuts to the chase too quickly, making things clearer for the reader but removing the pleasure the reader might take in coming to live with a character's complexity. One of his monologues begins by telling the reader about the character's state rather than allowing the character to do so in their own way: 'I cannot hope to win her', it reads.

Looking for Thornbury in Nunhead Cemetery is like wading through a chainmail sea, my feet slip into holes, branches fling back, vines wrap around my ankles. A grave in front of me has been split in two by a vine that then holds it in place: destroyer and sustainer. I spot the phoneme BUR on a half fallen stone, thinking this could be the penultimate syllable of Thornbury, and reach — heart racing — to pull back the vines on EUGENE BURNER. I gently place the vines back where they were. I look back to see how far I've come since entering the deep wood of section fifty-nine: less than fifteen metres. I feel like I've swum across a channel of bracken.

I stand up for a while and regain my breath. It's better to

think about shorter poems in this position and Thornbury's lyric pieces come to mind. These poems don't offer the immediate renewal that the form can offer and can be overly descriptive and awkward in expression, such as 'An October Fruit Piece':

> Look at the gold fruit hung
> Where the robin pruned, carolled, and sung;
>   Red through the green
>   Shows the nectarine.

('An October Fruit Piece')

The second line is too long here and the verb 'shows' is clumsy, making it unclear who is doing the showing. His poem 'The Dances of the Leaves' is more successful and suggests that it's within simple melody and form that Thornbury excels best, the repetition of words here echoing the sound of the wind:

> Now the sky is ever filling, ever filling,
> On such dark and rainy eyes,
> With unwilling, with unwilling
> Eddies of the countless leaves.
> They are sailing, they are sailing
> Round the wet and dripping trees,
> Mid the wailing, mid the wailing
> Groanings of the dying breeze.

('The Dances of the Leaves')

Perhaps the shortcomings I've found in Thornbury's poetry are also due to my tastes. I don't share his fondness for the ballad. It doesn't excite me as other forms do. His lyrics and monologues are accomplished but he doesn't bring that individual idiom, which he himself discusses, to the form.

There is one poem of his, however, included in *The Poets and the Poetry of the Century*, which shows why he earned his place, between George Meredith and Dante Gabriel Rossetti. It's called 'Smith of Maudlin' and is in the voice of a man who's imagining what will happen on the night he dies. The achievement of the poem isn't in the psychological insight or complexity of Smith — though there is a Prufrockian quality to the character — or in any great stylistic invention; its success lies in the contrast of the quiet individual and the ongoing forward movement of the city after he has ceased. Smith imagines the dons and coachmen, the London boats and boxing rooms, all containing a short exchange between people or at least an individual thought, in which Smith is remembered, before the city moves on, as it must. Through the refrain of each stanza in which someone says his name, 'Smith of Maudlin', the reader comes to sense that even this wish for a short moment of remembrance is more an aspiration on Smith's part. The city is cold and unfeeling when it comes to individual deaths:

> Wine-parties met, — a noisy night,
> Red sparks are breaking through the cloud;
> The man who won the silver cup
> Is in the chair erect and proud;
> Three are asleep, — One to himself
> Sings, "Yellow jacket's sure to win."
> A silence; — "Men, the memory
> Of poor old Smith of Maudlin!"

There are two lines in particular here that reveal a gift for condensed poetic expression, two lines which beautifully meld together the image of wine and clouds in the reader's mind, which show how the expanse of our short lives is momentous and — under the expanse of the skies — also just the popping of a cork:

> Wine parties met, — a noisy night,
> Red sparks are breaking through the cloud

It is for writing like this that Miles had included Thornbury in his *Poets of the Century*, and although I don't fully agree with his assessment of Thornbury's poetry, it is important to see how highly esteemed Thornbury the poet was. Miles asserts that his work 'Contains nothing poor in style, is replete with colour, and is the production of a writer who has achieved a distinct individuality ... his pen more often seemed laden with pigment rather than ink ... they have a tone and style which can at once be recognised as that of Thornbury and of no one else.'

There is a further connection with Thornbury and the poetic myth I've found myself inside, a link with *The White Goddess* and the map of poetic discovery that has written itself into the past years. Thornbury, like Graves, translated from *The Book of Taliesin*, including a poem called 'The Wind': 'Thou art a spirit whom we may not bind — / For mighty is the wind'. Perhaps more than any of the other poets in Nunhead Cemetery, Thornbury was fully immersed in the lore and language of previous poetries and responded to the questions left on the wind by the poets who had come before. He wrote a series of poems in response to Welsh legends which suggest that he had travelled to north Wales and into the ancient land of the White Goddess:

Some wreck of Druid times;
Where men poured out the human gore,
In cups of rock, in days of yore,
So say the runic rhymes.

('The Demon Oak')

Thornbury's poetry resists the platitudes written for Queen Victoria that we see in the writing of Richardson and Bennett. As Robert Graves argues in *The White Goddess*, Queen Victoria didn't incite the stirrings of lyric and muse-inspired poetry that Queen Elizabeth did; Victoria, in his view, led with a Thunder-God approach of war-mongering, giving much of Victorian poetry an element of 'didacticism and rococo ornament'. By looking further back in time — finding his inspiration in medieval and early modern literature and history — Thornbury appears less dated than those of his contemporaries who attempted to appear modern but failed to rise beyond the Victorian status quo.

As I walk out from under the canopy of sycamores a pug with what look likes human ears has tracked me down and stands a few yards from me, barking. Once the dog catches my eye it refuses to stop barking, its ears floundering as it looks at me. I stand there, unsure what to do, hearing its owner say to someone 'he must have spotted a squirrel'. If I could climb a tree I would.

Thornbury is the real find amidst Nunhead Cemetery's lost poets. I fear his poetry is not the revelation to me that his London prose has been, but then perhaps I need to balance out the gains I've made from my expectations. 'Smith of Maudlin' is a great poem, one that should be republished and enjoyed by new generations. Thornbury is a gift at this stage of my journey, a rich and mercurial talent to have found in Nunhead Cemetery. My work against the canon demands his reinstatement as a London chronologer; and Dickens was also right in realising his talents as a writer of place. In his introduction to *A Tour Round England,* Thornbury addresses Dickens directly:

> My Dear Mr Dickens, It is now nearly two years ago since you first suggested to me the writing of a tour through England. Starting from London and making straight for the sea, you advised me to branch 'as the crow flies', alternately north, south, east, and west, and to pick up from a bird's-eye point of perspective as I passed any beautiful or memorable place ...

It was due to Dickens' commission that Thornbury was able to travel to Amsterdam, Palestine, Rotterdam, the Iberian Peninsula, European Turkey and the United States. His *Criss-Cross Journeys* (1873) details those trips.

I won't give up on finding Thornbury's memorial. A few weeks later I'm back, with Tim Stevenson, to try and bring the memorial of Nunhead's most interesting poet back to the light. Tim wants to give it a go and has brought the crushed leaves of an elder tree to keep the Cemetery's notorious insects at bay — and strong yellow gloves to give some purchase against the undergrowth.

The headstones that aren't split by branches have been blanched into erasure with sunlight. Words remain faded or concealed under sun-patterned leaves. One seems to read WALTER BREAD. Give us this day. There are stones so enmeshed with bracken they're impossible to see. Proximity with bodies at such close range is beyond sociable. As I wind back through the burial ground, trying not to stand on any of the fallen monuments or flat headstones, I accidentally stumble back onto a grave and apologise, hearing myself say, 'Sorry mate' — as if I'm in a pub at last orders.

Somewhere back in the world, on the main path, an American woman is walking, explaining to the person she's with that, 'The movie was really bad and it got, like, nominated for all these awards and I thought *Noooo*.' It's then that I see a headstone which resembles the description given to me by Ron Woollacott: Thornbury's small headstone is not easy to see as the front of it faces towards Ivydale Road. *The inscription has faded but you can still make out his portrait which is carved in relief.*

I call to Tim, who's deep in section fifty-nine, moving back dried-out vines from any stone which happens to be less that waist-height. The stone I've found is not only facing Ivydale Road but starting to slant towards the ground. There is also a figure of a head on the stone, a silk-green patina of moss covering the face beneath it. Tim arrives and we start to gently wipe away the moss, using a softened stick to preserve the stone, and the letters appear one-by-one, spelling out the name: THORNBURY. It's like a form of magic writing in which the writer's mind and art — all I've known of him until now — is suddenly grounded in the fact of his death. Just to read a poet is to keep them alive but here the corpus is reclaimed by the earth. We stand back from the headstone to find that a tree, an ash, has grown straight from the ground that he's buried in, its roots clutching down towards the remains of his chest. Writers like Thornbury never die.

Thornbury's headstone being de-mossed

Monday 6ᵗʰ April 2015

*We seem to have a new tradition, which started last year, of Pavel dressing
as a cowboy to spend the day at a fairground. Last year it was a local fair
on Newsham Park, this year the fair is slightly further afield. We read the
destination on a poster on a barber's window:*

Fairground, Hawthorne Road, Bootle.

*Hawthorne Road: the road my mum grew up on, where she was living when
she first met my dad: the reason we chose to plant the hawthorn last year.
The symbolism of Blake's tree is now coming to find me.*

*The bank holiday bus clattered towards Bootle, stopping to pick up
dog-walkers, drunks, kebab-eaters and teenagers: communal Bank Holiday
celebrants. We went past Parish Walton Church where a taxi driver once
told us that a plaque marks the spot where Cromwell was shot at. Today the
bus drove us past the Clock Tower and the new mental health hospital — it
felt strange to drive past where my mum lives and not get off the bus to go
and see her. I told Pavel about his Nan living on the road we're going to,
when she was a girl, and he shrieked out on the bus: 'We're going past Nana
McCabe's twice, her old house and her new one!'*

*When we got there, Hawthorne Road wasn't what he was expecting;
it turned out to be a Dis of unused wasteland and scaffold. The entrance to
the fairground was alongside a carwash. Pavel confused the price for the
carwash with the fee for the fairground. We stood in the long queue to get
in, waiting for people to come out to make space for the new, breathing in
the smell of chips and candy floss, grease and cream soda. Everything's free*

once you've paid, the sign says. MEGA is the buzzword.

    The fairground, like every one I've ever been to, was structured with stalls from which transparent globes swung as if lit with flashing orange bulbs — the winnable goldfish. Pavel mentioned the two goldfish that we had for a week — Shakespeare and Dickens — who both died on Good Friday. They floated to the surface together: moustachioed bloodbrothers defending their place in the canon. Julienne carrots with bloodshot teddybear eyes who have yet to resurrect. But today these were new fish: a family walked away from the stall swinging a bag of three.

    The language and iconography of the rides was Gothic mixed with contemporary pop: Frankenstein pimping Rihanna. Fenced-off rides vied with deep basslines as middle-aged men provided the voiceovers from perspex booths. Pavel dragged me towards a ride called Twister: we pulled down the bar as it swung us in and out, close to queuing children, their dirty faces furred with candy floss. I'd never seen Pavel so excited: his face a fierce red ball of expectation. As Twister spun us around, he told me I've got to put my hands up in the air for it to work properly and that the louder we scream, the quicker it goes. I could see from the ride that the site for this fairground was wedged between a Spotmix dumpsite, the carwash and a Shell garage. A fringeland adventure land just a few hundred yards from where my mum grew up. Twister pulled me in to the centre of the metal claw, away from the dirty faces of the children, towards the dumping ground, then back to the Shell garage. It was absurdly nauseous.

    When we got off the ride the ground was a mush of woodchip, cigarette stumps and broken white bread. Hotdogs that had jumped — like scalded men overboard — from the canoes of their buns. We watched a man topping up the goldfish bags by scooping the fish from a bucket with his hand.

    After the ride we tried to win the fish. There was no way of losing.

For £2.50 the woman handed us a stick with a hook on, to hook a duck, with each duck having a number underneath. The least we could win was a fish. Dickens and Shakespeare had cost us £1.20; these new ones would have to live for two weeks to break even. Pavel hooked, lifted and checked the underside: a winning number. We looked in the bags to select the one we wanted and they stared back — luminescent Calibans — at these new faces plotting to take them from their island.

The last ride we went on took us to the highest point of the fairground. We looked one way to the south end of Hawthorne Road, my mum's childhood home — the disused cranes of the docks — then the other way towards the Clock Tower, my mum at home in recovery, the site of the Victorian workhouse and the hospital. We — or was it just Pavel? — made a decision to go and visit her — and we left the fairground for the two mile walk to the Clock Tower.

We walked carrying a plastic bag of fish each. We have the same faces, we've been told, me and Pavel. He was still wearing his gold stetson. When we got there my mum was in her dressing gown with a blue bandana wrapped around her head. She was pleased to see us, but tired. We placed the fish bags in a bowl and the pockets of air floated to the surface, twists of orange below, blurred through a slow light. My mum took off her bandana to show us: stubble, the first signs of hair growth following the radiotherapy. When we got back home we put the fish in the same tank that Shakespeare and Dickens had been in and watched them swim in gregarious loops.

My mum sent a text: 'I hope they last longer for him.'

Pavel with a stetson

This Place is Not Real: In Nunhead Cemetery with Charlotte Mew

Now I will burn you back, I will burn you through,
  Though I am damned for it we two will lie
  And burn, here where the starlings fly
  To these white stones from the wet sky –;
  Dear, you will say this is not I –
It would not be you, it would not be you!
  Charlotte Mew, 'In Nunhead Cemetery'

Tim grabs the tools from a corner of the cabin: gloves, secateurs and a spade which I mistake for a guitar. This is no time to be serenading the dead. As we walk, the gravel crunches underfoot. We turn right at the Anglican chapel, looking back at a Hindu family who are burning incense in the Cemetery. Log posts have been sawn down from a fallen tree. Tim recognises the tree that they came from. The Cemetery has its own ecosystem maintained by the Friends and the landscape staff. A man in an orange workman's jacket says 'Good Morning' as we pass. I look at my watch: 9.02am. The Cemetery is buzzing.

 I tell Tim that Mew had a favourite joke: a hearse driver runs over a man and kills him, and a nearby conductor on a bus shouts, 'Greedy!' Mew is a blessing and, perhaps, a curse at this stage in my journey; on the one hand here is a poet who was both of and beyond the Victorian period, but, on the other hand, this raises the bar — like a hydraulic coffin lift — on the great work I've found by Nunhead's dead poets. But then no book about poetry and Nunhead Cemetery would be complete without trying to find the grave of Charlotte

Mew's brother, Henry, who is buried here. Due to the unstable nature of the rest of the family Charlotte had taken control of the funeral arrangements and subsequently visited every year on her brother's birthday, 22nd March. The emotion harvested from this experience was the driving source for Mew's poem 'In Nunhead Cemetery'. I've brought the poem with me today but now I'm fretting that the other dead poets here will cower from the corrugated glare of its brilliance. I tuck it inside my jacket pocket.

Mew, like any poet who has snagged in the starched linen of their historical epoch, stands out for being many poets' favourite overlooked poet. Little has been written about her. The Poetry Library press cuttings for Seamus Heaney runs to three whole conservation boxes; the few loose pages on Mew are discreetly conserved in an A4 sleeve. She is a known poet on the fringes of being lost, or perhaps a lost poet who is always vying to push into the main canon of the twentieth century.

Tim pulls a hand-drawn map from his pocket which includes details on where to find Henry Mew's headstone, passed on to him from Ron Woollacott. Ron found Henry Mew's grave thirty years ago and, like all good historians, kept hold of the maps — you never know when an inquiring poetry obsessive is going to rock up. Tim holds up the page: a red rectangle has the word 'Mew' written at the centre. We follow the other boxes which direct us to the memorial we're looking for: Bisley, Jenkins, White ... then turn left along a path.

If my search is for a *lost* poet, then Charlotte Mew isn't quite that, and I give Tim the anecdotal evidence. The National Poetry Library in London observes an annual ritual: each member of staff takes a poem to the Christmas dinner and places it in a bag for everyone to pick out at random. A Secret Santa without the expense. Last Christmas I put my hand into the bag — into the fractals of folded edges — and pulled out Mew's 'In Nunhead Cemetery'. Evidence A: here is a poet who's sufficiently prominent in the thoughts of readers of poetry to be worthy of being offered as a festive gift. And what festive gift could be better than one that describes a bereaved man standing at the graveside of his fiancée, spitting at social norms, enraged by the prevailing hegemony of happiness? Behind this poem is Mew the survivor, the survivor amongst siblings sunk into the mental illness. Here, monologue poems return again and again to dispossessed and mentally sidelined characters. Yet there is also Mew the trapped Edwardian — the lesbian who never found the experience, or language, to live comfortably inside her own body. Her formative years were middle-class Victorian but she wrote her poems as a Georgian — dying with valid modernist credentials. She would be hailed by Virginia Woolf as the greatest living female poet.

Tim walks onto the grass in front of me, winding between the headstones, looking for Henry Mew's memorial. A gently arching, domed headstone has been pushed back by a tree which may have since died: the force through the green fuse has now gone the way of the wooden coffin beneath. A vine has stitched itself to the surface of the stone, but the name HENRY is visible. Tim removes the vines: HER, then HERNE becomes visible. This is it. Then MEW appears last, like freshly pressed type: HENRY HERNE MEW. Given the suffering in Henry Mew's life, the IN PEACE on the headstone was perfectly chosen.

Henry had died in the Lunatic Asylum in Peckham and as a result

Charlotte, like Browning, Tom Hood and Marian Richardson before, would have known Peckham too. Three of Mew's four brothers had already died in childhood and Henry, the eldest, was confined to Peckham hospital when he began to show signs of mental breakdown. After his death the registered details on Henry were 'no occupation or calling'. This was in 1901, the final year of Queen Victoria's reign. Henry's death can be seen as the beginning of more significant fractures in Mew's mental health. As Penelope Fitzgerald writes, Charlotte 'had come to terms with Henry's madness, but not with the idea of his dying mad.' Mew's sister Freda had also suffered a breakdown and was sent to the Isle of Wight, where she lived longer than any of her siblings. Perhaps as a result of this claustrophobic experience, Mew consistently wrote about deranged characters, compressed into claustrophobic, multi-perspective monologues. Through the technique of the dramatic monologue, broken, sidelined individuals are depicted with the kind of knotted intensity that Mew knew from her own experience.

Charlotte would have stood where I'm standing now, unable to get out of the way of the raw grief that, a decade later, would transform itself into 'In Nunhead Cemetery' — one of the best poems of the early twentieth century. The transformation of Mew's experience in this poem is strange: her personal grief for her brother becomes the grief of a lover standing over the grave of his dead fiancée. It is Nunhead Cemetery itself — the fact of the place in Mew's life and in the writing — that connects together the experience and the poem. The style of Mew's poetry pushes organised form to the point of breaking down. 'In Nunhead Cemetery' shows how Mew makes the ragged inner experience bear the truth of her life in the very form of the poem, a form which won't stay still but mutates

Henry Mew's headstone

through different stanza and line lengths.

Due to her awareness of the family history of mental illness Mew had agreed a pact with her sister Anne: that they would never marry and have children, thereby preventing the genetic slowworm passing the history of madness further into the family tree. By this stage Mew is likely to have known that she was a lesbian and that children would not be a priority — the deal with her sister was convenient on more than one level. But there is defiance in this gesture too: the limits of the age were obstacles that Mew would find her own way around, albeit with an unsteady balance of style and nervousness — like a cigarette in the eye after a casual flicking of her bowler.

Val Warner has described Mew's poetry as defined by 'passion unfulfilled by the loss of youth, by death, by the working of a malign fate, by the dictates of conventional morality, by renunciation and even by the glorification of renunciation of all love into itself a kind of passion.' Penelope Fitzgerald adds guilt to this list. Following the death of Mew's father in 1898, which was followed by Henry's death in 1901, Mew took to the fin de siècle period with textbook aplomb: she had her hair cut short, walked around London on her own, smoked hand-rolled cigarettes and wore a black velvet jacket with a tie. Broken, vulnerable, but determined enough to break ground for women that later writers like Radclyffe Hall would tread on further. Between spring 1912 and spring 1914, Mew experienced a surge of creativity which produced some her best poems including 'The Farmer's Bride' and 'In Nunhead Cemetery'.

Mew, a woman in a male-dominated poetry scene — standing upright at four foot ten — could easily be overlooked. She has been described by Kathleen Hughes as 'a tiny, crabbed spinster' and her friend Mrs Dawson Scott wrote in her diary that Mew was 'an Imp with brains'. If her friends thought this, then what did the rest of the world think? There's something in Mew that seemed to know all this and which made her all the stronger for knowing it and not caring. In every photograph taken of her she tries to look past the camera as if it is some kind of rabid dog. Her smile — if the twisted expression around her lips could even be called that — tries to pacify the camera-dog that she knows is out to get her. The great heave of energy involved in posing for the camera results in an expressive strain above her eyebrows, which arch in stressed acknowledgement that the pictorial evidence will result from the whole uncomfortable, dangerous experiment of being. Her hands get in the way of her pose: agitated, she clings to the lapel of the jacket. Her suit slopes off the shoulders as the bow tie — in an exaggerated loop — sags down towards her navel. Even a black and white photograph has a tinge of yellow.

At the time of Mew's 1912-1914 creative flowering the wider scene of poetry was beginning to break into separate camps between the modernist Imagists and the more formal Georgians. This was the beginning of the split between what we now know as the avant-garde and the mainstream. Mew, like many of the best poets of today, fell between both camps and received neither the popularity that the Georgians might offer nor the kudos of the modernist alliance. Edward Marsh, Winston Churchill's secretary, had edited *Georgian Poetry 1911-12* which — like Mew's later collection *The Farmer's Bride* — was published by The Poetry Bookshop. The anthology sold 15,000 copies and the revenue proved extremely useful to Harold Monro's running of the shop. What is interesting — and pertinent to today's poetry scene — is that it wasn't a straightforward case that the Georgian anthologies represented the old school and the experimental poets existed elsewhere, in isolation. As Helen Carr argues in *The Verse Revolutionaries*, Rupert Brooke had spearheaded the idea of the Georgian poetry anthologies as a way for a new generation of poets to define themselves against the Victorians and Edwardians that came before; Brooke saw the volume as 'the herald of a revolutionary dawn.' Despite *Georgian Poetry* running to five anthologies, Mew was never published in any of them. Apparently Marsh went out of his way to find a woman for the third volume and when Monro suggested Mew, Carr writes, 'Walter de la Mare pooh-poohed her and Marsh's courage failed.' Not for the first — or last time — in poetry, the middle-of-the-road male pooh-poohed the brilliant female.

Much of the avant-garde energy of this period was collected within the Imagist movement. Mew fared moderately better with the Imagists who, somewhat bizarrely, were also gathered together in an anthology published by The Poetry Bookshop which came out in 1913. Ezra Pound, the Great Lafayette of literary modernism — more likely to pull a shaven mouse than a bunny from a hat — had been shown Mew's work by the novelist May Sinclair, and published her poem 'The Fête' in *The Egoist*. Yet — in a twist that sees one of the greatest poets of her time shot from both sides — none of Mew's poems was selected for any of the Imagist anthologies that followed. Perhaps her poems were too long and the voices of her characters too rambling and idiosyncratic to fit with the Imagist ideal of salami-slicing all verbiage? Perhaps the more populist Georgians saw Mew's work as too ragged — too unpolished in its verses — for inclusion in their pristine sect? The Georgians could have given Mew the exposure her work deserved, while the Imagists could have offered everything that Brooke's claim for 'revolution' lacked: kudos and international reach. But Mew was distinctly doing her own thing — and, like many idiosyncratic poets, paid the price for it. Admirably for Mew, she didn't seem to care and seemed genuinely surprised when anyone wanted to read her poems — not because she didn't believe them good enough, but because she knew she was different. She described Pound and the Imagists as 'choosy young gents'.

So, despite sharing the same publisher, Mew was included in neither anthology. On the Imagist side this is an example of how a poet who takes great risks in their work — but doesn't fully align herself with the ethos of a radical movement — can be missed by the extremists. Only one poet was included in both the Imagist and Georgian anthologies, a man: D.H. Lawrence. It's hard to believe that if Mew were a male writer, her work would not have been published in one or other — or both — of these anthologies.

The distinctions between the movements, when they're considered closely, were not as entrenched as the groups themselves made out. The Imagists embraced the now forgotten Skipwith Cannell — who used the new reductionism to cover up his uncalculated haikus — and Georgians such as Rupert Brooke could very often write through using 'no superfluous word, no adjective, which does not reveal something' (Ezra Pound, 'A Few Don'ts by an Imagiste'). Of course, intention is behind the selection too; the camp which the poet chose to align themselves with was also significant. Mew seems to be both silent and ambivalent on where she saw her work fitting best, if anywhere at all. There were enough fractures within herself without risking wasted energy amidst the false rigours of coterie poetics. She would have happily stepped aside to see the two groups fight over her work, except they never did.

Eavan Boland further defines the in-between attractions of Mew's work:

> Mew is not a lyric poet. At least, not a conventional one — and certainly not in that era of lyric poets. She is something different and far more unexpected in a time when there was still honey for tea: she is a pre-modernist narrator, gathering her world into lines which tumble off the edge of the page with the strain of holding it together. Cemeteries, asylums, sea roads and broken dolls clutter these lines. The cast of characters is strange and estranged. While the Georgian poets of that era were seeking out small pastorals, she marked disharmony. She stands in the middle of the Edwardian

landscape, not to be framed by it, but to signal its danger, like a
fire-swallower at an otherwise sedate country fair.

There have been revisionist anthologies since which have tried to
locate Mew in a particular place in this period; for example, she is
included in *The Georgians 1901-1930,* published by Shoestring Press
in 2009. There have also been many critics and poets who have since
tried to elevate her to the ranks of modernism. But Mew has fallen
through the fault lines of poetic taste, despite the qualities of her
work. The period she lived through had forced her into writing such
strange and memorable poems, yet the same period failed to allot
her a straightforward 'place' — if you put your ear to Mew's poems
you can hear the growing pains.

We've got lucky I think as Tim points out Henry Mew's
headstone: a low lying sun is slanting through the brambles
directly onto the memorial. We notice the lead-lined lettering on the
gravestone. Much of the text on the headstones around us have been
erased by time. I think about Mew in the context of the dead poets
of Nunhead Cemetery. Like many of them, Mew was published in
her lifetime but also she had the advantage of having remained in
print since her death. She might not have caused anything like a stir
when she was alive, but her unique style did catch the attention of
those willing to read her work closely enough. Alida Monro, the wife
of Harold Monro, had been so impressed with Mew's poem 'The
Farmer's Bride' that she invited her to come as an audience member to
The Poetry Bookshop (the organisation that published the Georgian
and Imagist anthologies — as well as individual poetry collections
— and ran a twice-weekly reading series) in Bloomsbury. Alida had
been so struck with Mew's poem that she had already memorised it

and hoped that the poet might have more poems that were just as unique. Mew — known to be a recluse — surprised Alida by turning up at the Tuesday evening reading. Alida later wrote of how Mew had emerged into the poetry scene that evening, just a road away from where Dylan Thomas and, later, Ted Hughes would both live:

> Let me try to describe her. The Bookshop itself was a small room about twelve feet square, lined from floor to ceiling with books, and opening on to a dark slummy street off Theobald's Road in Bloomsbury. There would be a number of people wandering about looking at the shelves before going up to the reading room. The reading room itself was a converted workroom that had been originally used by the gold-beaters who occupied a large part of the street: and the gentle thud, thud, of their gold-beating hammers rang in the ears of all those who lived there, from morning to night, every day. At about five minutes to six the swing-door of the shop was pushed open and into the room stalked Charlotte Mew. Such a word best describes her walk. She was very small, only about four feet ten inches, very slight, with square shoulders and tiny hands and feet. She always wore a long double-breasted top-coat of tweed with a velvet collar inset. She usually carried a horn-handled umbrella, unrolled, under her arm, as if it were psychologically necessary for her, a weapon against the world. She had very fine white hair that showed traces of once having been a warm brown. Her eyes were a very dark grey, bright with black lashes and highly arched dark eyebrows. Her face was a fine oval, and she always wore a little hard felt pork-pie hat put on very straight. The whole time she was speaking she kept her head cocked at a defiant angle. When she came into the shop she was asked: 'Are you Charlotte Mew?' and her reply, delivered characteristically with a slight smile of amusement, was: 'I am sorry to say I am'.

Mew would have stood on this spot, where I'm standing now,

watching the mud fill up around her brother's coffin. That moment which poet Maggie O'Sullivan has described memorably of her own brother's internment: the earth entering into him. The ground becomes alive, the earth moves: all hopelessness is bound in the passivity of the body. Knowing Mew's later struggle and the fact that she stood here, at her brother's funeral, makes it difficult to dissociate her grief from the grief of the narrator of the poem — even if that happens to be a man who is in mourning over the death of his fiancée. The poem is saturated with sadness. Mew repeatedly experienced the agony of unrequited love. For Mew emotion was the driving source of poetry and the monologue the method by which she could turn that emotion into art: 'The quality of emotion is the first requirement of poetry,' she wrote. 'For good work one must accept the discipline that can be got, while the emotion is given to no one.'

Writing itself is an act of exorcism brilliantly hewn into the form of the poem. 'In Nunhead Cemetery' is incredibly odd, as if both Mew and the grieving lover are captured in one figure, both inside the crucible of the poem itself. Mew can be in her poem and watching herself at the same time. The poem has the perfect de-centeredness for the time it was written and for Nunhead Cemetery itself, on the edge of London. The opening line pulls the reader straight in to the physical reality of London burial: 'It is the clay that makes the earth stick to his spade'. London burials are subject to contraction and movement due to London clay, a resistant blue substance that turns orange-brown — a kind of umber — when weathered. It is already heavily fossilised with the remains of the past: new bones take their place in the Eocene sediment. Slate-grey winters saturate this once tropical earth. This has never been optimum burial ground — the non-commuter rush of the dead downwards is less stable than the underground Tube system. London as a cryogenic puppetshow: blink and the structures melt.

The geography of this part of London is also central to the grief expressed in the poem: central London becomes *other*, the thriving metropolis of present moments, down below the melancholia of the hill this Cemetery is built on. In the poem, the narrator tells us, the other mourners have left — 'there's nowhere else to go'. The speaker's nihilism and despair with London gives the poem a searingly modern edge — many of the poem's assertions and images would have jarred against the poetic vernacular and societal values of the period in which it was written: 'There is something horrible about a flower,' the narrator says, before pushing this discord with the world further: 'There is something terrible about a child.' We find that the death of the narrator's fiancée has been completely unexpected — only a week before they had experienced central London as lovers:

> We were like children last week, in the Strand;
>   That was the day you laughed at me
> Because I tried to make you understand
>   The cheap, stale chap I used to be
>   Before I saw the things you made me see.

There is no psychological torture worse than that of momentary relief before pain returns with force. The narrator must not only return to the 'stale chap' he was before but a stale chap who now knows the jouissance of being a lover, reflected back to him in London's unfading landmarks. Beneath the narrator's gaze the illuminated landscape of London is visible in macro but the micro details play out in his mind on a past tense reel of moving images.

Mew's genius in this poem comes about through how she updates the dramatic monologue for the twentieth century: she removes the *dramatic*. Browning's brilliance was in finding the expression of the flourishing idiosyncrasies of character, but Mew's speaker has been ravaged by experience to the point where he wants to disappear into the earth he describes, as if his character might best be erased by experience. This aspect of despair brings the poetic form of the monologue into the modern era, captured in the inconsistently ragged lines of the poem which Penelope Fitzgerald describes as 'like jets of blood from a wound':

> you used to care
> For the Lions in Trafalgar Square,
> Who'll stand and speak for London when her bell of Judgement
> tolls –
> And the gulls at Westminster that were
> The old sea-captains souls.
> To-day again the brown tide splashes step by step, the river
> stair
> And the gulls are there!

It is hard not to conflate the voice of the narrator here with Henry Mew, who had spent his adult life suffering from dementia praecox — what we now know as schizophrenia. As Nelljean Rice argues, 'it is almost as if his voice is blended with Charlotte's in the words of the poem'. This could also be Mew's own psychotic disorder used as creative force here. Mew was familiar with the sensation of having a divided self. One evening she had a fantasy that the front-door bell would ring and felt that if she answered it she would see herself, waiting outside, in the street. 'It is a queer uncertain mind this of mine,' she wrote. In the poem the imagery pans from the suburban Cemetery to central London and then back again. Flowers — and people — only have a chance of living when they are dug up. What feels odd, standing here, is that Mew could have easily changed the location of the poem to another cemetery — just as easily as she changed narrator — but she chose not to. The use of multiple perspectives in art was a modernist tool that would later be embraced by many different poets, in many different ways. This oscillation of perspectives is Mew's default position — she is most comfortable being in many places at once.

Peter Ackroyd has written that there's nothing like London to make us feel personally historic. The opposite could be said of London's Victorian cemeteries — situated in the old suburbs — where it's easy to feel forgotten. Mew paces out the silence of Nunhead with the attuned, idiosyncratic musicality of her poem. Penelope Fitzgerald suggests that Mew's metrical ear was often amiss because she counted by the syllable and not the stress. I would refute this. The poem measures out its lines with a range of alternating stresses, allowing Mew complete control of where she chooses, at each point, to place emphasis. She intuitively breaks her lines when she senses a heave towards the beginning of the next line, maximising the implicit pause before the next rangy, multi-stressed line begins. This has the effect of making the regular end rhymes unexpected and lively as the 'day of judgement tolls'.

Sometimes it's hard to know if I feel Nunhead Cemetery to be the realest place I know, a place that has grounded me in a difficult time, or something of an endless forest that has all the properties of dream:

This is not a real place; perhaps by-and-by
I shall wake — I am getting drenched with all this rain:
To-morrow I will tell you about the eyes of the Crystal Palace
train
Looking down on us, and you will laugh and I shall see what
you see again.

The Great Exhibition was relocated after 1851 from its home in Hyde Park to Penge Peak — alongside Sydenham Hill. The train that passes through the Mew's poem went through the old Nunhead Station, knocked down when the station was relocated in 1925. The narrator's glorious summer in Hyde Park seems far removed from the sleepy hills of Surrey. The landmarks of London appear as afterimages in the grieving lover's mind. When Mew was here, at Henry's funeral — and perhaps on visits many times afterwards — the height of the Cemetery would have given her an even clearer view of London than today. She would have looked down, as her narrator does, as if the few past loves and joys she'd had were still attainable in the present, down below. Time and space fold back on themselves. The narrator is aware that by the time he made it to the Strand the past would have moved on:

I shall stay here: here you can see the sky;
The houses in the street are much too high..

The poetic force of my Dulwich map has led me to this poem: the poem in which the hinge of the old and new in poetry is played out in the present of the Cemetery. The trains still run between Peckham and Sydenham though the Crystal Palace has, like Mew, vanished.

The poem in my hand remains.

'There's something in that poem,' Tim says, 'that's troubling: the confusion over who's talking.' He's right: the speaker of the poem seems to shift between 'I' and 'You', as if Henry Mew is trying to speak — channelled through his sister. This is akin to that other part of Mew — the one she saw outside her own front door — breaking through any sense of fixed entity that the poem might try to attain. When Mew stood here, mourning the death of her brother, she would have known that her struggle was going to be in not dying the same way, at a similarly young age. Her family was dying one by one and she knew she would not add to the family line with children of her own. Mew is disembodied, split between her private and public worlds. Now all we have of her are her poems, refracted through perspectives and layered voices. Despite creating other identities in her poems, these characters are split by inner divisions. Outsiders are central to Mew's poetics, her distanced self becomes central to creating her cast of deranged minds located in fringe places.

Mew's poem is, significantly, written *in* Nunhead Cemetery: her own dissolution in the poem only serves to affirm the absolute physicality of the place. 'In Nunhead Cemetery' is a poem that on the one hand is tight and formal but only as the casket is to the inert pupa waiting to emerge. In Mew's poetry the inert pupa is the modern mind: troubled, probing, lost. This is a poem that oscillates so freely through unstable perspectives that its centre has been wormed-out enough for the reader to climb inside: 'I shall see what you see again.' Now that we can place the poem — and Mew's experience — against the social fabric of the early twentieth century we can see the poem as a true imago: the fully developed original.

This ground I am standing on is the ground that seeped upwards, amplifying the moodboard of Mew's grief after the long decade had passed since Henry's death. The decade it took her to write 'In Nunhead Cemetery'. Like the tree's root that goes down into Thornbury's grave, Mew's grief twisted into a multi-stem, creating the persona in the poem that draws at the source of her grief. Deeper in the Cemetery I can hear a baby crying and — beyond that — the sound of a chainsaw. There's a scraping sound on the other side of the woodland. I enter back into daylight: a toddler in a pink helmet is trying to drag her scooter along the stones: 'Mommy,' she says, 'wait for me.' 'It's too hard darling,' her mum says, 'wait until we get to the park.'

Mew is neither a Victorian poet, though she emerged from its tail end, nor a Georgian; she breaks the expectations in form and meaning that applied to the Georgian approach. Neither, though, was she defined by the collective assertions of the Imagists. Mew is indisputably her own poet. 'In Nunhead Cemetery' still squirms and pulsates, refuses to settle, expresses its discomfort and out-of-its-time awkwardness each time it is read. It sits in the canon of early twentieth century poetry like Caliban picking his teeth at the Victorian hearth of the refined Anthologists.

Mew lived for many years after Henry's death and a further fifteen after writing this poem. There is something in her death that is true to the trapped emotion of 'In Nunhead Cemetery' and true to the awkwardness of her life and work. In a nursing home on Beaumont Street near Baker Street, in 1928, she drank a quantity of Lysol — a cheap poison — which she had earlier purchased for herself. There was no graceful sliding from the earth after this shredding of the internal organs that had sustained the body she could never accept.

One of the exhibits at the 1851 site in Hyde Park was The Tempest Prognosticator, a barometer that used leeches to forecast a rain storm. As a storm approached the leeches would rise, agitated, their movement striking a small bell. Here we are inside Mew's mind: the brilliance of her poetic devices are watertight and stable, her mind both liquid and shell, exposed and concealed. As Thomas Hardy put it, she is a poet 'who will be read … when others are forgotten'. Yet the reality of poets who are not praised in their lifetime is that they're always tanned by the grave they lie in: they are the unrecognised,

Charlotte Mew

underrated, unacknowledged that have to rise like revenants to take their place, after death, with the canonical poets flying on chariots of air. Poets like Mew become known for not being well known enough. A typo in a death announcement in a local Marylebone newspaper immediately set out the levels of recognition that her work had failed to receive and would always struggle to receive. 'Charlotte *New*,' the obituarist mistakenly wrote, 'said to be a writer.' The italics are mine, emphasising the fluked tribute to her originality.

I walk around to the clearest vantage point over London, which is down below, like a flattened globe of electrics, its surface racing with invisible streams of light. Nunhead Cemetery has brought me in contact with one of the great poems written in English, written by a poet buried ten miles away in Hampstead Cemetery. The rest of my dead are over the river, on the north side of the Thames, claiming me as poetry claimed their own lives — all their lost existing poems, like Mew's, waiting to be read — as she knew one day it would.

All 'my damned immortal work,' she called it.

9th April 2015

As I picked Pavel up from school I was told that in a few months the Victorian structure of the school would be demolished and replaced with a new building on the field where I first saw him take part in a sports day race when he was only four years old. Over the years the bricks have turned to black, the tiles have slid from the Gothic gables.

He was excited to see his Nana. We waited for the bus outside Kensington Library where I had worked in 2000 before moving to London: Sarah and I in the first months of our relationship, my dad adjusting to the first stages of his illness. One afternoon he took me for lunch at his favourite Chinese restaurant, the one we'd all gone to as children. It was only later I found out that he'd taken my sister and brothers there separately too, over those months, as if saying goodbye to us all individually. I'm so glad that we could all be there together, later, when he died.

My mum was at the bus stop outside the Royal Court, standing where we always meet. Pavel ran to her. We walked to our favourite pub for dinner, The Shakespeare, where each of the burgers is named after a character from one of the Bard's plays, The Falstaff being the ultimate. We sat at a table with a window view, looking out at the fountains, pigeons dunking in the water, clattering to dry themselves. I like the view from there, out over Queen's Square: The Playhouse opposite and Radio City Tower (St. John's Beacon) which rises (Wiki tells me) to 486 feet. The 32nd tallest building in the UK. My parents took me to the top when I was a baby, to visit the restaurant that was there — the restaurant which closed in the same year of my birth, for health and safety reasons. It reopened as a Buck Rogers space-theme restaurant but closed again in 1983 due to lack *of business. Radiowaves fly from it now — across the city — into offices, kitchens, cars.*

Against the backdrop of the city Pavel played with his toy aliens. Curled up against the glass like rubber foetuses; one gold, another silver. We laughed when my mum called them babies. She corrected herself: 'They're like foetuses,' she said, holding one up against the backdrop of Queen's Square. Between us, pensioners sat with their pints, smokers of all ages, children running through the fountains. A man stood at a kiosk of red and blue football scarves. People staring for hours at loops of water. Redundant flags slackening, words rippling in the breeze: LIVERPOOL IS LIFE.

Food arrived. After months of surprising us all by devouring meals fuelled by her steroid intake, my mum has now hit the wall: loss of appetite, nausea, iron deficiency. She ran a fork through a plate of chilli, white rice bunkering spicy meat and peppers. The steroids had been masking the ill effects of the chemotherapy for months. I finished my caesar salad and eat the food left on her plate. Sympathy eating: I did the same when my dad was ill, wading with him through multipacks of custard cakes.

We had an hour until the appointment and decided to sit outside in the sun. Pavel ran bedlam through the water before spotting an offer in a shop on certain ice creams he wanted to try. I took him to buy a box. He counted out how many were in the box and how many there were of us: one, two, three ice creams; then on the other hand for us: one, two, three. We ate them in the sun with a karaoke version of Elton John's 'Your Song' carried on the wind from Sweeney's Bar. I looked across to see the stage and microphone for the karaoke overlooking the square, the singer — lacquered with lager — projecting the barely recognisable notes into the crashing fountain.

Two white blots appeared on Pavel's coat and my mum's right knee: *seagull shit.* 'It's good luck,' I said. 'It friggin stinks,' my mum said. She wiped Pavel's coat before she wiped herself. Then, from nowhere, she pulled out money and gave it to me, knowing that payday is a week away and Easter has wiped me out. We looked at the clock: 30 minutes to the appointment. We rang a taxi.

The car cut through Liverpool towards Bootle. Pavel sat in the back reading the **Time Out** I'd brought back from London. We slowed down alongside Kirkdale Cemetery, watching a man inside, wearing a workman's orange jacket, walking his dog. Pavel nodded to my mum: 'Graveyard,' he said. 'There's people in there.' She nodded. 'Hundreds and hundreds of people must have died in the world,' Pavel told her. My mum said, 'That's a really old cemetery.' He turned back to his **Time Out** and said, 'Look! There's a fairground coming to London too!'

    The glass entrance to the Clatterbridge hospital at Fazakerley reflects those walking into it: no escaping the fact of being here. In the waiting room we picked up a **National Geographic**: whales, dolphins, seabirds, seals and sharks drawn to South Africa's annual sardine run along the Indian Ocean coastline. A shark lunged into a silver swarm of tentacle and fin.

    A nurse came out and asked my mum if she had a gown then led her into a room. 'Where are you going?' Pavel asked. She hesitated for a second: 'for my treatment'. 'Oh,' he said. 'Can I come?' My Mum explained that she'd be back soon, and walked into a room. The two of us sat and watched **Granada Reports**, which was showing a feature on trench warfare. Footage of a Flanders cemetery accompanied by a commentary: how soldiers who were never found are never forgotten. Artefacts presented from the mud: a ring, a pendant, a boot. The cemetery is in Ploegsteert, it turned out. Two men from the Lancashire Fusiliers have recently been found and will be reburied with their comrades.

When my mum came out Pavel spotted a mark and a plaster on her chest. 'What's that?' he asked. 'It's where I got my treatment,' she told him. It looked like a burn. 'It's quite hot,' she said, and quickly followed up with, 'but not sore.'

In the taxi, driving back to the Clock Tower, Pavel had a question.

– When are we going to see Grandad McCabe's grave again?

– In the Summer, my mum said, we'll go and see how the tree's getting on.

– I'd forgotten about the tree!

As we drive I tell them that I'd read that hawthorns can grow up to fifteen metres and live for 400 years. The day of planting the tree, last year, comes back to Pavel: the digging, the stories, the party afterwards.

– Did you ask them if we could plant the tree there? He asked.

– No no, we just planted it, I told him.

– But isn't it wrong to plant a tree without permission?

– They never said yes or no, I told him. We didn't think they'd mind. Sometimes things just grow without permission.

I pictured the hawthorn as the taxi drove: a maverick sapling in a public land.

Sometimes things just grow without permission.

22nd April 2015

After my grandad, Ronald Bunting Bennett, had died, my mum and dad tried to find a box he had kept, a box that they thought contained the things he never talked about. They never found it, or worked out what it was they thought it might tell them. A handwritten paper that spells out the missing pieces of who he was and how he got here? Everyone becomes mysterious after death. I imagine that box as stained yellow with tobacco and containing shreds of racing forms and used betting slips. Maybe a name. A date. A cause. The answer.

23rd April 2015

Despite his middle name Bunting — with its echo of the great modernist poet Basil Bunting — the box, I am sure, did not contain poetry. I can remember my granddad coming to our house each Sunday afternoon and asking to borrow books from my dad's own collection. He returned them dog-eared and satin-ringed.

25th April 2015

She's been baking again. Like she did when we were children. A circular fruitcake that weighs more than a Spartan shield; fairy cakes in frilled holders and a sponge cake that came out oddly like a pancake. I said: We're supposed to be looking after you? No, she said, I like to keep busy.

4th May 2015

Sarah, Pavel and I spent the May Bank Holiday in Dulwich, walking Vanessa's dog Bertie. Bertie stole a ripped tennis ball from a brown Labrador whose owner had to keep it from eating snails, whole delicacies that it snaffled beneath its wet nose in one go. I told Pavel about the River Peck and we followed it from the adventure playground until it appeared — with some force — in the middle of the Rye. A river that exists out of sight and underground, we followed it in our minds, lost, together, in the discovery. When Sarah joined us, we went for breakfast in Nunhead. Pavel pointed to a parachute-like kite on the Rye, turning red and blue figures of eight.

We walked past Linden Grove, past the Cemetery. Not today. The bakery I wanted to take them to was closed, refusing bank holiday business, though the greasy spoon delivered. We sat outside with Bertie as the trains *clattered overheard towards London or further south towards Sydenham.*

Pavel sneaked food to Bertie under the table: shreds of boiled ham and tacky medallions of fried egg blotched with ketchup. Afterwards we bought ice creams and walked across Peckham Rye – past the frisbee-throwers and the sun-bathers – to collect our bags for the return journey to Liverpool.

Cenotaph South: Mapping the New Peckham

The dead I praised. To everything a season; a time to rend, and a time to sew, a time to keep, and a time to cast away. I praised the dead who lie sleeping beneath the trees.

Alfred Döblin, *Berlin Alexanderplatz*

We make the return visit to check on the hawthorn we planted two years ago. This time it's just me, Pavel, my brother David and my mum. The feeling is one of trepidation over whether the tree has taken root and continued to thrive — but at least the road to the wood is open this time.

We cut through the estate on Fox's Bank Lane and Pavel, slightly ahead of us, shouts back.

— Toy Penguin!

We look at what he's pointing at: a dead magpie on the road. He realises his mistake as we spot another magpie on the bank behind us. The one on the road is face down in a pool of dried blood; the one on the bank is looking blankly up at a streetlight. Two for joy, even though they're dead?

We wind our way through the estate towards the wood, feeling our way by memory along the path. We find ourselves back in the hollow where we sat to tell each other stories and there it is — my dad's hawthorn. There is relief to be found in a living tree, thriving: it's small but its green trefoil leaves are reaching up to the light. We take out the picnic things: no stories today but togetherness, sharing. Pavel's dug out some Haribos from his picnic bag. A small red jelly man goes overboard from the packet and lands in the long grass.

Pavel's first to spot the tiny hawthorns that have taken root in the grass all around us, small saplings that are growing within ten feet of our tree. The buds must have flown out from our hawthorn and taken root. Mayblossom for future years guaranteed. After lunch we walk through the wood, finding hawthorns everywhere. What we had thought *we* had introduced was already native here. I walk ahead with my mum talking about the reconstructive surgery which she has scheduled for the Autumn. The breast that was removed will be remade from other parts of her body. By Christmas all the surgery will be behind her.

On the way back we cut through the estate again and the two magpies have disappeared, as if they were playing dead all along and then decided to fly back to where they'd come from.

And poetry in Peckham is thriving. All throughout my map of the area new activity is taking place. I recall how Peckham reached much further, geographically, in the late nineteenth-century than it does now. The ward of 'The Rye' is now subsumed in what we now know as East Dulwich. As the river Peck went further underground there was less cause to retain its name and the area willingly broke away from the harsh hacking K sound of *Peckham*, opting for the softer cadences of *Dulwich*: new luxury houses appeared and the artisans arrived. Patricia Doubell says that the area became less welcoming to poets in the 1980s, the readings at the Crown and Greyhound ceased around the same time that the prices of the properties began to soar. Margaret Thatcher — on being forced to buy a house outside Number 10 for tax purposes — chose a place to live at the edge of Dulwich Village. When she retired, she joked that she was replacing number 10 for number 11: she had bought 11 Hambeldon Place, in a gated community, with her husband Denis. He liked the nearby Dulwich and Sydenham golf course.

The 1980s did not, as Doubell feared, kill off poetry in the area. The culture of poetry is rhizomatic: it doesn't grow in hierarchical roots but connections formed in spontaneous clusters, sudden rootstalks that claim their own space — as Gilles Deleuze and Félix Guattari put it in *Capitalism and Schizophrenia*:

> In this model, culture spreads like the surface of a body of water, spreading towards available spaces or trickling downwards towards new spaces through fissures and gaps, eroding what is in its way. The surface can be interrupted and moved, but these disturbances leave no trace, as the water is charged with pressure and potential to always seek its equilibrium, and thereby establish smooth space.

This image is truer of poetry than any form of cultural activity as the kinds of cultural spasms that emerge in poetry are always on the surface of an underground river, where those with power and influence would fail to detect it even if they tried. In Peckham there are still affordable places for artists to live, venues that can be used for free, and poets with the belief in language to mark the climate with their art.

The invitations for poetry evenings in Peckham start to arrive. Poets I know tell me they are moving to the area — or grew up there — and I start to see living poets amidst the deadwood of bus stops. Not so much waiting as watching. Goldsmiths poets set up a reading series under the slick, anaesthetised name of *clinic*. In November 2015 I go to the Peckham Literary Festival, to a poetry event in the Review Bookshop on Bellenden Road. The restaurants, pubs and bookshop make Rye Lane's staring, dead-eyed fish — bedded on shales of ice — seem very far away. Burned-out shops still remain as they were left after the 2012 riots — events which made it into many contemporary poems. A poet I know took part in the rioting, though mostly watched, absorbing the friction: documenting.

At the Review Bookshop that night the audience took plastic cups of warm white wine down into the windowless bunker of the reading room to listen to young black poet Caleb Oluwafemi reclaim Peckham as his own in his poem 'The Rye':

> You will not take this place ...
>
> We gave adrenaline to wheezes architecture
> Bowing dried crayfish atoms under slab slips
> Beating torque into day
> This here is patented
>
> This quotient of sky is ours

Then I go to visit artist Tom Phillips on Talfourd Road. A huge Victorian terrace with the usual Victorian façade of the area, behind which Phillips paints, collages, erases text, reads, makes music. Inside is a living archive of his past and current projects; time is written into the process. He shows me a work that has been made by glueing his shaved facial hair to a series of tennis balls, the various lengths of hair giving each of them a different shade. I use the bathroom, or Samuel Beckett Memorial Bathroom as it's called, noting the poetry collections that are piled up around the house and — in the time-honoured fashion of the jobbing poet — stacked beside the toilet.

It's time for Phillips the artist to be held up as a poet too.

Phillips cites Van Gogh and Blake as inspirations, both of whom walked the same streets of Peckham where Phillips first found the source book for his epic lifetime project in 1966. In a furniture repository facing Peckham Rye, Phillips picked up a copy of W.H. Mallock's Victorian novel *A Human Document* after declaring to a friend that the first book he found for threepence would 'serve a serious long-term project'. Where Blake was looking up into the trees for angels, Phillips was amongst the deadwood of old furniture, trawling the books abandoned after furniture removals. For an artist whose whole practice has thrived on chance, this synchronicity is not lost. Blake's fusion of word and image (as well as the decision to make artworks that would find their home in illuminated books) is as much a presence behind Phillips' work as the explosions of colour to be found in Van Gogh and Cézanne. Phillips compacts the words 'Human' and 'Document' to coin new lexis: *Humument*. This process of reforming Mallock's language is the process by which Phillips creates the collage poems of his fifty-year epic. Language is fallow ground: dead earth can yield new fruit.

 A Humument is one of the most significant cross-arts projects since the output of Blake and, later, David Jones. A Gesamtkuntswerk: a complete work of art across forms. Phillips' creative process involves painting, drawing or collaging over the original pages of text of the novel — placing the fiction under erasure — until just a little of the text is visible through the new images on the page. Words determine the visual direction. In one sense this is a parallel to what a poet does, choosing words from the language — or the book of the language, the dictionary — to create new work using their preferred order. In the conventional approach to the poem, all of the unused words are invisible, their invisibleness determining the impact of the words chosen on the page. In *A Humument* words are selected only from those that are available for selection in the pages of the novel, though sometimes Phillips chooses to leave words semi-visible beneath paint or lightly sketched over with pencil.

Phillips appears to me now as a magus, a cavern-dwelling eccentric who divines the future through Victorian text. I look at the new pages for the next edition of *A Humument*; they are perched on the nineteenth-century fireplace in this room at the top of the house. There's a kinship with my project: obscure Victorian literature is re-mapped, remade as only it can be at this point in history. In the most recent edition of *A Humument,* Phillips was able to find language that had no calculable semantics when he first started his project. 'Facebook' and 'nine eleven' were already written into Mallock's novel long before social media and aeroplanes existed in the world. Language can do that, making the bizarre seem inevitable all along.

Phillips has given up smoking and now vapes like a Godfather don as we talk. There's something of Blake about Phillips, the same tension of harvested cantankerousness fuselit with sheer delight in the world around him. The man inside is led by the child he refused to put to sleep. 'An artist is a child,' I've heard Phillips say in an interview. 'He doesn't have to put his toys away, can make a mess. So you carry on being a child, really. Seems like a good idea.' He hands me a fifty pence coin which he's designed for the Royal Mint. 'Go on,' he says, 'keep it.' I take it, wondering if I should go and spend it later on sweets or ice cream.

We talk about the place that contemporary poetry has in his practice, in his life. This artist-poet who remakes dead prose into artworks that have prismatic, minimalist poetry at their core, is also fed on contemporary poets like David Harsent and Anne Carson.

This confirms his skill as a poet is no accident — like all poets that mine for gold, Phillips' poetry is honed on hard work and acute observation of other practitioners. There's something alchemical in how Phillips appropriates and illuminates a Victorian novel that would otherwise be dead and lost. Read, see fresh, make new: lost literature is cut from the branch and re-hewn for contemporary times.

All poets speak across space and time to the other: it's inevitable that I've ended up here, at the end of my map. 'The ruins of time build mansions in eternity,' Blake wrote. What would have happened if Phillips had picked up a different book by chance on that day in 1966? A whole different oeuvre in language would have been created, his own artistic career remapped in an alternative way. Place determines what we do and how we do it. I think of my map of dead poets across London that was always, in a sense, already there — just waiting to have its node-points pinned down. Location and personality synchronise in ways that seem to be obvious. We are defined by our own maps: look closely and we appear as gritted Lowrys in the online grid references of our lives.

'I'm very attached to south London,' Phillips says. 'It's uneven and pockmarked and relatively unspoilt in one sense and ruined in another.' There's nothing to do in most of south London *other* than work: no seductions of pretentiousness. Each spring since 1973 Phillips has walked a nine mile circle in Peckham taking photographs of twenty specific places. These photographs are taken from the same spot, facing the same direction, using the same framing. Each of the sites is within a half-mile radius of Phillips' original home. 'It's nothing glamorous, they're all humdrum places,' he says. 'It sounds boring but actually urban change, recorded in detail, is quite beautiful.'

I gather Phillips in to the poets mapped around Nunhead Cemetery, reclaim him as a poet for his metrical skill, his Imagist precision: 'A / sung / song / done / of / emotion   gone / lost / like the ghost of a poem.' The found, after all, is what brought me here: the poets I've discovered were there all along, already a part of London's past, waiting to be read whenever somebody cared to find them. And it's in the new version of *A Humument* created for tablets — in which the pages light up like church windows or Blake's Illuminated Books — that I come across Phillips' own map of Peckham, with a circle placed around the roads that have been there so long they've become like holloways harbouring the channels of his creative work. I look closely and see that Bellenden Road is on the map — the energies of contemporary poets re-chanelled into Phillips' Victorian divining of the future.

We gather at my mum's house. While the rest of the family arrives I go with my younger brother Ste to have my tarot read. He asks me to focus on one issue in my life that I'm trying to resolve, something that I'm thinking about enacting some kind of change towards. Easy, I think: finding time to complete this book.

He draws my cards: the Five of Cups, Temperance, Nine of Swords, Ten of Swords and Eight of Wands. The tarot pack he's brought is composed of Victorian imagery. On one card a man lies passed out on a bar as a barmaid brings fresh cups; in the background two goblets of red wine are spilling onto the floor and a fin de siècle sign reads above: LIQUOR. On another card a man lies flat on his back with ten swords above him, a bag alongside him and — in the distance — London is burning. A woman lies in bed covering her ears with a candle lit next to her and eight swords hovering above. Another card shows a sergeant major character firing eight rockets from a cannon, only two of which are truly lit. On the final card Temperance has one foot in a stream and another in a desert landscape; she's balancing a stream of water which is flowing from one hand to the other.

My brother talks me through the arcane signs and signifiers of the cards. Excess. Balance. Creativity. Change. My idea to find time to write this book should be pursued. I ask him if the pack has a figure which fits the description of the White Goddess? Yes, he says: The High Priestess or possibly The Empress — but both have failed to show for me.

It looks like I'm ready to move forward without the Muse-goddess now.

When we go back downstairs my mum tells us that her hair's been growing back and she takes off her wig to show us. It's more than the bristling skinhead cut she's shown to us before — this is real hair in growth. It has the downiness of a chick, the flaxen back of a basking otter.

It feels like Pavel's hair when I first touched it, on the day he was born.

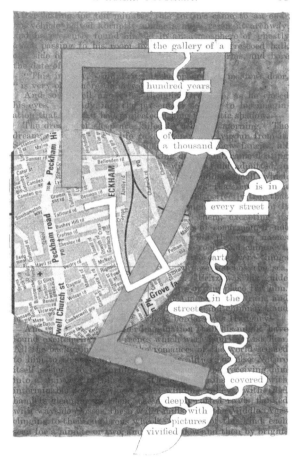

Tom Phillips, *A Humument* (page 53)

SELECTED BIBLIOGRAPHY

Peter Ackroyd, *Albion*, London: Chatto & Windus, 2002

Peter Ackroyd, *Blake*; London: Vintage, 1999

Paul Batchelor (editor); *Reading Barry MacSweeney*; Newcastle: Bloodaxe, 2013

William Cox Bennett, *Baby May: Home Poems and Ballads*, Oxford University, 1875

William Cox Bennett, *Poems: A New Edition in One Volume with Portrait and Illustrations,* London: Routledge, Warne and Routledge, 1862

William Cox Bennett, *Queen Eleanor's Vengeance and Other Poems*, Chapman and Hall, 1857

William Cox Bennett, *Shall We Have a National Ballad History of the English People?,* London: Macmillan & Company, 1866

William Cox Bennett, *Songs by a Song-Writer*, London: Chapman & Hall, 1859

William Blake, *Blake's Poetry and Designs: Illuminated Works and Other Writings* (Selected and edited by Mary Lynn Johnson and John E. Grant), New York, London: W.W. Norton & Co, 2008

William Blake, *The Complete Illuminated Books*, London: Thames & Hudson, 2009

William Blake, *The Complete Poems*, Harmondsworth: Penguin, 1981

William Blake, *Selected Poems* (edited and with an Introduction and Notes by G.E. Bentley, Jr), London: Penguin Books, 2005

Tom Bolton, *London's Lost Rivers: A Walker's Guide*, London: Strange Attractor Press, 2011

Ian Brinton; private correspondence with the author regarding

Barry MacSweeney

Robert Browning, *Sordello*; Bristol: Shearsman Books, 2012

Helen Carr, *The Verse Revolutionaries: Ezra Pound, H.D. and The Imagists*, London: Jonathan Cape, 2009

Gaius Valerius Catullus, *The Poems of Catullus* (translated with an introduction by Peter Whigham), Harmondsworth: Penguin, 1966

Geoffrey Chaucer, *The Canterbury Tales* (edited with an introduction and notes by Jil Mann), London: Penguin, 2005

Tom Chivers and Martin Kratz (editors), *Mount London: Ascents in the Vertical City*, London: Penned in the Margins, 2014

Cuthbert Collingwood, *A Vision of Creation: A Poem*, Edinburgh, William Paterson, 1875

Cuthbert Collingwood, *On the Scope and Tendency of Botanical Study; an inaugural address delivered before the Liverpool Royal Infirmary School of Medicine*, London: Longman, Brown, Green, Longmans & Roberts; Liverpool: E. Howell, 1858

Cuthbert Collingwood, *Visit to the Kaliban Village of Sano Bay, North-east Coast of Formosa. Including a Vocabulary of the Dialect*, S.l: s.n., [1867]

David Cooper, 'Telegraph Hill' in *Mount London*, Op. cit.

John Xiros Cooper, *The Cambridge Introduction to T.S. Eliot*, Cambridge: Cambridge University Press, 2007

Richard A. Davenport 'The Dying Druid' in Esther Le Hardy, *Agabus or The Last of the Druids: An Historical Poem*, London: William Pickering, 1851

Richard A. Davenport, *Sketches of Imposture, Deception and Credulity*, London: William Tegg, 1861

Daniel Defoe, *A Journal of the Plague Year*, New York: Dover

Publications, 2003,

T. K. de Verdon, *The Converted Jew: A Poem in Four Cantos*, London: Printed for the author, 1833

T. K. de Verdon, *The Veil Lifted from Israel: What Israel Ought To Do, and Hymns and Melodies for Israel*, London: S.W. Partridge, 1876

Gilles Deleuze and Félix Guattari, *A Thousand Plateaus: Volume 2 of Capitalism and Schizophrenia*, Translated by Brian Massumi, London and New York: Continuum, 2004

Patricia Doubell, *At the Dog in Dulwich: Recollections of a Poet* (edited by Clive Murphy), London: Secker & Warburg, 1986

Andrew Duncan, interview recordings with Barry MacSweeney (access given to the author)

Pierre Dupont, *The Legend of the Wandering Jew*, illustrated by Gustave Dore and translated by George W. Thornbury

Morris Eaves and S. Foster Damon, *A Blake Dictionary: The Ideas and Symbols of William Blake*, Dartmouth: Dartmouth College Press, 2013

T.S. Eliot, *Ezra Pound: Selected Poems, Edited with an Introduction by T.S. Eliot*, London: Faber and Faber, 1971

T.S. Eliot, *The Letters of T.S. Eliot: Volume 4: 1928-1929* (ed. Valerie Eliot and John Haffenden), London: Faber and Faber, 2013

T.S. Eliot, *The Letters of T.S. Eliot: Volume 5: 1930-1931* (ed. Valerie Eliot and John Haffenden), London: Faber and Faber, 2014

Iain Finlayson, *Browning: A Private Life, London: HarperCollins,* 2004

Friends of Nunhead Cemetery, *Nunhead Cemetery: An Illustrated Guide*; London: Friends of Nunhead Cemetery, 1995

John Gibbens, *Collected Poems*, London: Touched Press, 2000

Alexander Gilchrist, *Life of William Blake,* London: Macmillan and Co, 1863

Peter Gizzi, *In Defense of Nothing: Selected Poems, 1987-2011*, Connecticut: Wesleyan university Press, 2014

Robert Graves, *Selected Poems*, London: Penguin, 1986

Robert Graves, *The White Goddess: A Historical Grammar of Poetic Myth*; London: Faber and Faber, 1961

Alethea Hayter, *A Sultry Month: Scenes of London Literary Life in 1846*, London: Robin Clark, 1992

Christopher Hibbert, *Queen Victoria: A Personal History*, London: Harper Collins, 2001

Daryl Hine and Joseph Parisi (editors), *The Poetry Anthology: 1912-1977: Sixty-five years of America's Most Distinguished Verse Magazine*, Boston: Houghton Mifflin Company, 1978

Thomas Hood, *Selected Poems*, Manchester: Carcanet Press, 1992

Thomas Hood, *The Headlong Career and Woful Ending of Precocious Piggy, illustrated by his son*, S.l.: London, 1859

Tom Hood, *A Practical Guide to Versification, a new and enlarged edition...To which are added Bysshe's 'Rules for English Verse Making'*, S.l.: London, 1877

Tom Hood, *Excursions into Puzzledom: A Book of Charades, Acrostics, Enigmas, Conundrums, by the late Tom Hood and his sister*, London: Strahan & Co., 1879

Tom Hood, *Fairy Realm: A Collection of the Favourite Old Tales*, illustrated by the pencil of Gustave Dore, London: Ward, Lock and Tyler, 1865

Tom Hood, *Griset's Grotesques; or jokes drawn on wood, with rhymes by Tom Hood. One hundred quaint designs by E. Griset. Engraved by the Brothers Dalziel*, London, 1867

Tom Hood, *Jingles & Jokes for Little Folks*, illustrated by C.H. Bennett, W.Brunton, Paul Gray and T. Morten, London: Cassell, Petter and

Galpin, 186

Tom Hood, *The Daughters of King Daher: a Story of Mohammedan Invasion of Scinde: and other poems*, London: Saunders, Otley, 1861

Gerard Manley Hopkins, *The Poems of Gerard Manley Hopkins*, London: Oxford, 1970

Richard Hort, *The Kilmainham Pensioner's Lament, Illustrated by Eight Engravings on Stone*, Dublin: W.F. Wakeman, 1834

Christopher Howard, *Peckham Rye Park Tree Trail*, S.l.: s.n., no date

Stephen Inwood, *A History of London*, London: Macmillan, 1998

William Irvine and Park Honan, *The Book, the Ring and the Poet: A Biography of Robert Browning*, London: The Bodley head, 1975

B.S. Johnson, *Well Done God! Selected Prose and Drama of B.S. Johnson*, edited by Jonathan Coe, Philip Tew and Julia Jordan; London: Picador, 2013

Peter Jones (editor), *Imagist Poetry*; London: Penguin Books, 1972

Anthony Kenny, *Arthur Hugh Clough: A Poet's Life*, London: Continuum, 2005

La Fontaine, *The Fables of La Fontaine*, with illustrations by Gustave Dore and by George W. Thornbury

Anne Lohrli, biographical entry for William Cox Bennett published in the Dickens Online Journal

Malcom Lowry, *Under the Volcano*, London: Penguin, 2000

Emma McGordon, *The Hangman and the Stars*; Newcastle upon Tyne: Blacksuede Boot Press, 2000

Barry MacSweeney, *Barry MacSweeney at Dulwich College*, London / 29.iv.2000; recorded by Colin Still; London: Optic Nerve, no date

Barry MacSweeney, *Elegy for January*; London: The Menard Press, 1970

Barry MacSweeney, *Horses in Boiling Blood*; Cambridge: Equipage,

2004

Barry MacSweeney, 'Mary Bell Sonnets' published in *Tears in the Fence* magazine and further unpublished poems provided by Ian Brinton

Barry MacSweeney, *The Book of Demons*; Tarset: Bloodaxe, 1997

Barry MacSweeney, *Ranter*; Nottingham: Slow Dancer Press, 1985

Barry MacSweeney, *Wolf Tongue: Selected Poems 1965-2000*, Tarset: Bloodaxe Books, 2003

Paul MacSweeney, in correspondence with the author

Hugh Meller and Brian Parsons: *London Cemeteries: An Illustrated Guide & Gazetteer*, London: The History Press, 2011

Charlotte Mew, *Collected Poems and Selected Prose* (edited with an introduction by Val Warner); Manchester: Carcanet Press, 1997

Charlotte Mew, *Selected Poems*, London: Bloomsbury Publishing, 1999

Charlotte Mew, *Selected Poems* (edited with an introduction by Eavan Boland); Manchester: Carcanet Press, 2008

Alfred H. Miles (editor), *The Poets and the Poetry of the Century*, London: Hutchinson, 1893

Thomas Miller, *Picturesque Sketches of London, Past and Present*, S.l.: s.n., 1852

Alida Monro, 'Charlotte Mew — A Memoir' in *Collected Poems of Charlotte Mew*, London: Gerald Duckworth & Co. Ltd, 1953

Pamela Neville-Sington, *Robert Browning: A Life after Death*, London: Phoenix, 2005

Jeremy Noel-Tod, *The Whitsun Wedding Video: A Journey into British Poetry*, Powys: Rack Press, 2015

Olson, Charles; *The Collected Poems of Charles Olson: Excluding the Maximus Poems*; California: University of California Press, 1987

Caleb Oluwafemi 'The Rye' in *Reading / Review*, London: Tangerine
    Press, 2015

Samuel Pepys, *The Concise Pepys*, Hertfordshire: Wordsworth
    Editions, 1997

Tom Pickard, interview with the author, 31st August 2016

Tom Pickard, *Mores Pricks than Prizes,* New York: Pressed Wafer,
    2010

Ezra, Pound, *The Cantos*; London: Faber and Faber, 1975

Marian Richardson, *The Talk of the Household: Poems*, London: S.
    Straker & Sons, 1865

Joshua Russell, *Poems*, London: self-published, 1819

Joshua Russell, *The Christian Sabbath; The Way of Life and Other
    Poems*; London: Houlston and Stoneman, 1853

Joshua Russell, *Journal of a Tour in Ceylon and India Undertake at
    the Request of the Baptist Missionary Society in Company with the
    Rev. J. Leechman, M.A. With Observations and Remarks*; London:
    Houlston and Stoneman, 1852

W. Sharp introduction to the *Delphi Complete Works of Robert
    Browning*, S.I.: Delphi Classics, 2013

Iain Sinclair, *Blake's London: The Topographic Sublime,* London: The
    Swedenborg Society, 2011

Paul Talling, *London's Lost Rivers*, London: Random House Books,
    2011

Alfred Lord Tennyson, *The Works of Alfred Lord Tennyson*, London:
    Wordsworth Editions, 2008

Donald Thomas, *Robert Browning: A Life Within Life*; London:
    Weidenfeld and Nicolson, 1982

Walter Thornbury, *A Tour Round England*, S.I.: Hurst and Blackett,
    1870

George W. Thornbury, *Art and Nature: at Home and Abroad, in two volumes*, London: Hurst and Blackett, 1856

Walter Thornbury, *Haunted London*, London: Hurst and Blackett, 1865

Walter Thornbury, *Ice Bound*, London: Hurst and Blackett, 1861

Walter Thornbury, *Lays and Legends, Or Ballads of the New World*, London: Saunders and Otley, 1851

Walter Thornbury, *Old and New London, Vol. 1*, London: Cassell, 1897

Walter Thornbury, *Songs of the Cavaliers and Roundheads, Jacobite Ballads &c*, London: Hurst and Blackett, 1857

Charles Godfrey Turner, *The Happy Wanderer: Being Some of the Writings of the Late Charles Godfrey Turner*, edited by Ethel M. Richardson Rice, Liverpool: The Literary Year Book Press, 1922

Henry Vaughan, *The Complete Poems*, London: Penguin Books, 1976

Meryn Williams (editor), *The Georgians 1901-1930*; Nottingham: Shoestring Press, 2009

A.N. Wilson, *Victoria: A Life*, London: Atlantic Books, 2014

Ron Woollacott, *More Nunhead Notables*, London: Friends of Nunhead Cemetery, 1995

Ron Woollacott and Michèle Louise Burford, *Buried at Nunhead: Nunhead Notables Volume 3*, London: The Friends of Nunhead Cemetery, 2014

Ron Woollacott, *Investors in Death: The Story of Nunhead Cemetery and the London Cemetery Company and its Successors*, London: The Friends of Nunhead Cemetery, 2010

Ron Woollacott, *Ron Woollacott's Nunhead Notables*, London: Friends of Nunhead Cemetery, 2002

ONLINE RESOURCES

BBC article on the Leysdown tragedy: http://www.bbc.co.uk/news/uk-england-kent-19096670

Gordon Burn, 'The Drunk Poet's Society', *The Guardian*; 26 August 2006, https://www.theguardian.com/books/2006/aug/26/featuresreviews.guardianreview

Paul Cox, 'Lost Rivers from Above: The Peck', *Londonist*: http://londonist.com/2009/01/lost_rivers_from_above_the_peck.php

Sarah Crown, *The Guardian*, 'Blake's Vision Tree Returns to Peckham Rye', 20 September 2011: https://www.theguardian.com/books/booksblog/2011/sep/20/william-blake

Dickens Journals Online: http://www.djo.org.uk/

Maps of Southwark: http://www.southwark.gov.uk/info/200212/egovernment/1776/old_maps_of_southwark

Londonist, '1848: London's First Electric Light Festival' http://londonist.com/2016/01/electric-lighting

Tom Phillips interview with Susannah Frankel in *The Independent*, 6 October 1992: http://www.independent.co.uk/life-style/when-success-is-a-routine-matter-tom-phillips-is-nothing-if-not-a-creature-of-habit-susannah-frankel-1555936.html

Jay Rayner, 'How a toy shop closed to pay for pupils at Dulwich College (and Alleyns and JAGS)': http://www.jayrayner.co.uk/news/dulwichcollege/

Time Out article about Nunhead: http://www.timeout.com/london/things-to-do/streets-of-london-nunhead-lane-se15

INDEX